Praise for The Pursuit of Life, Money, and
Happiness After Graduation

*"A book for anyone fresh out of college, high school, or just in need
of some general life skills."*

Dr. Veronica L. Thomas

"Perfect tone – funny and factual. Love the stories!"

Dr. Vanessa G. Perry

*"A lot of the stuff in this book is definitely stuff that I learned im-
mediately after school or at least realized that I needed to learn."*

A Gen Z-er

The Pursuit of Life, Money, and Happiness After Graduation

The Pursuit of Life, Money, and Happiness After Graduation

*Essential Tips for the 20 Something
That You Don't Learn in School*

Philippe Duverger, PhD

Published by PhD Consulting LLC

Copyright © 2021 by Philippe Duverger
Illustrations by Philippe Duverger
All rights reserved
ISBN 978-0-578-90308-8 (paperback)

Published by PhD Consulting LLC
First paperback edition

I dedicate this book to my parents,
my wife, and my children.

TABLE OF CONTENTS

ACKNOWLEDGMENTS

I want to thank my mom for keeping me in (some) school rather than letting the system kick me out at 13 into the wilderness. I want to thank my dad for introducing me to so many different adventures, such as judo, spear fishing, scuba diving, DIY projects, and many more.

I want to thank my wife, Sylvie, for supporting my creative mess and for being one of the first readers of this book.

I want to thank my daughter, Frédérique, for being my official editor and for the many Beyoncé and Michael Scott references throughout this book.

A particular thank you to Vanessa Perry and Veronica Thomas for some good ideas and early suggestions.

Thank you to all the early readers and critics of this book: Sylvie Duverger, Kristin Lamoureux, Plamen Peev, and Toby Porterfield.

Thank you to my Gen Z and Millennial students for their time, their comments (in italics throughout the text), and their experience used throughout this book: Ali, Brad, Crystal, Kim, Matt, Neal, Rachel, Taylor, and more.

Gen Z POV

Throughout the book you will notice quotes in italics under the title "Gen Z POV." Gen Z Point of View (POV) are quotes from interviews with Gen Z-ers. The quotes are verbatim (with their exact words) and therefore, it is the Gen Z-er's POV.

INTRODUCTION

"If you have a college degree you can be absolutely sure of one thing... you have a college degree."

It is customary to say congratulations to the class of [insert your year] and to wish you luck in your new endeavor, after the usual words of advice, a sprinkling of buzz words such as: "leadership," "continuous learning," "cherish failures," "fail soon and early," blah, blah, blah. You know the feeling.

Then, you move your tassel from right to left, and bam! You are a graduate. Good luck, and don't forget your alma matter...

I am sure, for having practiced it many times over, that some of you start thinking about a job or a career right at this moment. You would not believe the number of students who ask to connect with me on LinkedIn on commencement day. Most don't have any professional pictures of themselves and their job title is "student looking for a job." As the music is playing and you are proceeding out to rejoin your family and take pictures, you are asking yourself: "I got my Bachelor's, now what?"

Well, for starters, you're late. Yes, you are late. Life is not a game you play sequentially. You've got to multitask (if that's even possible) or at least play the circus game of plate spinning–warning: metaphor– where each plate is a project that you move along in the grand scheme of your life. Don't be too sad, though, if you haven't done much on that front yet because it's not too late after all. That's the good news. The bad news is that you might need a lot more luck, motivation, or both, if you want to "be all that you can be" given your late departure on that race that some gcall a rat race (I know I can be cynical at times).

> *Gen Z POV: "My goal was to always have a job before I graduated. I am like super OCD about things."*

The purpose of this book is to give you my experience from having practiced life for a few decades now, and for having observed young adults like you plenty of times. And, although I have a Ph.D., it is not in life coaching (it is in business). Yet, I have spent 20 years in the corporate world. I started at the bottom of the ladder and climbed my way up to managing hundreds of employees and multimillion dollar budgets, before retiring as an educator, or, as I like to say sometimes when I am in a better mood: giving back to the community.

I noticed, with my educator's cap, that young adults are not fully equipped for the race that is to come. And there are many reasons for that. The education system is not teaching life skills, such as interpersonal relationship management (i.e., how to deal with your significant other, your parents, or your co-workers). Your parents don't share much with you, mainly because they're your parents and you don't want to listen to your parents; who does? Your bosses don't want to share too much with you, maybe because they don't know, or they're afraid you would be successful, or more likely, because they think, they assume, you know what you need to know since you have just spent the same amount of money on your education that you could have spent on a townhouse.

So, where are you going to learn what will help you become all that you want to be? (Hint: in this book, at least in part.)

What do you need to know? Well, for starters, you need to understand the world around you and understand where you are in that world. Life is a strategic game you play against 7 billion other players. It has rules that you need to know. For instance, do you know what a FICO score is? Do you know what equity is? Do you know how others perceive you? Can you effectively gauge a person you need to hire? Can you give constructive feedback to a person working on a project with or for you? Can you fire someone, and as a result make them more successful in their own career? Do you know where your beliefs come from? Are you in charge of your own beliefs? Can you explain to someone, without judgement, accusations or insults, your political views and have the patience and respect to listen to their—sarcasm alert—bullshit? You get the point.

The book you have in your hands is organized into nine chapters because as Jack Black in School of Rock says: "9 is a magic number." I used to believe in numerology. Incredible right? Not really when you know my life story. But, even though numerology is bullshit, many adults still believe in it, so let's not ruin it for them, yet.

Each chapter can be read independently, however, I tried to follow a certain logic. The first five chapters are designed to answer some of the concerns you probably have right now: the need for a job, a career, a higher degree, things (i.e., clothes, shoes, cars, furniture, fitness club membership, etc.), and the biggest of all, a house. Most young adults are content with these five things. They might even define the American dream for them. A few young adults want more; they want money, lots of it. They want adventure, thrills. They want a family (and a dog/cat). They want happiness (remember that constitutional law class?). The second part of this book attempts to give pointers to these broader concepts. Ok, ready for the ride? Let's go!

CHAPTER 1

Get a Job

*"Some people are willing to work, only if
they can start at the top and work up."*

I remember my first job. I was an "extra" in a restaurant. An "extra" is an added person to the regular staff, often for a day or for a particular event, like a wedding, where you're paid a flat fee. Mine was as a waiter on Easter Sunday where lunch was going to be pretty busy with lots of families coming out, and a wedding scheduled for that evening. I was 15 years old and in my first year of vocational school (the best I could do given that I was terrible in pretty much every subject in middle school except maybe math). The restaurant did not hire me because I was a seasoned waiter; no, they hired me because they wanted to evaluate me since I was supposed to work for them during the summer practicum. [note: Keep in mind, if this all sounds a little bizarre, summer practicum, vocational school, etc., that I grew up in France where the education system works a bit differently.]

I guess they wanted to see if I'd fit in. The summer practicum–July and August–consisted of two shifts a day. The morning shift started at 8 am and lasted until after lunch, around 2 pm. Then, the evening shift started at 6 pm and lasted until 11 pm or later if there was a wedding.

Six days a week, one day off. The pay was a whopping 500 francs per month, which is somewhere close to $100 today, which broke down to 34 cents an hour.

[**Side note**: there are roughly 2,000 working hours in a year–52 weeks per year times 40 hours per week is 2,080 hours. So, an annual salary of $40,000 (pre-taxed) breaks down more or less to $20 per hour: $40,000/2,000 hours. If you lose the three zeros after $40 in $40,000, then divide $40 by 2, you get the same result. So, an annual salary of $30,000 is $15/hour ($30/2 = $15). Similarly, you can reverse the calculation to get an annual salary from an hourly wage. A job that pays $12.50 an hour is the equivalent, if you get 40 hours per week, to an annual salary of $25,000 ($12.5 x 2 = $25; adding three zeros behind that will get you to $25,000].

I remember getting more in tips than I did in pay, which allowed me to purchase my first cassette tape collection of classic rock music. Sweet memories. I guess waiters today can relate (except the cassettes of course).

In the few years after that Easter gig, I would have many other gigs. All of them would pretty much end up being some sort of mix between Germinal (Emile Zola's depiction of coal miners' exploitation in 1860's France) and my own realization that it takes two to tango. What I mean is that if I was exploited and underpaid for working 12 to 15-hour days, it was also partially my own fault. I first realized this when I saw a couple of my buddies getting better jobs than me. One was an extra, as well, but got gigs that paid five times more. Another followed me to the job I had on the French Riviera, and in a matter of a day, driving from place to place along the coast, he got a job that, at first, I wouldn't take because it was a bar waiter's job–you know, the guy with an apron carrying a tray with drinks and ice cream cups under the sun to clients in swimsuits lounging on the terrace overlooking the beach–no, not for me. I was too proud (and an idiot). Yet, he was making five times what I was making.

What was different between them and me?

In hindsight, I think that there were two main differences. First, I was a pushover. I know, surprising for those who know me today. Call it shy or quiet, but the result was that I would rather quit the job than argue with the owner for what I thought was unfair pay. The second reason that I ended up with sub-par gigs or jobs was my superficial view on the fit between my personality, my skill set, my views on the restaurant trade, and my perception of what a good job and a bad job was.

You see, when you go to a vocational school to learn to be a waiter, and when you're 14 or 15 years old, you're influenced by your professors' views. I was not going to rebel or have my own views because of who I was. I took it all in and internalized my professors' views as my own. Thus, a good waiter's job was in a good restaurant, regardless of pay. A good restaurant meant one that has a Maître d', white tablecloths, a menu that looks fancy to my parents, a good reputation. A bad restaurant would be one that was on the side of a high-traffic road, a "routier" in French, where truckers and door-to-door salesmen would eat lunch, or worse, a "café," where the main attraction was horse race betting while drinking wine at the counter, with the occasionally ordered ham and butter sandwich (the famous "jambon-beurre").

In today's America, the equivalent of bad places to work in the eyes of public opinion, would be in a fast food or in a night club. No parent wants that for their kids and no kid who listens to their parents want that either, unless they're the rebellious kind.

Yet, all my gigs and summer jobs taught me things that shaped me for the rest of my adult life. (Warning: I use a lot of marketing metaphors because, as a good Marketing Professor, I know that "marketing is everything and everything is marketing.")

1. You are the product. What I mean is that the person trying to hire you has as many preconceived ideas as you have. You need to anticipate that and present yourself in the best light to them. You are the product.

2. You are not the only product on the shelf. Yes, you are in competition with many other job seekers. You need to be special, different, unique, better–all of the above–in order to stand out and be picked, or at least pass the five second selection that is bound to happen at each level of the selection process (read "Blink" by Malcolm Gladwell).

3. Jobs aren't going to knock on your door. Yes, some parents are going to be more involved than others (right or wrong) and send you job advertisements they think you should apply to or talk to their friends about offering you a job. That's fine, and can even benefit you, but it's not going to make you stronger in the long run. Looking for that job yourself is what you've got to do. It's a jungle out there. You have just stepped out of the reality survival show's pickup truck on the side of a dirt road and your mission is to get through the jungle and survive, because the job is on the other side of it. Good luck!

Gen Z POV: "I would have never planned on being in that job, but in terms of getting it, it was because of networking. Networking a lot through friends. I found opportunities and places where I could talk to people, and I am a fairly social person, so I did not use much of the professional network like LinkedIn. It was, in the end, a family friend that got me that job, so it was a different type of networking."

You are the Product

You are the product. This is the first thing you need to understand. Employers see you as a mean to get things done. You are the resource in human resource before you are the human. They need skills and productivity, but they also want the right fit. Fitting in the organization is a matter of skills, but more importantly, a matter of personality, attitude, and look. Yes, look. Just like a box of cereals. You are going to be picked from the grocery store shelf because: (a) you are at eye level and consumers are lazy and people of habit; (b) your packaging is flashy ('cause that's what consumers like for a cereal box), but it is more (or differently) flashy than the competitors' brand next to you; (c) the price is right; and, finally, (d) the product in the box is to your liking.

So, what does it mean for you?

A. Being at eye level is the equivalent for a job seeker to having a good online presence and a timely response to job offers.

B. Having a flashy packaging for a job seeker does not mean having a flashy suit and a very elaborate résumé. It actually means the opposite in most cases. You need to be dressed in a narrow understanding of conservative. Your résumé needs to be professional looking in some predetermined "Word" format (See Chapter 8).

C. The price is right. That means that you need to know what to ask for as a salary and you need to know what the job pays so that you might or might not negotiate. Check out Salary.com.

D. The product is to your liking. Here we are talking about the skillset. You need to have the skills the job asks for (but not as much as you think; more on this later) and you need the right personality. This is often determined during the interview and is confirmed during your probationary period. Employers talk about "fit".

You are the product. Ok. But what need are you fulfilling? Cereals are for breakfast (although many would argue you can eat cereal all day). They fulfill the basic need of providing nutrients and giving you energy (and heart disease, cholesterol, diabetes, obesity, etc.). The job you are seeking is going to give you a way to make a living and buy those expensive cereals. Viewed from the other side, the side of the consumer, i.e., the recruiter, you are the product that will solve their problem. They need more workers to produce more stuff, or they need to replace a worker who has left. In that sense you should think about the type of job that you are best for, given the type of worker you are. It takes two to tango (I know, I repeat myself). What are you best at? What skills do you have? What flexibility do you have in terms of re-location, hours to work? What salary expectations do you have?

When I started to work, I did not have a car, nor did I have a driver's license. So, for me jobs had to have access to public transportation, other-wise, I had to ask my parents to drive me to work and pick me up. Not too cool for a [INSERT YOUR AGE] year old. Yet, they did it a few times–thank you mom and dad but drop me off at the curb down the road, please.

Eventually, I got a driver's license and a car. That's independence. The fight was no longer how to get to work, and where to look for a job. The fight was to leave home and having to watch your mom on the sidewalk waving you off to that job far, far, away in another galaxy.

How far are you willing to go for a job? Is the world your play-ground?

Understanding the Consumers and the Competition

Picture yourself in a very large pool (still a marketing metaphor, but with a little hospitality twist). In the center is a bar. You are thirsty. The bartender rings the last drink bell. You are swimming with an-other 1,000 thirsty friends. At the center of the pool is some kind of gateway to another pool where the bar is located. That pool is smaller and the water is warmer. To get there you need to swim faster than your 999 friends and maybe elbow your way through the small gateway. When you get into the smaller warmer pool, a bartender is in the center of that smaller pool and you and nine new friends are now trying to get the bartender's attention for that last drink.

The job market is like that pool you are in. Lots of people are there. And just a few lucky ones can make it to the interview (the bar). Yet, an even smaller number will get the bartender's attention, i.e., will get the recruiter to notice, remember, and select you. So, what do you need to do? You know you are a good "product." But, before you figure out how to market yourself, you need to understand the market, that is the competition and the recruiter.

The Competition

In the marketplace there is you and there are the others that want the same thing you want. The pool analogy. A lot of people want to get to the bar, but only a few will. And out of the few that get to the bar, only one will get the attention of the bartender. You want it to be you. Knowing your competition means that you need to understand who is going to apply for that job. Yes, more likely than not, people like you will apply since you are applying. That part is easy. Look at your peers in school. Look at the students in your class. They will all apply to your job (I call it your job even though you don't have it yet, but that is the attitude you need to have. It is your job to get). You need to know their strengths and weaknesses. The second layer of people that will apply to your job are the people that graduated last year and the years before. What? Yes! These people are not happy in their current jobs and they want to move. Whatever the reason, there will be more seasoned, more experienced applicants to your job than you. That's your competition. Forget the overqualified applicants and the very experienced ones, they have less of a shot than you at that entry level job.

The Recruiter (The Consumer in the Analogy)

In the cereals analogy the recruiter is the consumer. The recruiter has a clear (not always) idea of the job requirements. What skills are needed, what type of job seeker experience would be required, what other jobs and responsibilities should the job seeker have, what diplomas or certifications, and, while not legal, most recruiters have in mind a particular age range, gender, and other nonverbal clues (e.g., the way you dress, the way you look) in mind that they try to guess from your résumé and online presence, then confirm during the interview. Ideally, the right job seeker looks like the other co-workers, but not always. Some nontraditional firms like diversity not only because it is politically correct, but also because they truly believe that it makes a difference in terms of creativity, synergy, teamwork, and more. Most companies tend to be more conservative and hire "people like them." In the 80s the IBM person had a certain look, a certain navy-blue suit, a certain winning attitude. We all have seen movies where the FBI agent looks the part. Think Sandra Bullock in *Miss Congeniality,* or Will Smith in *Men in Black.* Today we picture someone working in Silicon Valley and any tech firm to look more like Justin Long in the ad, "I'm a PC; I'm a Mac." Untucked, unbuttoned shirt over slacks, maybe even a T-shirt, and a hoodie. This is all fine and dandy, but most recruiters don't expect that. They want you to be more in the middle. For you guys, that means a suit, dress shoes, shirt and tie, clean shave, no jewelry, no apparent tattoos. For you ladies, that means a suit, or a blouse and skirt, dress shoes with either a small or no heel, and discrete make-up (I mean wear what makes you confident but stay away from looking like you are going clubbing after the interview) and a little amount of jewelry or accessories, no apparent tattoos.

In other words, you need to look like FBI agents, minus the gun and the shades. That goes for any job, from McDonald's to Facebook. Ok, there are certainly exceptions, but don't really count on those. More likely than not it is safer to have the recruiter say: "you know, next time we see each other you can lose the tie; we are a business casual type of place," than not say anything at all and not call you back because you showed up without a tie (believe me, I know, I did that as a recruiter).

The recruiter will judge you in a matter of a seconds and in two distinctive phases. First, your résumé (and online presence). Second, your interview. Each phase is an elimination game. It is the first pool to the gateway of the middle pool (i.e., the résumé and online presence); then it is the interview phase where you get a pass to the next phase, or you get passed over. See Figure 1.

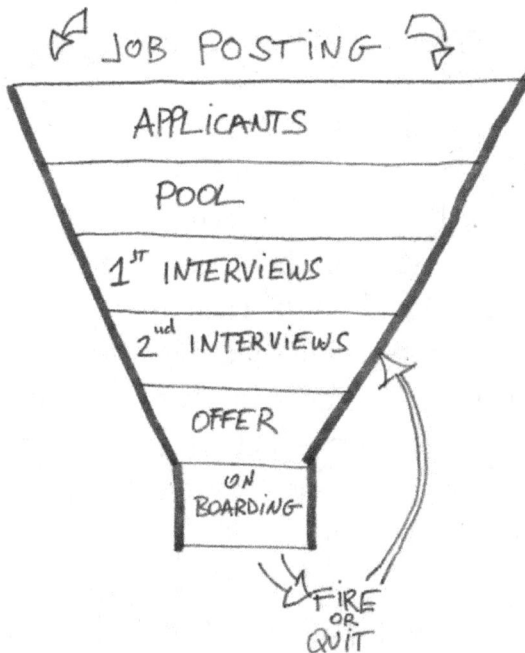

Figure 1   The job search pipeline/funnel (from the recruiter's point of view)

Bottom line: you are in a strategic game competing against other similar contenders for the one prize, that holy grail you are after; the iron throne can be yours, winter is coming and you are ready to take down your opponents (enough with the mythical fantasy drama analogy, you get the point). Yet, again, don't get fixated on that one job. There are many jobs, and you should not put "all your eggs in the same basket," right?

Market Yourself

I don't know if you realize, but in the pool example you start with a pretty good chance of 10 in 1,000 or 1 in 100 to making it to the bar. Then, once you're at the bar, your chances are even better at 1 in 10. The combined probability of you making it through in that situation is 1 in 1,000 [foot note: combined probabilities of events that depend on each other need to be multiplied, so [10/1,000] x [1/10] or 0.01 x 0.1 = 0.001 or 1 in 1,000]. Not the best odds, huh? Therefore, you need to apply to a lot more than just one job. It is a numbers game. Just like a door-to-door salesman, or any other marketer for that matter, you need leads, lots of them, and you need to call on them one after the other despite the frustration that a large amount of rejections will trigger. Remember that even the best athletes make it more or less "only" 30% of the time. Beyoncé faced rejection 46 times when she was nominated for a Grammy, but she's still considered one of the greatest singers and performers of all time. Whether it's losing to Taylor Swift for best album of the year, or losing three-pointers in basketball, or strikes in baseball, 70% of the time the best athletes fail. Don't be afraid of failing. That means, expect to get rejected a lot. That's OK. Just focus on getting your quota of applications every day and every week.

Focusing on Getting your Quota

Assume that each business receives 1,000 applications for each job they advertise. And assume that your chance of making it to the interview is fair (meaning not biased in any way). That means that you have more or less the same chance as the other 999 applicants of being selected. Now, how do you increase your chances? How do you make it an unfair game for your opponents? How do you tilt the odds in your favor? Several strategies could be applied.

1. It's a numbers game. As a rule of thumb, set yourself a goal of ten applications per week (that's a minimum) for four weeks. That will allow you to test the market response. For instance, if out of your forty applications you get twenty rejections, nineteen "nothing" (i.e., the company does not even send rejection letters/emails), and one interview followed by a "thank you, but we have hired someone with a better fit" type of rejection, then you've got something. I know, it is not a job, but it is something. Read on. The point is to apply until you get an interview. That is step one. "Why should I care if I don't get the job anyways?" You should care because you now have somewhat of a beginning of a pipeline [note: a pipeline and the funnel are the same basic concepts]. You know that it takes forty applications to get one interview. You can increase the precision of that trial by either increasing your weekly applications, say 100 applications per week, or running your experiment with forty applications per week for eight weeks instead of four weeks. In the end, you get a probability (a percentage) of getting an interview based on the time and number of applications. You have transformed a process of hope into a scientific

machine (yeah!). See Table 1 and try your own pipeline with the worksheet in Table 2.

Now, think about the interview process. Maybe you get interviews where you get no feedback. And you get other interviews where you get feedback like, "you are one of our top contenders," or, "it is between you and another candidate," or, "we hired someone else." Whatever the case, treat a feedback as a better interview than the one with no feedback. If you get ten interviews and three give you positive feedback but no job, then you could say that you were a better "fit" in three out of ten, or 30%, of the interviews.

Being a better fit is what you want. One of these interviews is going to land you that job. Thus, the more the better.

Put it all into a pipeline/funnel format (see example Table 1), then work it backwards. You are going to set yourself a goal of 10 interviews with positive feedback. You want to do that over several weeks. You believe that once you get 10 interviews with positive feedback, then one of these will become a job offer. How many interviews do you need? Well, if a third of all 1st interviews are positive, as in the example, then to get 10 of these you need 30 interviews all together. How many applications will get you 30 interviews? If 400 applications get you nine 1st interviews, then to get 30 interviews you need 1,332 applications. 30 (your goal) divided by 9 (your experiment result) is 3.33. Thus, you will need 3.33 times more applications than in your experiment. 3.33 x 400 = 1,332 (easy, right?). In Table 1 you can see that to get 1 job offer it took 400 applications, thus if you have a goal to get 2 job offers, then working backward, you would need 800 applications. It's a numbers game. Now it is your turn. Use the worksheet in Table 2 to record your successes with getting interviews and set yourself a goal for interviews with a thank you, and a goal for job offers.

2. Time is of the essence. How fast do you think you should answer an application? Put yourself in the company's shoes. What is the human resources manager or recruiter thinking? They probably want to get a feel for the quantity and quality of applications within a few days, and let the ad run for a week, sometimes more, then start the selection process. So, you have a week. On the other hand, you have limited time yourself. Maybe you are working on some other project, maybe you are finishing school. Maybe it's finals week. Who knows? The point is that if you open your favorite job posting website (think Indeed or Monster) and you see 100 jobs that fit your profile, how many should you apply to today? The answer is 100. Time is of the essence and it's a numbers game, remember?

> *Gen Z POV: "I had like 47 interviews. I'd say work your connections. I got my job through a guy I connected with on LinkedIn. One day I was driving, and he contacted me, and we talked for a little while; then one thing led to another and I told him I was looking to make a move, and he said ok we have a couple different positions, and that's how that happened."*

3. Position yourself for success. Positioning is what brands use to "own" an idea in your mind that gets associated with their brand. It allows brands to be unique or different than the competition in the mind of the consumers. You know what Walmart's positioning is? "Everyday Low Price." We know

that because of the constant advertising and in-store displays. You can probably figure out the positioning of McDonald's, BMW, Nike, and many other brands. What is your positioning? How do you get one? Why would you want one? I often see students, seniors mostly, creating their LinkedIn profiles and connecting with me in the last weeks of school, or even the first week after commencement. That level of procrastination in itself is problematic as we saw that it will take many applications to land an interview. But equally problematic is the positioning that these students advertise on their profiles. I often see no picture, or if there is a picture, it is a recycled picture with someone cropped out (sometimes not even cropped out). Sometimes I see the student in full regalia, robe, and mortarboard. LinkedIn is a professional website that acts as your online "augmented" résumé. It is your résumé, but it is also a way to network with other users. In that sense, it is a social network of professionals. You can do many more things on LinkedIn such as post updates, search the network, create groups of interests, and more. Keep it professional. Would you go to an interview in regalia? No. Then don't post that picture. Would you go to an online interview and not have your camera on? No. You need and you want the interviewer to see you.

Table 1: Job Search Pipeline/Funnel Example

	Weeks	# of Applications submitted	# of Rejections received	# of 1st Interviews	# of Thank You emails received	# of 2nd Interviews	# of Thank You emails received	# of Offers received
Example	1	40	2					
	2	40	5					
	3	40	4	1				
	4	40	8		1			
	5	40	8	2	1			
	6	40	2					
	7	40	5	2		1		
	8	40	6	4	1			1
	9	40	4					
	10	40	0					
Total		400	44	9	3	1	0	1
If you want 2 job offers, how many applications?		800	←------------					2

Table 2: Job Search Pipeline/Funnel Worksheet

Weeks	# of Applications made	# of Rejections received	# of 1st Interviews	# of Thank You emails received	# of 2nd Interviews	# of Thank You emails received	# of Offers received
Your turn 1							
2							
3							
4							
5							
6							
7							
8							
9							
10							
Total							
If you want X job offers, how many applications?							

Gen Z POV: "Usually when I get a LinkedIn request for internships or jobs I usually go on their profile. I have reached out to a few people and gave them suggestions on how to improve it. 'Cause some people have a very plain, and not appealing LinkedIn, and I think it's very important. It's basically your résumé nowadays."

Another one of my pet peeves on LinkedIn is what is called the profile headline what shows just under your picture and name, and the "about" section, which includes a few lines explaining who you are (i.e., your positioning) to the reader. I see students' headlines that say: "student at [blank] University," more often than not. Sometimes it is "seeking a job in business." My advice is to write something that tells the reader/recruiter who you are, but definitely not that you are a student. First, we are always all students of something, so let the recruiter figure out if you are a junior or a senior or if you're out of school. They can do it by looking at your education and having that fact so obvious and up front might be a negative when it comes to screening applicants quickly. Remember that the recruiter will have 1,000 applications to go through in one week. You do not want your otherwise perfect application to be discarded because of some perception issue, whether it's right or wrong. You are not a "student at [blank] University," you are not "seeking a position in business;" you are a "Digital Marketing Specialist" (you can substitute that title for whatever fits for you). Now, be careful and don't overdo it. The positioning statement needs to fit the bill. What I mean is that your picture, how old (read experienced) you look, and your positioning statement need to be coherent. McDonald's' "I'm lovin' it" fits because you see young people smiling and enjoying their McDonald's meals at the same time that you hear the Justin Timberlake jingle. I see twenty-year-old something pictures of folks with positioning such as "sales expert". That might come across as a little cocky.

> *Gen Z POV: "Make sure your LinkedIn header is not, like, active student or student seeking a job."*

In the "about" text box write something that differentiates you from the other "Digital Marketing Specialist" (or whatever job you are going for). For example, what you achieved at your internship, or what school clubs you're a part of, or what certifications you've earned. I know that these might be repeats from your actual résumé but think about the recruiter. They are looking at the first page of your LinkedIn "above the fold" (the first page showing without scrolling down). That is your opportunity to give a really good elevator pitch that will trigger interest so that the interviewer will scroll down and read the facts of your experience, education, interests, etc. You won't have another shot at it. So, something like "Data-Driven Digital Marketer with four years of experience building an integrated digital marketing strategy with a specialization in paid search, website analytics, and market research" or "Experienced Sales Manager with a demonstrated history of working in the luxury hospitality segment," will lure the reader into wanting more information and, thus, scrolling down your page.

> *Gen Z POV: "Treat LinkedIn like your most prized social media. Be active, comment/like peoples' posts. Engagement is key; try and build virtual relationships. Always reply to recruiters, even if you're letting them know you're not interested. Recruiters can see your response rate/percentage of you responding. Don't miss out on an opportunity because a recruiter decides not to reach out due to your low response percentage. You should at least be browsing/skimming LinkedIn once a day."*

How should your résumé read? Do you need one? Yes, you do need one; it needs to be in a PDF format, and it needs to be ready to be emailed. Create it with a simple Word format, then save it as PDF. It needs to have the same content more or less than your profile on LinkedIn. The dates of employment do not need to be precise to the month or day. You can say "2019-2020" even if you worked from June 2019 to February 2020. You will be giving the exact information if needed when you get to fill out your formal application. The "formal" in formal application is where you do not want to "puff" or embellish reality. On LinkedIn or your résumé, it's not a big deal. Treat that as a positioning statement, a piece of advertising to get you to the next level whether it is an interview or that second interview with the decision maker. For the love of god do not list your GPA. That serves no purpose. It is schoolish. We get it, you got a gold star, but unless you were on the Dean's List or Latin Honors, there's no need to say my GPA is 3.86.

What format should you use for your résumé? Can you be creative? Unless you are in some kind of artform industry, I suggest sticking to black and white, 12-point font, Word template-style résumé. You can get a little creative with the font, maybe use Garamond instead of Times New Roman, for instance. Clarity and the use of proper key words early on in the résumé is paramount to the recruiter who is battling getting through 1,000 résumés before their deadline. As a rule of thumb, you should have action words (i.e., created, managed, achieved) and a short description of your achievements. What have you done at this internship that was different or impactful?

Now, not all jobs are for you. You have to target your efforts. The same way the recruiter is targeting a certain profile of applicants, you need to target certain jobs and/or companies. Most of the time, this won't be a problem. For instance, if you are a business major graduating with a Bachelor's Degree in Marketing, any job that needs a "marketer" is good for you. Maybe you want to think about that twice. For example, a door-to-door sales job or a lead generation (cold calling) job might not be for you. A digital marketing job might be for you, but a branding job might be what you want. Should you look for jobs that are offered by small companies employing less than ten people? Or should you look for jobs at very large companies where there are 500 employees or more? The two companies' profiles will be very different and your career (See Chapter 2) might be very different as well.

Let's assume that you know what kind of company you want to work for and what kind of job and job description you believe your skills will best serve. It is a good idea to show that you are targeting these job offers by adapting or arranging your communication based on the job ad content and company website. For instance, if your résumé shows two or three bullet points of achievements for a particular job, then position the first bullet, which will be read first, to be the most relevant achievement based on the job ad text. If the job is looking for a social media manager, and part of what you have done in your previous job is managing the Twitter account, then put that first. You can also do the same thing on LinkedIn in the "about" box where you can position yourself as more of a social media manager.

The place where you will be able to really position yourself exactly like the job ad is in the cover letter, or email, you will send with your résumé or application. That letter needs to hit all of the points in the job ad and how they relate to your experience. It is crucial that the recruiter gets a sense that: (1) you have read the ad; (2) you fit the profile; and, (3) you have achieved something in at least some of the requirements of the job (i.e., you are not just a graduating student with no experience).

You positioned yourself well, you targeted all job postings that match your skills and interests. You've submitted 100 applications a week for several weeks. You just got your first interview. Now what?

The Interview

Think of the interview as a seduction opportunity. The company is trying to show you their best angle so that you will accept the job at the conditions they are ready to offer, if you are selected. And you are trying to show your best angle as you want to be remembered and selected for the next round, be it a second interview or a job offer.

There are three phases in an interview. First, you only make a first impression once. Within the first few seconds of the initial meet and greet, the interviewer will have an impression of yourself, whether it's positive or negative. It will be based on nonverbal cues such as your look, hair style, face, dress, posture, but it's also about the first physical encounter such as the way you stand up and walk towards them, the handshake, and the way you sit in the interviewing room.

Your hair is not quite groomed or looks as if you're going out for a night on the town. Your dress is not conservative enough. You sit on the edge of the chair. You are slouching, you are keeping your briefcase or handbag close to you, you look around with big eyes, you look down. You stand up in an awkward way as if your legs were sleepy. You stand up too fast showing how nervous you are. You walk too slow or too fast toward the recruiter, and your handshake is either too hard or too soft. You follow your interviewer too closely, or you do not know if you should get into the office first, second, or wait until you're asked to sit. In a word, you are awkward. It is clear that this is your first interview. You are not the confident, assertive Digital Marketing Specialist that was advertised on LinkedIn. You aren't "on brand." There is a disconnect between your positioning, your image, and the real you. So, get feedback, tape yourself, practice. It is just like being on stage playing a role. The role of yourself confident and assertive.

The second part of the interview is the "meat and potatoes" of the interview. It is what you have prepared for (hopefully). Questions are fired at you by the interviewer and you reply to them the best you can. The problem is that you did not anticipate these questions. For instance, the interviewer asks you tell them about yourself, or they ask: "If I would ask your best friend (or colleagues or boss) to describe your strengths and weaknesses what would they say?" What you prepared for is to recite your résumé and to fill in the blanks when necessary. What you should be prepared for is to sell yourself. You should be able to sell yourself to someone in the time it takes to take an elevator from one floor to the next. The proverbial "elevator pitch". For each job you had you need to have an example of what you have achieved and how it contributed to the success of the company you work for. For instance: "In my current job I manage the social media pages, which includes creating and posting ads, answering customer comments, boosting previous posts," and then quickly add, "for example, I did a campaign that had a goal to get 200 new likes and....[explain what you did]."

Handling negative questions or questions that ask about your weaknesses is not very complicated, although it can be disarming. The recruiter might ask: "Tell me about your weaknesses," or "Tell me about a problem you had in your previous job and how you handled it." The first question is easy, and a little "cliché" these days, but some recruiters might still ask. You basically have no weaknesses. Right? Wrong, everyone has weaknesses. So, pick something that could be seen as a strength as well. For instance: "I was told that I am a perfectionist once. I spend too much time on a task and maybe I should know when it is good enough." If you feel up to showing a little more vulnerability, then pick a weakness of yours and tell the recruiter how you are working on bettering yourself. Just don't be too critical of yourself. As for the second question, it is an opportunity for you to be specific about how you handle roadblocks. Keep in mind that the recruiter wants you to describe an issue that is not too small—"I misplaced my stapler once (*office space*, anyone?)"–but, not too big or unbelievable—"I was facing bankruptcy and the Feds were closing in on me." Something like: "I had to tell my boss that the project was not advancing as fast as we thought. So, I procrastinated a few days, and then took my courage, and told my boss. She was a little mad at first, but it was not a last-minute type of conversation, and we still had time to fix things. My boss helped me think about a different strategy to meet the deadline, and in the end we did it." Or, "We had an issue with too many customers coming to the restaurant during brunch, which created service issues. So, I thought about it and I proposed an idea to simply inform customers that peak hours were from 12-12:30pm, and that if they could arrive a little earlier or later, they would be served faster. That did relieve some of the pressure at the peak time and worked out well." In the first issue/solution you are saying that you know your limits and know when to ask for help in order to meet company deadlines; in the second issue/solution you are showing that when confronted with a problem you are creative. So, in the end it is all positive for you! So, be prepared and have some examples ready in case you are asked. Be a good actor, and do not answer the questions too eagerly, showing that you had prepared. Instead, be smart and fake a little surprise by the questions.

The third part of the interview is where you have the opportunity to ask questions. It goes without saying that before the interview you need to do your homework. You need to go on the company's website, search for recent news, look at the employees' profiles on LinkedIn and be prepared to ask questions. These questions should not be idiotically obvious such like: "What is your company doing?" or, "Do you have locations in [fill in the blank]?" But rather, they should be related to your field of work or your future responsibilities. When in doubt, read the job ad again. More than likely, it lists all of the information you need. For instance, if the ad said: "As a social media coordinator, we expect you to be up-to-date with the latest digital technologies and social media trends. You should have excellent communication skills and be able to express our practice views creatively. Ultimately, you should be able to successfully manage our social media presence. Ensuring high levels of social traffic and patient engagement." Then you could ask clarifying questions that should show your interest in understanding the particular "problem" the company faces and propose solutions that "only" you could offer. "I see in your ad that I will be (assume you have the job) managing the social media presence. I looked at your presence on Facebook, Twitter, and Instagram (because you did your homework), but I didn't see much presence on LinkedIn. Would I be expected to create a presence on LinkedIn?" or, "Your ad talks about "patient engagement." What constitutes good and high levels of patient engagement for you?"

If you feel inquisitive, use questions that are about the interviewer him or herself. Try: "what do you like most about your company/job? That will definitely put the light on the interviwer and show that you are skilled at interviewing and motivated to get that job and fit within the company.

What about salary talks during interviews? It depends. If you are at interview #1, don't ask. If the recruiter does ask you: "what are your salary expectations?" it is a trap to see if you are out of the company's range, so do not answer a number. Rather answer something like: "depending on the responsibilities and goals I am thinking that somewhere between $30,000 and $50,000 will be fine." Give some range based on your research about what the job pays. See Salary. com. If you are at interview #2, then that is a different case. You have passed the elimination game. So, you need to sell yourself and ask for the maximum you think the job pays. Say you figure that it is $50,000. You can say: "given my experience and the responsibilities of this job I think that $50,000 will be an acceptable level of compensation." The recruiter might say: "we were thinking something more like $40,000." You are negotiating. So now depending on how flexible (desperate) you are you might say: "$40,000 could work for me depending on other benefits. For instance, can you tell me about potential for growth within the company? Or tuition reimbursement if I pursued a Master's?" Or maybe: "$40,000 is much lower than I had in mind for the level of responsibilities of this position; however, if you are willing to meet me in the middle, considering all other benefits the company is offering, I think that could work." You get the point.

Before you leave the interview, it is perfectly ok to say something like: "Thank you for your interest in me and your time today. Can I ask about the process? Will there be a second round of interviews? Besides yourself is there another decision maker? When will you be making a decision?" Asking any one of these questions shows your interest, but make sure you don't overdo it.

Today, more likely than not, you will have an online interview (think Zoom, WebEx, Skype) as your first interview. What does it mean in relation to what we just said? Not much. Everything is pretty much the same, with some obvious, or not so obvious (from my experience), differences. For instance, you will be judged on your appearance and the appearance of your background. Your appearance needs to be professional (we just talked about that), but so does your background. Do not interview in your bedroom, or if you do, make sure it does not appear as a bedroom. Change the camera angle so that the sun through the window is not behind you, that the lighting is not too low or too bright, and that the wall behind you is either empty or sends the proper message. For instance, if you have shelves behind you, then the books and knickknacks on the shelves should tell your story the way you want to tell it. No Star Wars Chewbacca doll next to a Mexican Painted Skull ashtray or worse, some home-made bong. No angle that shows the ceiling. If you can use a virtual background, do it. Yet, be careful because if you do not have a green screen, then the background software will cut off some of your head, your hand, or something. Best to try that with a friend first and to record the session so you can see how you look. If you are doing an online interview you also want to make sure that the room you are in is going to be quiet, meaning that you wouldn't hear your neighbor mowing their lawn, you wouldn't have any interruptions from your mom asking you a question while barging into the room, or that kids wouldn't come into the room unannounced during the interview. You obviously need to test the camera, microphone, and speakers ahead of time. Disable all sound alerts from your emails and social media that will pollute the interview at random times.

Another pet peeve of mine is the business suit. I see a lot of interviewees take a more business-casual approach in this video conference setting than I see in face-to-face settings. I assume it is because when you are at home, you feel that the interview is more relaxed–don't. You need to take the interview seriously whether it's in person or virtual; you're still making the same first impression. Finally, make sure you have a good Wi-Fi connection. Don't blame your failed interview on your bad Wi-Fi. Nobody cares. If you do not have good Wi-Fi, get good Wi-Fi. Last resort, go to the Starbucks and sit in your car, use a virtual background, and pretend you are at home. Whatever it takes.

After the Interview - Thank You

It looks a little fake, but you need to do it. It is proper etiquette to send a thank you email (I have seen handwritten cards, which I think are too much) after the interview. Don't be too laconic or too talkative. Personalize the thank you as much as you can. A simple "Dear Mrs. Smith (don't use their first name; and use their title if the recruiter is a Doctor, as in Dear Dr. Smith), Thank you very much for the opportunity to interview for the Digital Marketing Specialist position at your company (maybe Mrs. Smith does many interviews and will not remember you or the job you interviewed for). I enjoyed our conversation and learning about the company. I am very interested by the position. *Here is the paragraph where you would personalize and bring it back to your résumé and skills.* I particularly enjoyed our exchange on the metrics you used to gauge customers' engagement and I believe that my HubSpot certification and my current experience in the area will allow me to help the company achieve its goals. Do not hesitate to contact me if you have any further questions. I look forward to hearing from you in the near future. Best regards, [your name, email address, phone number, link to your LinkedIn profile]." Be careful in using the correct spelling of names! I have seen thank you emails that misspelled my name, title, or company. That is a no-no for me. Perception is reality. If you are sloppy with a simple task, you will be sloppy with a big one.

Is it ok to email if you do not hear anything from the recruiter? I say yes. If the recruiter said that a decision would be made in two weeks, then two weeks later, if you have not heard anything, send an email. Something like: "Dear Mrs. Smith, I wanted to reach out to you to find out if you have been able to fill the Digital Marketing Specialist position for the company. I wanted to let you know that I am still very interested by the position. Best Regards, [your name, email address, phone number, link to your LinkedIn profile]." Either Mrs. Smith has made an offer to someone else, and she might tell you "thank you, but no thank you." Or she has made an offer but will want to keep you "warm" in case the offer is rejected. In that case, you are at the "top of their mind" and might actually make it back to the short list (See the pipeline in Figure 1). Or the job is still open, and by showing your interest strongly, you might make the cut. Ok, you might also see that in a negative nagging way; however, if you send one reminder email, that should be enough, and you've already done more than most of the other candidates.

Chapter 1 Appendix: Questions for an Interview (in no particular order)

For each of the following questions, reflect on what you will say during the interview. Prepare by brainstorming and make sure you think of examples that are positive and make you look good, even when describing difficulties and failures you have encountered. After all, you are perfect for that job!

- Why do you want this job?
- Why should we hire you?
- Tell us about yourself.
- Describe a time where you had to learn a new skill.
- What accomplishment are you most proud of?
- How do you deal with stressful situations?
- Why do you want to work in this field?
- What are your goals?
- What are your strengths?
- What is a weakness of yours?
- Describe a time you disagreed with a teammate or a supervisor.
- Tell us about a time you failed.
- What specific skill set do you bring to this job?
- What type of people annoy you?
- What kind of culture are you looking for in a company?
- Describe a time when you stepped out of your comfort zone.
- Tell us about a time you planned and accomplished a challenging goal.
- When have you had many tasks to accomplish and a short amount of time to accomplish them?
- Do you value creativity or efficiency more?

- How do you set priorities or manage time?
- Do you prefer to work alone or on a team?
- How would your best friend describe you?
- Do you have any questions for us?

CHAPTER 2

Pursue a Career

"Life is a journey, not a destination."

I got my first "real" job after I graduated with an Associate's Degree from a hotel management school in Bordeaux, France (yes, that's where you can drink fantastic wines). The job was in a Palace Hotel, in Versailles of all places. A Palace is a luxury hotel. Famous people would stay there. Everything was fine china, silver, flamboyant flower arrangements, and oil paintings on the walls. I was a cashier. I know what you're thinking: Associate's Degree - cashier; it doesn't make sense. Well, it didn't for me either, but not for the same reasons you might think. First, an Associate's Degree in France in hotel management was the norm. Out of a vocational school, the highest degree you could get was an Associate's Degree. I was very proud of it knowing that I had failed middle school and went to vocational right off the bat. I had to pull myself up by the bootstraps in order to slowly climb the different levels of vocational school and cross all of the educational bridges that allowed a guy like me to "make it" to the top, albeit a small "top." In France, once you fail regular school, you're kind of doomed. Folks and the system they've created, label you, making it so that you can't really get anywhere. So, for me to have been able to navigate that system, made me proud of myself, even maybe a tad cocky (a lot, actually). Yet, all I could get for a job was that of a cashier–not an Accountant, not a Cost Controller, not a Manager, not an Assistant Manager, not even an Assistant to the Manager (*The Office*, anyone?). A cashier in France is a person that would type menus on an old typewriter (think Tom Hanks typewriter collection old) and print them in mass quantities with an even older reprographic machine (the Neanderthal relative to the photocopy machine). The process is a little difficult. You first had to type the menu on the typewriter and center it (those of you who have done that can sympathize; for you youngsters, though, I know you don't get it). You had to use parchment paper (bible style), so that the typed text would puncture the paper, and thus you could then use the reprographic machine to ink the menus through the paper-typed holes. For its time this was antiquated, big time. But that was the way they were doing things in that hotel since World War I (and before). I say WWI because the Treaty of Versailles between Germany and France and its Allies was negotiated – dictated – by Clemenceau (check your history books) in the main ballroom of that hotel. A plaque hung commemorating the event. Accounting was done manually in books using red pencil for deductions and blue pencil for additions. Anyway, I am not this old...really. After typing and printing the menus of the day, the job of the cashier was to sit at the entrance of the restaurant where the cash register was and wait for the waiters to bring their menu order sheets so that the bill could be started. Once everything was added to the bill, the waiter would collect payment and the cashier would close the bill, give change, if needed, and then close out the entire lunch, or dinner, or afternoon tea cashing process by reconciling the cash, credit card stubs, and checks. After lunch I would have a break until 6pm before dinner started. I loved the place, the people, the smell of fame and riches. But my job sucked. I was bored out of my mind.

Would I see myself here for the next ten years? Even five? What could I do after that job? There was no "chief cashier" position for me to have.

I started looking for other things to do, and naturally I wanted to prove to the Hotel General Manager that I was a valuable employee with ideas and motivation to change things up. As any 20 something, I thought I knew it all and that everyone five years older than me was an idiot who didn't have a clue about the cutting-edge management techniques I had learned at school and what I was reading in business magazines and books (Yes, you need to read; it's not an activity only for the liberal art colleges).

So, I took it upon myself to write a financial report, including management insights and proposed changes to the operations that would bring more profit or more sales or both. I went to the city records to dig up financial information and I looked at the historical books at work. I did what today we call a "forensic accounting research." The results were a recreation of the balance sheets with profit and loss statements for the past several years.

Note for the non-business students: a company – more or less just like a family – has money coming in (sales for a company, salaries for a family) and money going out (expenses, salaries, taxes, rent, mortgages, interests on loans). Every year the money coming in minus the money going out is how one can find out if the company made a profit or if they had a loss. A loss is when there is more money going out than coming in. That is what you can read in the document referred to as a "profit and loss statement," or P&L for short (See Figure 2). On the other hand, the same company starts with some money and equipment before they even make their first sale. That initial money is brought in by the owners and is called "equity" and serves mainly to buy buildings and equipment needed to run the business. The value of the equipment and buildings are collectively called "the assets." On the other side of that equation resides what is called "the liabilities of the company." The liabilities are made of money owed to the banks, think mortgages and loans, and money owed to the shareholders/owners, the equity. Both sides, assets and liabilities, have to be equal. We say that they are balanced, thus, the name of that particular statement is the balance sheet (See Figure 3). This is also where we derived the term "balancing the books." When a company makes profit, the profit goes to the balance sheet as an asset in cash and is eventually given back to the owners in the form of dividends (money given to shareholders) as a reward (think of it as interest) for risking their equity. When a company has a loss, the money also goes out of cash (somebody has to pay the expenses due) and is financed by the owners having to put more equity in the business, or by a bank that will make a loan with interest to the business. Congrats! You just passed Accounting 101.

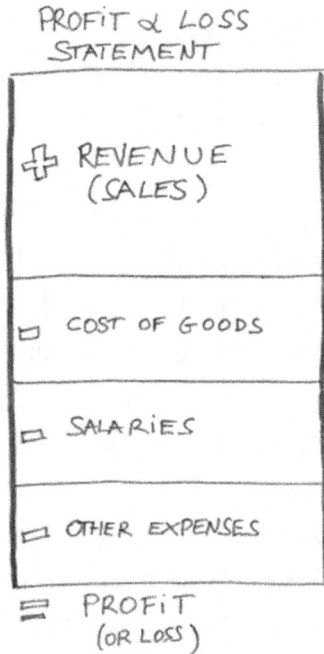

Figure 2   A Crude Profit and Loss Statement

The Palace Hotel was not a public company. Thus, they had no obligation to share financials with the public, and internally the company owners were pretty secretive, as well (the owner's representant was the brother of a past President of France). So, for me to be able to make any recommendations to management in terms of sales or profit I had to recreate the books. Which I did. Then I looked at sales and expenses and started to make an assessment and propose changes. All of that was packaged into a report that looked as official as a financial prospectus would (a prospectus is the info you get before you buy shares of a company). I slid it below the General Manager's door one night after my evening cashier's shift. Pretty lame if you ask me now. I didn't have the balls to knock on his door and say: "Mr. Bacus [not his real name], I prepared a report for your review. Please read it and let me know what you think." Nope, instead I slid the report under his door like a criminal would slide compromising pictures to ask for a ransom.

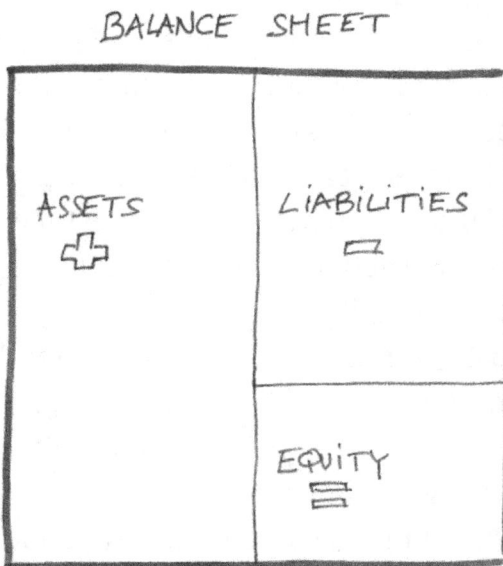

BALANCE SHEET

ASSETS

LIABILITIES

EQUITY

Figure 3   A Crude Balance Sheet Statement

The General Manager, Mr. Bacus, called me into his office the next day. He was impressed by the information I was able to recreate. He told me that he read the report very carefully and asked me how I did it. He thanked me, and that was it. Back to my job as a cashier.

At the same time, a friend of mine, who was in my same cohort at the hotel management school, had taken a Breakfast Maître d' job at a 3-star Parisian chain-owned hotel located in a touristic Montmartre area in Paris downtown, near the "red light" district. He was doing hands-on breakfast shifts managing a wait staff.

He and I had been friends since vocational school and now, we both lived in Paris. There were plenty of things to do in Paris and we were experiencing the town together. As we were exchanging our job experiences, it dawned on me that maybe my path was going to be a very long way to the top (as AC/DC would say) where his possibilities seemed endless and almost effortless. A chain of hotels grows and needs people all the time. A stand-alone hotel, palace or not, doesn't grow much. Thus, one needs to wait for someone to retire or look for a job at another hotel. That was my exact situation.

After my failed attempt at high jacking my way to a management job with my financial report, I spent my down time at the cash register thinking about my options. There was plenty of time to think at the cash register, let me tell you.

You need to know that as a 20 something, just like most of you readers, I had no fears, and I had high hopes that my goal of becoming a hotel General Manager by 30 was achievable. Others had done that before me. So, why not me?

I think it is important to give yourself goals, ambitious goals, when you are 20. When will you do that if not at 20? On the other hand, you need a dose of reality and some perspective on the context you work in to be able to set somewhat achievable goals. You need a coach, a mentor, or a hero.

What Have My Heroes Done Before Me?

I had several heroes, or mentors, who served me well when I was 20, as well as a little earlier and a little later. These people were either examples because they had been able to do what I wanted to do, or they were able to explain to me what others had done and how I should be able to do it.

I was conflicted because some of my heroes, or mentors, were successful and had achieved a high level of success in their careers, but they were very different careers. My goal at 20 was to be a hotel General Manager by 30. My cousin was a hotel owner and manager. So, I went to see him and discussed how he had achieved that. It turned out that he inherited the "pension de famille," or family inn, from his parents and ran it with his wife for the past 10 years. He was successful and would work very hard all summer long. Then, by winter, he would go on vacations that seemed expensive and adventurous like exploring the jungle of the Amazon or trekking the desert of North Africa. His inn was small, less than 20 rooms, and had a large restaurant sitting 100 customers. Most customers were regulars that would come back year after year. My cousin was the Chef and his wife was the hotel manager and the Maître d' at the same time. I did not picture myself doing that, but our conversation was really good because it helped me clarify my thoughts. Some of my school friends had done that right after graduation. They went to see a banker, and with good credit and good professional backgrounds implied by the freshly owned diploma, they got enough money to buy or lease a small-budget hotel which the couple (it was often a couple) would manage for what seemed a lifetime.

The second example I had was Mr. Bacus. He was closer to 40 than 30, but he was managing a 130-room Palace Hotel. What did he do to get there? I found out that he was a pure product of apprenticeship. He started as a busboy, then waiter, then assistant Maître d', Maître d', Food & Beverage Manager (F&B for short), deputy Hotel Manager, and finally, 20 years later, General Manager. His wife was the Housekeeping Manager. They lived in an apartment in the hotel. I could see myself managing a palace, but could I see myself "waiting" 20 years for that? No! I wanted it all, and I wanted it now! (Queen's reference, the Rock band). So, scratch that plan as well.

A third example was a hotel manager I talked to during our graduation ball. Each year the graduating cohort at the hotel school would organize a ball (buffet and dance) to celebrate their graduation, and also to raise funds to spend on a group vacation. Since the school worked only as a cohort system, the students took the same classes together for the duration of their time at school. The entire graduating cohort comes and goes every year, celebrating their rite of passage into the working life by taking a trip together. France does not have commencement ceremonies; thus, the trip serves as a sort of ritual. One of our hotel professor's husband was the general manager of a three-star hotel downtown. The hotel was part of a chain and was modern. It was a good level hotel, above the cousin's inn, but below the palace. Less amenities, a good restaurant, but not famous. Similar to a Hilton or Sheraton. A cut above your Best Western, but below your Ritz Carlton. I liked the look of that manager. I liked his suits and ties. Don't ask me why, but he embodied what it meant to be a successful businessman. He reminded me of a famous French businessman that did a lot of acquisitions and turnaround deals with companies, like Adidas. This guy was the picture of success (think of Richard Gere in *Pretty Woman*). He was the French Trump (the Trump from *The Art of Deal*). He was a celebrity, someone critically acclaimed on TV and in the News. A "winner," as Charlie Sheen would say. That hotel manager was a celebrity in my mind. The only "problem" was that he was "only" managing a three-star hotel.

I also had a mentor when I was at the palace, Mr. Lozelle. He was a Cost Controller. I did my graduate thesis on his job. The title was: "Profession: Cost Controller." I was fascinated by the way he used all of the tricks in the books to figure out which restaurant dish was most profitable, what the proper turnover of the wine cellar was, who was cheating on their cash out, if the bartender was free pouring or not (free pouring is when the bartender gives a free shot or oversized shots to a client in exchange for additional tips, i.e., s/he is using the hotel liquor to get more money; a form of theft). He took me under his wing and showed me everything. Some of the techniques I knew from school, some I discovered on my own. At the same time, he was about 30 years old, and I could not quite make out why he wasn't a general manager. He had worked for "American hotels," as he referred to the only Ramada Hotel in France, where he learned the "American cost control techniques." He was in a palace today only because profitability was the new motto for palaces. For many years, palaces were overcharging their way out of "quality," but now with the succession of oil crises and economic recessions, the bankers, also owners, demanded a little more control. So, he took the job and loved it. He was friends with the celebrity Chef and the staff respected him, mainly because they knew he could catch them should they try to pull a fast one. He told me what the best route was to become a celebrity Chef and I quickly realized that it was not going to be me. Apprenticeship starts very young, and I was already 20 years old. I should have stayed in the kitchen of a four-star restaurant starting when I was 15 years old, but that was not the case. Becoming a hotel general manager of a palace was extremely difficult as well, but doable. So why wasn't he one already? Two reasons. First, he had not climbed the food and beverage ladder. Most General Managers, like Mr. Bacus, had all been in Food and Beverage before. Very few were in Housekeeping or were Front Office Managers, and very few were Sales Managers prior to becoming a General Manager. I guess Food and Beverage is a multifaceted complex set of operations (banquets, restaurants, bars, room service), and if one is successful there, s/he can manage 80% of what's going on in the hotel. He was a Cost Controller, and that path was more on the accounting side than the operations side. He was a little sidetracked. And in palace terms, that is a difficult route to change. It is possible, but exceptional. Another friend of mine who graduated with me took that path and went from Accountant to General Manager of a Parisian palace. That is a very impressive career that took him 20 years. Mr. Lozelle's main problem, though, was that he really liked to spend time at the bar after work, which I found out when he and I went out together. That made things a little awkward to say the least.

I came down with three possible choices for my path to stardom. Should I be a budget hotel owner/manager now? Spend 20 years in a palace? Or "give up" on "quality" and settle for a "three-star chain" hotel so that I would have the option of being promoted from within? I managed to find a compromise. A four-star hotel chain in Paris was looking for a general cashier. I liked the fact that it was a four-star hotel, close to a palace, yet still a chain, implying the opportunity for promotion from within the chain. They had 20 hotels worldwide at the time, so I figured there were lots of opportunities. It was a trade off with my "standards" between quality (what I perceived) and opportunities.

What path do you have in front of you?

You have more than you think, of course. More than three. It is usually a way to reassure ourselves that we limit our choices in order to "make decisions" that seem rational. If you are a marketing major, for instance, have you put any thought into how many categories of marketers there are in business? For instance, you could be on the sales side. Becoming a Director of Sales could be a goal of yours (take a look at the movie, *Glengarry Glen Ross*). The path here might be to get a sales job, at a car dealership, in pharmaceutical products, in services, software, copiers, and so on. Then prove yourself by meeting and exceeding your allocated quotas, being a good company man, a good team player, and then maybe you will get a shot at being a Sales Manager, then Director of Sales, and why not, Vice President of Sales one day. Ray Kroc, the founder of McDonald's, was a Regional Sales Manager for a company that sold milkshake machines to fast food restaurants back in the 50s. Howard Schultz, the founder of Starbucks, was a Sales Manager for Xerox copiers before becoming a Sales Manager for a coffee machine company and then creating what Starbucks is today. Alternatively, you might not like sales, and think that you are better at branding or product development, or digital marketing, or analytics and research. Whatever the path, you need to think about it, and you need to evaluate what would motivate you to get out of bed and work hard every day.

Gen Z POV: "My first job, I can definitely say, taught me what I don't want out of a job in general, because the first job I took out of college I took because I was so excited to get a job. I thought like $35k, that's enough, to get an apartment downtown, and it was just not. It's like barely livable. But it taught me what to look for in my next job."

I suggest you write it down. I suggest you close your eyes and picture yourself in 10 years from now. Where do you see yourself? What type of life do you have? Do you have a home? How big? Where is that house?

Downtown or suburbs? Seaside or mountain? What type of car? What color? What family do you have? Picture yourself in all your glory, at 31, "being a success." What does it look like? Write it down. It could be something like: "I am 30. I live in a seaside resort town and work as a brand manager for a multinational company. I travel a lot; most of the week I am in a different state or a different country. I drive a silver Audi A6; I am not married; I golf." Put that in an envelope, seal it, and write "to be opened when I am 31" on it. Place the envelope somewhere safe.

Once you have that "vision" think about what steps you need to take on your path to success. If you want to be a Brand Manager by 30, then you have ten years to do that (assuming you are 20; if not do the math). What do you need to do before you get that manager's job? And before that? And so on. You have no clue? Ask a mentor, a professor, or look at LinkedIn profiles of people who are 30ish and are Brand Managers. What have they done? Think about what company they work for and how long they stayed until they moved to another job. Is that what you want to do? Can you do it? (See the visualization exercise at the end of this chapter)

Not too Fast, Not too Slow, Just Right

Be patient. I didn't achieve my goal of becoming a hotel General Manager by the time I was 30. Some of my school friends did, but most did not. While it made me feel like a loser, that wasn't the case. I was just a little slower, maybe a little less lucky, maybe not the right fit, maybe not at the right time or in the right place? Whatever the case, I got my first position as a General Manager at 34. So, everything panned out fairly well. Thus, my advice is not to panic and want to do things too fast. For instance, taking a job because of the title and the prestige but neglecting to see the reality of the job. Maybe the job is not going to allow you to move up further, maybe the job is not going to be as motivating as another job. But don't settle for a slow career either, unless you know that it is common practice in the industry, then maybe that's what you have to do. But, if you are in a fast-paced industry that prides itself on promoting from within and growing by double digits [double digits mean that the growth, the increase in percentage from one year to the next, has two numbers, as in 10%. 3% is single digit, 10% or 15% is double digits] every year, then you should be well positioned for a fast-paced promotion yourself.

My advice is to give yourself a little wiggle room to succeed, while taking your time or letting the chips fall, whatever you prefer. I am not saying change your goals. That would not be SMART (SMART is an acronym that stands for Specific, Measurable, Achievable, Realistic, and Timely), and will affect motivation (See Figure 4). What I am saying is don't be too hard on yourself if you do not achieve your goal. Slow down, reflect on what happened, think about what you could change, and go for the jugular. Put your energy in "pivoting."

Pivoting is a term used in new venture creations. The idea that you have to create the next killer app, or the new electric car, is what gets you to start a prototype, get some funding from friends and family, and transform your garage into a high-tech firm. Sometimes your original idea does not really meet the market demand. The consumers are looking at your prototype and they might say: "Yes, but it is not exactly what I need or what I want." They do not see a benefit for themselves. Marketing can change that, and a good campaign might make consumers see benefits and create an interest to try your product or service. But sometimes it comes to a crossroad between either giving up and quietly moving from being an entrepreneur to becoming an employee somewhere or changing and tweaking your idea to make it more desirable for the consumers. That is pivoting. So, with your career be ready to pivot.

I remember when I first pivoted (I've pivoted several times). I was that General Cashier, at this very large (more than 600 rooms) hotel in Paris. But my job became dull very quickly (again?). Imagine that. I started my day at 7am locked in a room that resembled a prison cell–7 square feet, double doors with a camera and buzzer, one small bullet-proofed sealed window, a very big safe, and lots and lots of cash from an international customer base. That meant handling many currencies: Francs, Deutsche Marks, Pounds, U.S. Dollars, Pesetas, Liras, etc. It was before the Euro thus, all European countries had a fluctuating currency exchange rate between each other, and it was also before the wide use of credit cards. Most customers paid in checks or cash. My job was to make sure that the cash drops from all 20 employees that worked the day before were correct in comparison to the computer report, then consolidating and depositing the cash to the bank, and accepting deliveries of new and fresh change so that it could be distributed to the employees at the start of their shifts. A large part of the job was to figure out the exchange rate of the day, post it at the front desk, and then make sure that the foreign currency on each day was exchanged at the correct rate.

This is where I realized that a bank, or an airport exchange bureau could make easy money. Imagine, for instance, that the official exchange rate of the day taken from the official newspaper like the Wall Street Journal (WSJ), is 0.9 U.S. Dollars to the Euro (or 1 Euro is worth $0.90 U.S. Dollars). That means that to get (buy) 1 Euro you would need to give 90 US cents. Similarly, to get 1 U.S. Dollar someone in Europe would need to pay 1 Euro and 11 cents. So far so good. The first thing that banks, exchange businesses, and hotels do is take a commission, a profit, on the exchange done. For instance, if today the official U.S. Dollar exchange rate to the Euro is $0.90 for 1 Euro (the WSJ), then the hotel will take a 10% commission and will say that the exchange will be $0.99 for 1 Euro, or $0.90, the official rate, plus 10% ($0.09 off of $0.90). Now the customer will need to pay $0.99 instead of $0.90 to get the same 1 Euro. The hotel will then deposit the dollars to its bank, the bank will pay the hotel in Euros at the official exchange rate of 1.11 Euro for 1 U.S. Dollar (to convert the exchange rate from 1 Euro = 0.90 USD to the value of a one USD in Euro you use that formula 1/USD exchange = Euro exchange. In our example 1/0.90 = 1.11). The hotel presents U.S. $0.99 to the bank and gets 1.10 Euros (0.99 x 1.11. Note: numbers are rounded). The hotel made 10 cents of profit in Euro (1.10 – 1.00). If the hotel would not have taken any commission, then the hotel would have exchanged the dollar with its customer at $0.90 for 1 Euro and presented to its bank the $0.90 to get 1 Euro back (0.90 x 1.11).

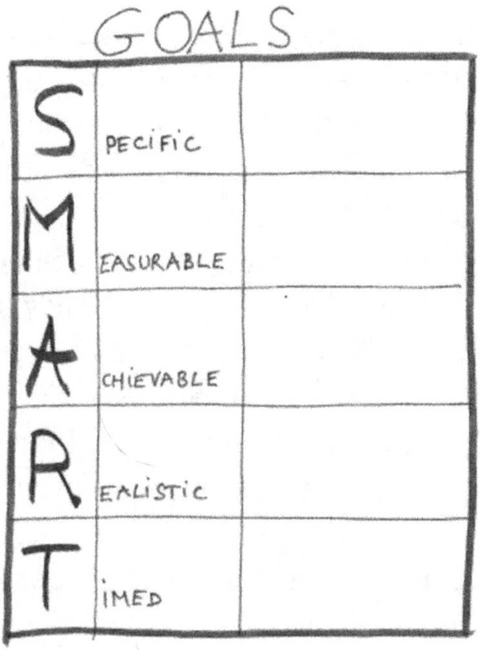

GOALS

S PECIFIC	
M EASURABLE	
A CHIEVABLE	
R EALISTIC	
T IMED	

Figure 4   SMART Goals Worksheet

You can easily imagine several scenarios here. First, the bank, of course, can also play the game of commission, and it does. So, the customer has to pay a commission to the hotel, and because the hotel will have to pay one to the bank, the hotel might pass on that commission, or part of it, to the customer by taking more than 10%. Then, exchange rates fluctuate every day (actually every split-second, but technically, unless you are a currency trader, you only look at the close of day exchange rate, which is the one printed in the newspaper the next day). If currencies fluctuate every day, what will happen if someone waits one day to deposit its currencies to the bank to get it exchanged? It depends, right? If the exchange rate has changed in your favor, meaning that instead of $0.90 U.S. Dollars for 1 Euro, it will cost the customer less and now $0.80 U.S. Dollars will buy 1 Euro, then the hotel and the bank will make more profit by waiting to exchange back its US Dollars into Euros. Let's look at the math. Assume today the hotel rate is $0.99 U.S. Dollars to get 1 Euro (official rate of $0.90 plus a 10% profit, like in our first example). And then assume that the hotel's rate the next day, based on the official WSJ exchange rate, is $0.80 U.S. Dollars to get 1 Euro. The $0.99 U.S. Dollars the hotel got from its customer should have been exchanged on that day for 1.10 Euro (example above), but the next day the exchange rate is now 1.25 (1/0.80 = 1.25). That means the $0.99 the hotel got from its customer is now worth 1.24 Euros (0.99 x 1.25). Waiting one day in that situation increased the hotel's profits from 10 cents in Euros to 24 cents, or more than doubled the profits in one day. Not bad. Of course, that game is dangerous and not played by conservative hotel managers, because if the exchange rate goes the other way, then the hotel will lose money. Not to mention that there are legal implications as well.

Spend All Day at Work and More.
Be a Company (Wo)man.

I know some of you (what's up millennials?) are going to say, "My job is not my life, and I am not spending more time at work than I am paid for. My personal life, my friends, my hobbies, my entertainment are more important to me." Ok, I get it. Me too. Except that "it is a rat race" (as we say) for the most part. Particularly if we are talking about a career rather than just a job. People above you, your bosses, will look down at their soldiers and will pick from the ranks the best and most loyal to the cause to be the next leader, the next boss, for when they will move on. You see, when you want to move on, it always creates a problem for the boss of your boss and for the organization. Who is going to replace the person leaving? What institutional knowledge are we loosing (institutional knowledge is the expression that means the skills and know-how that the person has and will take with them)? For instance, a person knows the history of all of the equipment and knows how to operate the machinery at work. When they leave, if they were the only one with that knowledge, then the knowledge is gone, lost. And the efforts to train a new person will be much more difficult and take longer, since even the boss of that person might not know what the person knew. Thus, most bosses like to have a plan. Sometimes at the Chief Executive Officer (CEO) level, or ownership level, they like to call it a succession plan (See HBO series *Succession*). If you want to leave and you go to your boss and say, "I quit," their first question might be, "Where?" But their first thought will be, "Crap! Who's going to replace her?" So, be ready with someone in mind. Someone from your team you have identified and groomed, if you have a team, or someone from the outside you know is capable and willing to take your job.

Out of boredom (when you're young, you get bored fast) I started finishing my General Cashier's work a few hours before the end of my shift at 3pm, so I stepped out of my Fort Knox office, and wandered into the accounting department. I belonged to that department and the Director of Finance was my boss. I asked what I could do to help? They had plenty of mundane tasks to give me. One that took quite a while was the bank recs' (short for bank reconciliations). A bank rec is an exercise that we all do, somewhat, at home when we look at our bank statement and we say to ourselves: "Geeze, I got some cash to spend this weekend!" only to quickly realize that, "Damn! My rent check hasn't made it to my bank yet, so really I have less money than what my statement says, and if I spend that money this weekend and rent clears on Monday, I'll be in the red with the bank, they'll charge me overdraft fees, and that's not good. So, maybe I can't spend frivolously this weekend after all." Ok, some of you probably don't do that, but you should. The fact that your bank statement does not match your reality is a factor of two things. First, a check or payment you make to someone might take time for them to deposit it with their own bank, and then their bank has to ask your bank for the money. During that time, the money is still in your account, but you've already committed to giving it to someone else, so it is not really available to you. That situation today is disappearing fast since we rarely use checks to pay anything, and money transfers are immediate on our bank account. But checks are still OK in a lot of businesses, so think about it. One day, instead of paying through PayPal or Venmo, pay with a check. By the time the check clears, if you have your paycheck coming to you, then you can use the time it takes to the business and the bank to your advantage.

The other reason why your bank statement doesn't look like reality is that banks use specific dates to credit (give you money) or debit (take money away) your account. In other words, they keep your money longer in order to "make it work," that is to say they use your money to make a profit. Scandalous, right? That's the banking system of "bank days" or "availability days." What it means is that under the pretext that it takes a certain amount of time for the bank to deposit or withdraw funds from one account and get the other bank to clear these funds, the bank has a policy (you can ask for it or read the fine print of your bank policy) that states that in order to get funds available for a deposited check of $500 or less it will take one business day. But if the check is more than $500 it will take three business days. Meanwhile, the checks you are making out to someone, say for instance your rent, today, might actually be taken out of your account yesterday! Yes, you read that correctly, yesterday! It seems obvious that when, in 1855, actual people somewhere in the middle of Texas had to handle a check drawn from a New York bank, it took days to transport the check from Texas to New York and get the confirmation that funds were available. These "bank days" policies were in place to protect the bank and the public. Today, of course, it takes a milli second to "see" if the funds are available. Even on a non-business day (i.e., a business day is also a bank definition. Some banks consider the weekend non-business days, and some banks consider holidays as non-business days) today the computer "knows" that funds are available; the transaction is done in a milli second, even between banks, even between countries. So why still have such a policy? So that the bank can safely use the money on hold between you and your landlord, or between your employer and you, and lend it to someone in need of a mortgage, or to buy stock on the financial market. The banks play with your money. Sometimes they lose, sometimes they win. They win more often than not, so you'll see your paycheck deposited a few days later, thank God! And you won't have to face eviction because your landlord did not get the check.

So, now imagine a business that has thousands of transactions a day back and forth between customers and suppliers. It creates a very long 20-page (yes, on paper; no electronic statements at the time) bank statement in the chronological order of the bank days, i.e., when the bank credits or debits your account. On the side of the business, you also log (in a computer, thank God!) each transaction on the day you are making them. So, you get the printout report form accounting with a long chronological list of checks made and checks received (and cash, and credit cards, etc.), and on the other side the bank statement. The two matches for the most part, which means that within a month most checks made by the business make it to the bank statement, give or take a few days difference. So, the checks made earlier in the month should be on the bank statement, and the ones made on the last day of the month are not there yet. My job was to "reconcile (def. restore friendly relations between)" the two reports. Armed with a highlighter I would look for a check on the accounting statement and find it on the bank statement, then highlight it in yellow, meaning it is on both statements. When one check was not on one statement, it would be highlighted in orange if it was missing on the accounting report and in green if it was missing on the bank statement. Many reasons beyond the bank days can make checks "disappear" from one statement. For instance, the check might be lost, not deposited because the supplier is not organized, or not sent to the supplier because the business does not want to send it yet. That last one is tricky. When you call a business' "accounts payable" to look for where your check is and they say, "in the mail," what it really means is that your check has been cut, and it is in an envelope with your name on it, but not in the mail, rather it is in the Accountant's right lower drawer waiting for him to "release it" when the business has funds, or when they feel like doing it. It is a very crude cash management system that every business, small or large, plays (don't ask me how I know). Thus, that check makes it to the accounting report, but not the bank statement.

The ongoing process throughout the month took a week off the next month. Today with electronic statements it is a little faster to do that, although not all banks are friendly in that manner.

Why would you do that anyway? First, the bank charges you fees for doing certain transactions like credit card fees, wiring fees, management fees, and gives you (very little) interest on short term deposits. So, you need to account for that in your accounting. Also, someone in your organization or one of your suppliers might have committed fraud and deposited a check with an added zero in the end, or some other mistake. Your bank rec is supposed to catch that. Finally, you want to know how much cash you have "on hand," available, and the bank rec is going to allow you to know that. The information is important so that you do not commit to spend more cash than you have, and thus, do not suffer from bank overdraft fees, or even have checks/payments bounce, which could negatively affect your credit rating. Fifty percent of banks' revenue is made with fees and interests. That's a lot of money that you should avoid paying.

From doing bank recs on my "spare time" to taking on more jobs that accountants would not, or could not do, I started to develop a better collaboration with my colleagues. And I started to show the Director of Finance, my boss, that I could learn new tasks and do them efficiently. So, when the Cost Controller quit to go work for another company, I applied for his job. I also suggested a friend who could replace me as a General Cashier. She was looking for work, and I figured that having someone else who could fill my spot was an additional argument in my favor because if she would get the position, then I could mentor her–what we call a "win-win-win." That's what happened, and that's how I became Cost Controller for that hotel.

I now had an open-spaced office, made a little more money, had more responsibilities, interacted with all of the departments in the hotel, and was visible to management. Perfect!

I was in that job for a year or so when a General Manager for a hotel that was being built in the nearby business district moved to the office next to me. He was in what we call "opening" mode. That means 12 to 18 months prior to the opening of a hotel the General Manager is hired, and his job is to organize the opening–hire the staff, come up with the strategic plan, the budget, the marketing actions, follow-up with the construction company, etc. It is a big job for one person. So, I started to engage with him and showed interest. Of course, I had an agenda. I would have liked to be hired in that hotel. Why? I felt it would be good to "do an opening" for my résumé, as it is often seen as a special opportunity that takes special people. Also, I figured that if I could get on the staff early maybe I would have a shot at a better or more visible position in that new hotel than in the current one I had. These where suppositions and it could have been better for me to stay in the current hotel and work my way up to becoming Director of Finance. But, as I said earlier, most General Managers are recruited from the operation side, not the finance or accounting or even sales side. And most are even recruited specifically from the Food and Beverage side. This General Manager was in Food and Beverage at some point before he got his first General Manager position. So, I wanted to see if I could help, in the hopes that I could maybe be the Food and Beverage person on his team. He needed someone to help with the budget. I had just acquired my first Apple IIC computer, and I figured that I could help him by showing him the power of spreadsheets! (Advice to everyone: get to know how Excel, Word, and Power Point works, or the equivalent. That will take you far.) Over the weekend I developed the monthly and year-to-date budget starting with revenues (revenues or sales are made of customers' transactions, i.e., rooms sold, and price paid. Price varies based on the type of client. Some clients pay full price, others pay discounted rates.) followed by the cost of sales (things you need to do for the business that cost a set amount for each client. In a hotel each client costs you food that is served to them, soap and shampoo they use in the hotel room, etc.), then salaries and benefits, then other costs, such as administrative costs, rent, financial costs, all the way down to profit (or loss). The beauty of the spreadsheet, of course, is that if you want to change one number, say for instance the salary of the Chef, then the entire profit and loss by month and for the year changes, and you can see the impact of that change on the bottom line (the bottom line is what is usually called the operational profit). The General Manager loved it (who wouldn't?) and of course used it a lot to create different scenarios. Since that was on my personal Apple, I was kind of indispensable. Nice play, my friend. Eventually the General Manager told me that the hotel was very high profile as the owners were some famous people, so he needed to get a very seasoned Food and Beverage person, i.e., not me. But he wanted me because I had resources he could use, and we had also built a relationship. So, he made room (with my help) in the budget to find me an Assistant to the General Manager position (in other words, I was Dwight Schrute). I spent six months prior to opening, and six months post opening putting all of the procedures in place, helping with everything. And now he would help me get a new job because, in part, my job was no longer needed, but also, he felt that he owed me a little help. That is how I got my job as a Deputy Manager in Marseille (largest city after Paris located in the south of France). By the way, I also helped hire another one of my friends for my Cost Controller's position. That made it easier on the Director of Finance to let me go.

Keep up with your friends in your network. You might hire them one day, or they might hire you. Use LinkedIn to get all of your friends at school connected with you. You never know who is going to need you, or who you will need one day in order to be able to leave for that new opportunity knocking on your door.

Should You Take a Job Downtown, In the Suburbs, or the Province/Countryside?

Over the years I have observed a perception that hiring managers share. For instance, if you are a Director of Sales in a suburban hotel and want to apply to a Director of Sales job in a downtown hotel, your chances of getting that job are less, not more, than if you are a Sales Manager in a downtown hotel applying to the same Director of Sales job. A similar observation can be made between perceived levels of quality. A Manager in a two-star hotel has less of a chance of getting the same job in a three-star hotel than an Assistant Manager in a three-star hotel has of getting that Manager's job. There is a stigma associated with the suburbs or the countryside and the same stigma with lower-perceived quality operations. In general, one could say that the suburbs' pace or complexity is lower than downtown, and that a budget hotel is less complex than a four-star hotel. And that would be true. However, how is one supposed to get that dream job if they have started on the wrong side of the equation? Several avenues are possible. First, you can look for a time when the job market is really tight, meaning that hotels or businesses have a difficult time hiring, thus, "they'll take anyone." And that might be you. You should not care that they will take you despite the stigma because you're going to prove them wrong and do a fantastic job. Just be cognizant of the stigma. Second, you could aim at a lateral move. A lateral move is getting the same job, in a similar setting, but downtown. If you are a Sales Manager in a three-star property in the suburbs, try to get a Sales Manager job in a downtown three-star hotel. Do not go down in perceived quality, i.e., taking a job at a two-star hotel AND making a lateral move at the same time. Third, get a job, say as a Sales Manager, in a hotel located in the suburbs that has other properties in downtown locations. Maybe the company owns several hotels, or the hotel is part of a chain. Whatever the case is, the idea is that people inside the company, the bosses, will get to know you enough to overcome the stigma, and offer you the "challenge" in the downtown hotel. There are probably other strategies, but you get the point.

Should you Take a Job in a Different Country?

That's a big one. First of all, I do not see many graduates who want to do that. Fear of the unknown, being far from family, not speaking the language well enough, and so on. All of these excuses are either in the way of your ambitions or keep you in check. I have always been fascinated by America (i.e., the United States of America). My youth was spent with Cowboys and Indians games (not very politically correct today), then I was fascinated by the size and speed at which things, anything, moved in America. Fast food, fast fortunes, fast pace of development, fast turnover of politicians (a French President at the time could stay in power for 14 years). English was creeping up in the French language and culture every day. McDonald's was present in every major town in France. The radio was playing more English based music than French; even French artists sang in English. That was "cool." Movies were 90% American, so much so that the French government had to impose quotas for French films on the theatres and TV stations and had to subsidize movie makers to produce French language movies in order to be able to play them on TV or in the theatres. With that in mind, America was the land of opportunity, where everything is possible to the one who can grab it. The picture of settlers running from the Appalachian departure line toward the West who had a stick in their hand to plant where they wanted and claim that land theirs, was fascinating to me. I found out later that there were many problems with that picture, but that is for another discussion. Today, American born friends often ask me why I came to the U.S. when France seems to be a better choice in their eyes. The answer is always: land of opportunity. The opportunity is in the eye of the beholder. This is how that adventure happened.

I was the Deputy Manager of a four-star hotel in Marseille, France, on the Mediterranean coast. I was 28. I could touch that goal of becoming a General Manager. I was invested in the city in different associations, doing my Public Relations for the hotel, but also making friends and getting to know the cultural landscape. Just as Louisiana's local culture is different from Massachusetts's, the south of France is different from any other part of France in its dialect, idioms, insults and swear words, cuisine, rituals, and so on. I was also representing the professional side of the hospitality industry at thesis defenses for graduating students at the local hotel management school. One day a professor sitting with me between two students' defense, asked me if I would consider going to the U.S. with the same hotel company I was working for. They had hotels in Chicago, Miami, Minneapolis, San Francisco, Los Angeles, and Houston, and "had big plans for professionals like me to fill General Manager positions at a group of three-star hotels they were developing." I said yes on the spot. I gave him my résumé and forgot about it. Then, in the very beginning of July I got a call at home from the General Manager of the Chicago property. She wanted to offer me a job! Would I talk to the Director of Food and Beverage? I did. I found out that the job was Maître d' of the fancy dining room, paid about what I was making in France as a Deputy Manager. Crossroads. I said yes (after consulting with my wife) and I moved there a month later after having sold all that we owned, including my very recent acquisition, a red Opel Corsa GTI, my golf clubs, and so on! My wife and 18-month-old daughter would join me a month after I would get there. My job was to get there, get a car, get an apartment, settle in, and then wait for them. What an adventure!

My preparation was going to be linguistic essentially. My English was ok, but quite schoolish, and my accent was not American, but rather Monty Python style. I started to read the American professional press in order to pick up some lingo, and I purchased a course on books and cassette tapes (I know) that specifically looked at business interactions, meetings, phones calls, sales calls, employee management, etc., through the lenses of international accents in English. All that effort took one month! And boom! I was there at O'Hare airport with a suitcase.

Whether you want to immigrate to another country or simply work there for a while, I suggest that you go somewhere for a few months and live and work there, among the people. No English pubs, No American movies or TV. Immerse yourself. Survive as an immigrant. Prior to my "going West" adventure, I went, as most French do, to the UK. That is a must for French folks. First, the UK is a little taste of America because it speaks English and has some cool music. Second, it is not far, and therefore cheap to get there, I drove there, and the immigration process is simple. I also spent three months in Pamplona, Spain, working as a cook in a big five-star palace hotel. This was during the San Firmin. You know, when the bulls run through town and you wear bandanas and berets running for your life in front of the pack (see *City Sleeker*, the movie). On both occasions, my appreciation of the cultural differences, and my command of the language went from schoolish to a low level of fluency in speaking, but it was great ear training. It is like listening to music a lot and recognizing songs in the same key by ear, not being able to play them on the guitar quite yet. In short, go to Mexico or Central or South America and immerse yourself in Spanish. It is so close and so beneficial. Get an internship there. Go for Spring break and ask to see the Manager of the restaurant/hotel. Ask for a job. What do you have to lose? The experience will pay off many folds. You can't do that? Then try to study abroad. I know it is expensive. But think of it as an investment in your future (at least sell it like that to your parents). I directed many study-abroad programs in France with American students (that is in my current Professor capacity). Every student came back not only with lifetime memories, but with French friends for life, and a new appreciation for a different culture and a different way to live your life. Some are not conscious of that a month after being back in the US, but I can guarantee them that they will think about it for the rest of their lives, and will use the experience in some form (ok, not all experiences are this glorious; as you know France's drinking age is 18 officially, but who cares, right? You can make your own decisions). So, clearly the benefits of going outside your comfort zone, to a new country, on your own, are numerous. When you come back, if you do, continue the training. It is like a skill; you need to practice it often in order to maintain some expertise level (it takes 10,000 hours of practice to become an expert at anything according to Malcolm Gladwell's "Outliers" book). Watch movies or series in their original versions, with subtitles or not. Read an article or book in the language. Pick stories from the town you have lived in to keep you engaged and interested. It is not easy, but you can do it, and it will pay off. Do not forget to capitalize on that experience, whether you study abroad, have an internship or work abroad, your résumé and LinkedIn profile must have that as an international experience. Employers will look at you differently than the friend who interned at their mom's business.

What Should You Do to Better Yourself?
In One Word: Read.

You think that you got your education at school because you have that diploma in hand, right? Wrong. You have been given the opportunity to get an education, and you have taken some or all, in exchange for some grade on a scale, but do you remember everything you learned? No. I did not. I definitely skipped some classes, and used the brain dumping strategy many times between classes. Many times, I had started to review for a test the day before or took a chance without reviewing. Who cares, right? My interests were cost management, new product development, and technology as in how to do certain things like culinary production, productivity in processes, computer coding, and so on. I was not interested in law, human resources, language (although I loved going abroad), French literature or philosophy, history, economy, microbiology, and many other topics that were part of the curriculum. Yet, I found myself very interested in law when I started to look at employment situations, or interested in human resources processes when hiring teams, or in microbiology when putting culinary hygiene control systems in place. I also wanted to further my knowledge in cost management and financial analysis, and in computer coding. Since I was out of school, I had to read, and self-educate. That's what I did. For a long time, my "relaxing" reading moments were spent with a finance book or a management book, even the occasional statistics book. Add to that the world knowledge and cultural knowledge that is necessary to understand what's going on around you and to be able to "intelligently" converse with friends that have not been on the same path as you have, and might have a more formal education, or just be more informed. As a Deputy Manager doing my rounds around the hotel talking to customers or going to town to clubs and association meetings, I did not want to be the "ugly little duck" without an education. So, I read the newspapers, and listened to TV programs, and read books. Do the same.

Be on a "continuous improvement" plan (continuous improvement is a quality control process method used to systematically look for defaults in a production process; think about a defective pair of jeans in a batch of thousand and eliminate the root cause of the defaults or errors in order to get a better quality output. The implied goal being 100% quality or perfection). Self-educate if you have not taken the time in college to learn and remember all that was taught. Even if you were an "A" student, keep up with the new stuff in your field, in your world. It is your responsibility, your duty to be an informed and educated consumer and citizen.

What if you do not want the career? Maybe you don't. That's ok. You do not need to "drink the Kool-Aid" (drinking the Kool-Aid refers to a really dark event in history when a cult leader had hundreds of his followers commit suicide simultaneously by drinking a poisoned Kool-Aid drink. Since then, drinking the Kool-Aid is used when describing someone in a corporate setting that accepts the words of management at face value without questioning it. A company (wo)man is one that follows orders and company ways of doing things without questioning too much. We say that s/he "drinks the Kool-Aid"). Maybe what you want is a job at a small business or in a small town and do the best job you can for many years until you retire. That is quite fine. Just think about one issue with that strategy though. If the small business is going belly up (i.e., bankruptcy or some other negative events that dries up revenues), then what will happen to you? So, even if you are content with a small business job, put yourself on the continuous improvement plan, be ready to protect yourself in case of a catastrophe. You do not want to be the one suffering the most during a plant closure, or during a pandemic. It will be your time to pivot, use your skills to stay agile in the face of adversity, it is your duty to stay relevant and well-informed.

Many people think about creating their own jobs by creating their own business. That could work, but it takes a whole different set of skills. For more on entrepreneurship see Chapter 7.

> *Gen Z POV: "Talking about the adjustment period post-graduation. I know to me it was a huge shock not having a Thanksgiving/Christmas/summer break. Having to take PTO (Paid Time Off) on Christmas Eve or having to take the day after Thanksgiving off if I didn't want to drive 6 hours back home after Thanksgiving dinner (thank God for WFH now). I also think it's a huge adjustment having to get up and go to work for 8 hours a day, 5 days a week. In college, if you don't want to go to class you might skip it; in the working world that's not an option. I see the weekends as really one day (Saturday). Friday you still work all day and boom-Sunday's a work night."*

Chapter 2 Appendix: A visualization exercise

Close your eyes and imagine yourself in a future where everything has gone right.

You have accomplished your goals, and as a result, you've become your *best possible self.* What do you see? What would your life look like? Who would be by your side? How would you spend your time? Describe what you see below in details.

_____

_____

_____

_____

Repeat the exercise but focus on imagining yourself 3 years from now.

_____

_____

_____

Repeat the exercise but focus on imagining yourself at the end of your life. What is the happy ending of your life?

_____

_____

_____

_____

CHAPTER 3

MBA or Master's?

"You are the only teacher you will ever have"

I had just been turned down for that General Manager's job, and I was over 30. What was wrong with me? What did I need to do for my boss to give me that promotion? I looked around me, and I saw that one of my colleagues got that General Manager's job. Of course, there was no comparison between me and him. He was a Harvard MBA grad. I was nothing. It's funny (Not! See *Borat*, the movie) how what you have done or accomplished in one cultural, or sub-cultural setting, can be ignored or overlooked in a different setting. In France I had a little status given my education (not as much as Harvard level, but a little); in the U.S. I had zero.

My company at the time was fond of personal development trainings. It was the company's mission to train people to later "promote from within." Most top executives in my company were once just like me. They had the same education, and today they were the CEO, COO, Country or Regional Managers, and of course, General Managers. So, don't worry, just follow the company's training and you'll be fine. When I was a mid-level manager, I was enrolled in a company two-year management training program that gave me all the practice in the world I needed in order to hire, train, manage, coach, discipline, and fire my employees. Then, I enrolled in a life-project training program that was designed to make me think about long-term goals and how to create a plan to get there.

The multiple team building retreats were designed to weed out the bad managers (that's my cynical self-talking here) and make sure the remaining ones were loyal and motivated to achieve long-term stretch goals and not just simply achieve budget. Then, as General Managers and Deputy Managers, we were enrolled in a specifically designed strategic management series of seminars at Cornell School of Hotel Administrations. That was the pinnacle of all training, and we got our certificates! Ok, the certificate was not much, but it was something that I held on to at the time, because of the University brand appeal, and the fact that all I had done in France was nothing in the eyes of American employers. In fact, it is a common experience for most immigrants (in any country) that what you have done before is basically inconsequential. I hired many recent immigrants that were doctors in their country, or engineers, and were seeking waiters' jobs hoping one day to get some American equivalency of their diplomas so that they could use their knowledge in some other way than simply carrying plates. I got quite lucky in the following year. I was gathering information on MBA programs, when I met with my company's Vice President of Human Resources and was able to clear up a lot. She basically said that an MBA was a good idea as it was "framing the street smarts" and that the company would (probably) support that initiative. I understood "pay for part". I was soon after named General Manager of a 130 room three-star hotel near Manhattan. I was ecstatic. I had just become father to my third child, I was enrolled in an MBA program, and I was in charge of a hotel that was losing millions with the goal to make a profit in 12 months or less. Bring it on!

To Be a Master, or Not to Be

As I was looking for MBA programs, without understanding the American education system as I was still a little green in the country, I did what anyone would do and contacted universities nearby. The first university I contacted told me I needed a Bachelor's. My French degree was equivalent to an Associate's Degree, so I needed to go back to school for two years to learn stuff that I either did not need or already knew. No way! After lots of research online I found a university in Canada that would accept my professional experience as "lifelong credit" and would allow me to apply directly to the MBA program. Perfect! It was one of the first online programs in the world and was similar to what was called the "Open University" in the UK. 90% of the courses were cohort based online, and in between sets of courses face to face seminars or practicums were offered. That was the best setting for me as I wanted to stay flexible (agile) in case my boss needed me in the middle of the MBA and would inevitably require me to move anywhere in the world, which by the way happened.

Picking the Right Master's Degree

What Master's did I want and for what purpose? That question came from a friend of mine. He had the right question. Did I want the Master's in Business Administration (MBA) to be like the other colleague that had a Harvard MBA? If yes, I needed to earn an Ivy League school MBA, not a Canadian open university. If I wanted the knowledge the MBA would bring me then a good, accredited university would do just fine. I sided with the latter as there was no way I was going to make it into any Ivy League program.

What Master's is right for you? I get that question often. I am the Director of the Master's in Marketing Intelligence (at the time I wrote this book) and a lot of undergraduate students think about "doing" a Master's after their Bachelor's at some point. I think that getting a Master's is important in today's world. It is not for everyone, but it is almost indispensable for those who want the career we talked about earlier. Today's Master's is yesterday's Bachelor's. I don't know who said that, but I think it says it all. As more and more people get access to education and can get a Bachelor's (thanks to mom and dad, and to the bankers) then the value of the Bachelor's becomes diluted. It is like most things; abundance of something makes the price (value) go down (See your ECON 101 course).

Should you do an MBA, or should you do a specialized Master's? A specialized Master's is by definition not an MBA, although some MBA's get an emphasis (mine was an MBA in General Management), but most MBAs are generic. You will learn a little bit of everything, in business of course. On the other hand, the specialized Master's dives much more into one particular subject matter. So, for instance, a Master's in Marketing will almost entirely cover marketing, and thus will not cover accounting, or leadership. Most non-business Masters' are specialized Masters. It is a common saying that if you major in psychology you wasted your money and will not get a job in that field unless you get a Master's in psychology. That, of course, is an anomaly and might not reflect every subject. But the point is that a specialized Master's might be what you need to get the job, and to get that career opportunity. This is why a lot of 30-year-old-ish's either take a year off before getting a Master's and pivot their career or start a Master's part time while working in order to expand their opportunities.

Some companies, usually the large corporations–think Walmart, Marriott, Stanley Black and Decker, GE, etc.–might have a tuition reimbursement policy as part of the employees' benefits package. It is somewhat the equivalent of the G.I. Bill for the military where your degree is paid for by your organization either as a benefit or reward, or as a retainer. A retainer is a mechanism by which a company gives you something, a bonus or benefits, and asks you to stay on board for a certain amount of time in exchange. If you don't, you might have to repay the company. So, if that is your case, then go to your Human Resources department and ask the question.

Not all is lost if you do not go straight from undergrad to getting a Master's, or you have passed the major 30-year-old bump. You can still do what is called an executive MBA. An executive MBA is exactly the same thing as the "regular" MBA but catered to the executives at large. So, people who are already managers, or pretty high up in the hierarchy and have not done a Master's can take these executive MBAs to get the same diploma. The difference is that classes are often in the summer, on the weekends, or quite spread out throughout the year to facilitate attendance. Sometimes the tests are a little easier or at least less academic if any tests are required. Case work and group work are largely used to evaluate executives, and pretty much everyone that attends (and pays) gets the diploma. Note that It is a lot easier for someone with a non-Ivy League Bachelor's to get into an Ivy League executive MBA program. Most of the time the threshold of admission is your career achievements more than your outdated Bachelor's, since the average age of an executive MBA student is around 40 years old. But you don't care too much about that because you are in your 20s!

For a business major, even with a marketing concentration or a management concentration, I always say the same thing: If you see yourself (your goals) as the CEO of a company one day, then an MBA is what you need. If you instead see yourself being a C-level executive (an executive sitting at the board table but not the CEO. The Chief Marketing Officer (CMO) or the Chief Financial Officer (CFO) are C-level executives), then maybe it would be best for you to dig really deep into your subject, i.e., a future CFO might want to pursue a Master's in Finance.

How about a professional degree like a J.D.? Just like a Medical Degree (M.D.) a Juris Doctor (J.D.) is the highest degree in one professional field, in that case, law. One that is extremely specialized and is needed, even required by the state to practice as an attorney. Some MBAs double up and pursue a J.D., as well. Often, they do not seek to practice in the courtroom as an attorney, but rather as consultants or legal advisors of sorts.

How about a CPA? Here is a little distinction. A Certified Public Accountant (CPA) is someone that has a degree in accounting equivalent to a Master's or a Master's in Accounting, and then takes a state exam (similar to a bar exam for an attorney) in order to get a certification (not a degree) that will act as a license to practice. It's complicated, but if you want to be an accountant, that's what you'd want to do. On the topic of certifications, do not mistake a CPA and a Certificate in Accounting as the same thing. Certificates are usually, but not always, not a degree, meaning that you pay to get a class, you take some sort of exam, usually fairly easy, and you get a piece of paper that says certificate on it. Think about a HubSpot or Google certificate. A CPA is much more rigorous and has the power of allowing you to work in the state. If you don't have a CPA, you can't work in that capacity. On the other hand, if you don't have a Google certificate, you can still work in digital marketing. So, certificates are a good way to stay up-to-date and add lines on your résumé and LinkedIn profiles. They're also usually very affordable and are better than nothing.

Some industries require licenses. Public accounting requires a CPA as a license equivalent, but Real Estate agents (those who help buy and sell houses) need a license; Financial Advisors need several licenses and certifications; Insurance agents need a license, Mortgage originators and so on.

Some industry certificates allow you to add letters after your name. You might have seen M.D. or Ph.D. after someone's name, which is a Medical Doctor or Doctor in Philosophy, titles earned through diplomas. But some certifications also have their set of letters that you can use to show people that you have some level of education or knowledge, even more expertise than the person without the letters. For instance, you can be a PMP (Project Management Professional), a CHA (Certified Hotel Administrator), or a CCNA (Cisco Certified Network Associate), and so on. Next time you see someone with letters after their name check it out and find out what it means. If that person is in your LinkedIn network and you aspire to become that person, then maybe that is something you'd rather pursue than a Master's.

GMAT or No GMAT

One thing you have to do if you want to go to grad school is to either take a GMAT, a GRE, a LSAT (law), or a MCAT (medicine). Watch "*meet the parents*" movie for some laughs about Gay Fockers' MCAT top of the class results.

A GMAT or any of the other grad standardized tests is like an SAT, but on steroids. The median GMAT score is around 550. My first time around I studied for three months and I got 550. I was accepted into the MBA program, but I did not impress myself.

Gen Z POV: "I go back and forth. I looked into master programs in my field, but it is the general sentiment that if you work for a Fortune 500 company like I do, it's not that you are lacking experience. Some companies that are smaller, maybe you would want to go to school to learn more, but I work with the latest technology. In my community, a master is not necessarily needed unless you want to teach. But businesswise I would consider an MBA, maybe that would make me stand out if I apply for a job. I think my path right now is to continue building my résumé. With different experiences."

When I returned to school later in life to get a Ph.D. I knew I had to retake the GMAT and I knew that I had to do a lot better than my mediocre 550. I studied again for three months, and I got every book you could get (I love books). I got a 660, which was not too shabby considering the score to be able to get into Wharton grad school (yes, that's where Trump went) is 660. However, I knew I could do even better, and I needed to do better if I wanted to get into a reputable Ph.D. program. So, I got a tutor. This guy was scoring the maximum (850) each time. And with a little work I got north of 700. Ok, I stopped there; that was enough.

They say there is a correlation between standardized tests and your IQ (intelligence scores), but I think it's bullshit (pardon my French) designed to sell you more stuff. Actually, today many schools have stopped requiring the GMAT, so as you read this you might not have to take the test. Don't take it if you don't need it.

What will you learn in an MBA?

What's the benefit of spending another year in college, or two years part time? You'll learn a lot of theory, and a lot of application of that theory on different cases. Most of all, a Master's is an opportunity to create or expand your network. Yes, going to Harvard or the university of your state carries a big difference over and beyond the "brand" effect. Your peers will also be graduating and getting the best opportunities, thus, that network will serve you at some point in your career. Wouldn't you wanted to have been at Harvard in 2004 with Mark Zuckerberg (Facebook creator)? Many Harvard grads hire newly fresh Harvard grads. There is a lot of "nepotism" when it comes to hiring. The university of your state will also have its network and its nepotism advantages. Only it will be different, and possibly less opportunistic than the Ivy League ones. That is where most of the difference in tuition cost resides (in my opinion). As for the core of what you will be learning, let's take a quick look together [note: I realize that if you are not in a business field today you might find learning about an MBA a little out of your interest, but think about the world that surrounds you. It is very business-like. Whether you are working at any job in a small business practice, a non-profit, or even a government agency, the business mentality, the business lingo, and the business approach (sometimes wrong) is omnipresent].

A typical MBA program will have most of the following topics covered: Leadership, Management, Human Resources, Teamworking, Accounting (financial and managerial), Finance, Information Technology, Manufacturing, Marketing, and Strategic Thinking. Sometimes leadership and management will be merged, and another "hot topic," such as operation management added. That gives each MBA school some differentiation against others. These courses would make for a 30+ credits degree; some will have a little more, some will be more "strategic" and will have every topic titled as "strategic" something, as in strategic leadership, strategic management, strategic human resources, you get the point. But in the end the idea is to give the student an overview of all the functions in a corporation (with most functions, legal is usually not taught, although some programs have a good emphasis on the legal and the ethical aspects of business embedded in all topics). You become a generalist, with some depth, and some knowledge, and it's up to you to dig wherever you feel you need to.

Let's review the main takeaways from each area. Remember that beyond the topics, a good MBA program will be hands-on, and practical, in the way that only group work and case discussions can be.

Take the following as a crash course, or an MBA in 5 minutes. Your attention span is shorter than that, some say, but I trust you are going to be engaged in the heavy learning that follows [note: this is only the tip of the proverbial iceberg folks; don't think that it's all you'll learn for your $30,000+ tuition].

Leadership

Numerous books have been written on leadership. Numerous people, often military, have written books on being a leader. Thus, we often think that a leader is someone that commands in the sense of ordering and directing. And, to some extent it is. But it is a lot more subtle than that to be a good leader. A good leader will first set the stage with a company's culture and values that will serve as a bedrock for establishing a company's mission (what the company does) true to the leader's vision (his/her mental picture of where the company will be in the future).

It boils down to the way the leader communicates with the stakeholders in general (stakeholders are the people that interact with the corporation: employees, customers, shareholders, people in the community, and to some extent, depending on how much reach the corporation has, the entire world. Think of the duty to ecology for chemical companies, for instance, and the global impact it can have). Corporate communication is key in setting a culture. That includes talks, memos, website, advertising etc., but also the way information circulates among employees, the rituals that are put in place in the corporation. For instance, celebration events for milestones achieved, employees' recognitions, Public Relations, and crisis management communication. One example of setting a culture might be that the leadership holds strong beliefs about promoting from within. That means that an employee entering the corporation at the lowest level might see an opportunity to grow and become a manager or even the CEO.

As an employee in that type of corporation I strongly believed that my future was there. I made that horizontal move from the palace hotel to the chain hotel in Paris for that reason. Upward mobility, promotion from within, whatever you call it, it was a motivator that would make me work harder and stay through thick and thin because the carrot was better than the stick, or in my case the smaller salaries. Looking at my career now, I think it was a great decision. Yes, sometimes I felt that I could have moved faster, or that my contributions were not rewarded properly, but in the end, my loyalty combined with my results were well rewarded. When my turn came to be able to change people's lives, I mean when I became a manager and was able to hire and promote, I did it with a lot of pleasure, actually quite a bit of pleasure. Several of my employees throughout the years became my peers, and even my bosses!

Leadership needs to set the culture, and often that becomes clearer when the leader creates a story. Very much like a mythical story, leaders sometimes like to tell the story of their life and business adventures that guided them to where they are today. Think of it as a biography but written by the corporation for the corporation and its shareholders. So, a little bias, thus, the myth. Symbolism is often used to make culture tangible. It is obvious in the company's logo, but it is also very powerful in the company's rules and regulations, employees' titles, and internal lingo. It is quite interesting to see how culture and leadership take form in corporate buildings for instance. Is the CEO's office at the very last floor of the tallest tower? How many barrages of people do you have to go through before you can talk to the leader?

One hotel I was managing was converting from being a run down to a brand new and fresh three-star hotel. I was the opening General Manager. I was able to impact the blueprints for the new ground level in a way that would impact leadership once the hotel was open. Instead of having my office in the back of the lobby tucked between the sales office and the back offices, I moved it into the lobby of the hotel. It was smaller, but I didn't care. I was able to hear any and all customer inter-actions with the front desk staff from my chair. If something was not going the way I wanted, I could jump in and deal with it immediately. Customers were able to pop-in and say hello or complain to the guy in charge. One day an angry customer knocked at my door. You're the General Manager, right? Yes, how can I help? He had an issue with his room, and I fixed it. I didn't do anything the front desk agent couldn't do, but the customer obviously wanted special treatment. After that, he was almost a friend and kept popping up "just to say hello."

Some corporate cultures are not very healthy even if they're some-how efficient in the short-term. Take, for instance, the GE Jack Welch method of assessment for employees. Separate employees in three groups: the top 20%, the next 70%, and the bottom 10%. Fire the bottom 10% every year. That may seem like a plan but think about the message and the culture GE sets. Why would you have hired the bottom 10% if it's just to fire them? What happened that made them perform this badly? Is it that the other 90% really performed better? The bottom line is that the culture can be perceived as fear based. Remember me asking you sales folks to watch the movie *Glengarry Glen Ross* earlier? In that movie the regional director of sales, played by Alec Baldwin, gives the local sales team a task. If they perform well, they will get rewarded, and if they don't, they'll get fired. The sales manager who performs the best will get a Red Cadillac Eldorado, the next one down the totem pole will get a set of steak knives, and the rest of them will get fired. That movie is fun to watch, but believe me, when you are in such an organization, you'll go to work every day with a knot in your stomach.

Management

Management is very much a result of leadership (or lack thereof). The term refers to the people in charge of how the organization functions, the "bosses," but more broadly it defines the way in which the leadership makes people (the staff) produce what needs to be produced in the way it should be produced. Management is an extension of leadership like in the examples from GE and in the *Glengarry Glen Ross* movie. By managing with the fear of getting fired, not only do the leaders of the organization get results (not always the best results), they also set the stage for that fear culture that might impact many other facets of employee-management relations and employee-customer relations.

Take the example of a hotel where the fear of making a mistake, possibly reinforced by a history of employees being fired for it, make the front desk staff terrified of taking initiative when alone in front of a customer with a problem (which happens often, particularly at night). For instance, what if a customer comes to the desk to complain that his room is not what the reservation person promised, and the hotel is fully booked? What usually happens here? In most cases, the employee will try to get the customer to go ask someone else or will defer to a manager if one is around. In this example, if there isn't a manager "on duty" around, the employee will probably say: "Sorry, sir, there is nothing I can do now, so may I suggest you talk to a manager tomorrow?" Not a very good practice. Ritz Carlton and Marriott (who owns Ritz) were the first ones in the industry to empower their front-line staff in order to exceed customers' expectations, particularly when an issue arises. For instance, and very pragmatically, each front desk employee has a certain amount of money, a few hundreds, they can freely spend, without pre-authorization, to please the customer. No questions will be asked. No one will be fired because they used the money on something deemed to be trivial. As long as the customers are happy, that's what counts.

Management decisions (hire, fire, promote, etc.) are often based on beliefs. At the top there is the belief that people are good, with some exceptions, or that people are bad, with some exceptions.

Some managers holding the latter set of beliefs might organize work and make decisions in a very different way than the managers holding the former set of beliefs. If you believe that most employees are bad, then you will set very rigid procedures for employees to follow in order to produce what is needed. Employees, as a result, might feel like children, leading them to ask management what to do each time a roadblock arises, which would prove that this way of managing was correct—a vicious circle. In fact, they were probably trying to avoid making a mistake, because management with these beliefs are often prone to managing by fear, with very harsh disciplinary actions. In this kind of management setting, "good" employees might not be noticed because no one is able to take initiative, and the definition of a good employee is one that does his/her job without complaining. Thus, that management style, although fairly efficient, is not one that creates a long-lasting feeling of love for the corporation. Employee morale might be low, and if the hiring market is good, employee turnover (the percentage of employees that leave the organization every year) will be high. In addition, when the organization faces hardship or a crisis, the employees are not volunteering to save the day and might organize more against the leadership rather than make concessions to help. This is a bad spiral.

The other broad belief is the more positive one—that most employees are good. In this case, management might delegate more decision making to the employee level, as in our Ritz example, trust that employees do their jobs, thus applying less control or asking employees to self-control. Rewards might be the main motivators, as opposed to fear of punishment. Employee initiatives might be encouraged, and as a result more innovative ideas might emerge from the employees that create better customer service, increase productivity, and increase profit in the end. This is a virtuous spiral.

The typical MBA student will learn many management concepts "packaged" into what is called a 2x2 matrix. I challenge you to open any business book and not find a 2x2 matrix. For instance, situational leadership (also called situational management) is the concept that incorporates different sets of beliefs and gives management an opportunity to increase productivity by adapting their own management style to the situation the employee presents measured by their level of maturity. Each employee is assessed on two dimensions: the ability to do the task, and the willingness to do the task. Thus, one employee can be "labeled" in one of four (2x2 = 4) unique boxes (See Figure 5).

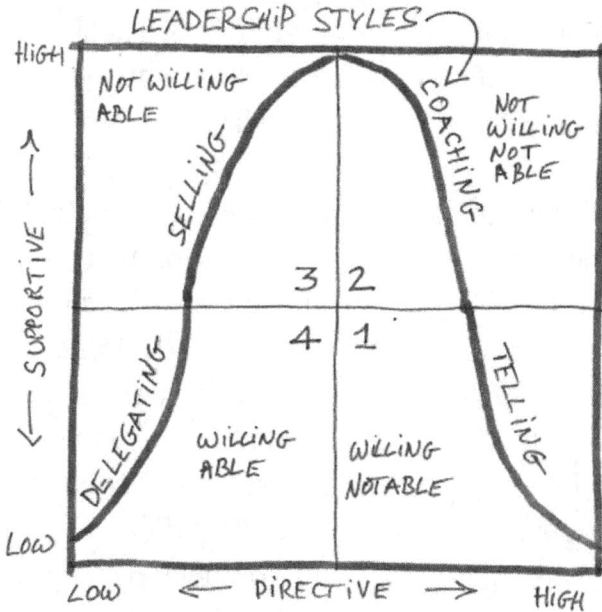

Figure 5   *Situational Leadership (Source: Hersey and Blanchard)*

Box 1: Willing but Not Able; Box 2: Not Willing and Not Able; Box 3: Not Willing but Able; and, Box 4: Willing and Able. Based on this assessment, which can be done for each employee in each manager's team, the manager will respond with a different style of management. The term "willing" here should be taken either at face value, i.e., the employee does not want to perform the task, or a little lighter, as the employee does not find the motivation to do the task. The term "able" here should be understood as the pertinent knowledge is not yet acquired, either because the employee has just been hired, or because the job has been retooled or is new to the employee. There are four styles of management (in this particular concept): telling, coaching, selling, and delegating.

Box 1: Willing but Not Able employees are your new employees. They should be trained and given clear guidelines. Their manager should use a directive style of management, *telling* employees what to do in order to build their knowledge and confidence.

Box 2: Not Willing and Not Able employees can be potential problems. But with proper management they, in large part, can be motivated to do a task that they feel they know little about. *Coaching* is the proper management style here. Coaching involves training to acquire the knowledge and some level of demonstration and on the job training. Then comes the motivational part where the manager has to communicate to the employee his/her vision and trust in their ability to achieve the goal/do the task. It is quite difficult to achieve as most managers are better at simply telling, or "delegating" in a laissez-faire or hands-off manner. Coaching must be finely tuned between these two approaches.

Box 3: Not Willing but Able employees are what is often called "dead wood" in a demeaning way. They can lack motivation or simply resist directions. They're able to do the task; however, if the manager uses a hands-off style like delegation, more likely than not the work is not going to get done properly or within deadlines. Here very often organizations don't recognize the issue, which I have often seen. And instead of using the *selling* style of management, they think employees are not able to do the job, thus, launch a new round of training because maybe they fear the alternative of having to fire the employees, or better properly manage them. It is often a waste of resources. The employee needs to be sold on the "why" things need to be done or done in a particular way, then they need to be left to do it without too much supervision. Yet, accountability needs to be reinforced.

I remember one day wanting to get a restaurant manager's job in Paris. That particular job was a fast-paced job, paying "six figures" and requiring me to work 15 hours per day. I passed all of the interviews and the last step was to try out for a day at a restaurant and get feedback from the manager on my performance and how I fit in. I went there all motivated and I knew I could get that job. At the end of the day, actually the night, because the job was from 10am to 1am the next day, I sat with the current manager and he told me "that job is not for you." He was right. Technically I did a good job, I got the management processes right away, and understood the service processes and the flow very well. I could carry plates and help the wait staff without missing a beat. What was wrong? I could not be the type of bubbly, ass slapping (you read correctly) manager they were looking for. We agree that was not me. I was not able, and not willing.

Finally, employees in Box 4: Willing and Able should be given ample freedom to do their job the way they feel it should be done best, given a set goal [note: goals need to be SMART; see Figure 4]. Their manager should *delegate* them the ability to make decisions, and step back. Here, the issue with most managers is that they feel they must solve every issue for their employees–a "helicopter parenting" view of management. Which results with box 4 employees demotivated because management does not recognize their willingness to help the organization and their ability to do it alone. It is quite difficult for a manager, often the first-time managers promoted from within the ranks, to delegate without thinking that this is a "laissez-faire or hands-off" style that does not make use of their skills. All managers need to do in that situation is make sure the employee has the resources they need to reach the set goals.

Human Resources

Human Resources (HR) designate the function in the organization that often is responsible for managing employee's "life" inside the organization. It is often looked at by the set of life events the employees go through such as hiring, orientation or onboarding as we say today, training and development, promotion, assessment or reviewing, reward and morale related events (i.e., Holiday Party, Employee of the Month), disciplining, and firing (also called separation in our Politically Correct (PC) world). It is also the department that sets policies with regards to all life events for use by management. It manages and sometime decides along with management the benefits that are offered to employees. How many holiday leave (with pay) can be taken, what health company and what health coverage should be offered to the employees, and how much should employees contribute to the cost. Policies set by HR have to be in line with the leadership mission, vision, and culture. For instance, if leadership wants to set a culture whereby employees feel they have hope to grow within the company and get promoted, then a promotion from within policy will be needed, and will need to be reinforced with managers each time there is a hiring need, each time managers sit down with employees for their reviews, and so on. In most organizations, HR uses marketing tactics to communicate internal policies to the employees and managers. That way they contribute in convincing and influencing employees' perceptions of leadership values and beliefs and, ultimately, they contribute to the motivation needed to get employees to achieve the set management goals.

HR is also in charge of employee morale even though usually, beyond policy making they do not impact much. In fact, the managers are the ones that should manage situationally as we have seen, and then use the policies appropriately and fairly. So, HR is really there to make sure this is happening and to train and coach the managers that are a little "green." HR's goal in a lot of organizations is to be the go-between leadership and employee representatives, often a Union. If there isn't a Union present in the organization, HR's role might be to avoid a Unionization of the workforce by either "fighting" the Union, or better yet, setting policies and their implementations that are fair and close to a Union contract. In other words, to make sure employees don't see a benefit in signing up for the Union.

I worked in organizations that had HR managers and others that did not. The problem with organizations without HR is that someone has to do it anyway. And that someone is either the accountant, and that's bad news, or the general manager, and that could also be bad news. The "it" that someone has to do is sometimes pretty administrative in nature, like filling out the forms needed to process new hires in the payroll, in the health plan, or the 401k retirement plan. Sometimes these forms have a confidentiality angle or even a very emotional angle to them. Think about a separation form (that is HR jargon to tell you that you're fired), or a loan on your 401k to pay for a home down payment, or a medical issue you would rather your boss not know. So, HR plays that role of confidants (although don't think they do not report relevant info to the boss, they do), but ultimately it is an expense that management rarely sees as strategic.

Teamworking

Setting the stage and the cultural framing of an organization, effectively managing employees that have a clear sense of what is expected of them is a step (albeit a big one) in the right direction. Creating a highly performing organization is something else. It is quite difficult to both pay attention at the individual level, and to also look at the entire organization as a group. In their book, Katzenbach and Smith (1994) suggest that employees grouped together as teams could be more productive if they would risk interpersonal conflicts rather than simply avoid confrontations. In fostering risk early on working groups could be more efficient.

Often, working groups are really a bunch of people working side by side, not really a team or a cohesive group, whereby teams have to support each other and find synergies in moving forward together. The risk that teams take will potentially yield a better performance than if the group would stay a simple working group (See Figure 6).

Team members need three sets of elements to produce growth and results. A team needs skills in problem solving, technical skills or interpersonal skills, then it needs commitment on the goal and common approach to achieve the goal. Finally, the team needs accountability. Each team member holds others to their words and set goals. If a team is armed with these elements it will outperform working groups.

However, if the working group call themselves a team but do not take risks together pursuing a collective effort, they might actually be a pseudo-team. After "forming," a real team will first take the risk to "storm" together by taking risks and failing together. Then the team will fix what needs to be fixed and rebound stronger in a "growth" phase that will produce outstanding results. Eventually, the team might "plateau" in its output and a shakeup (change of people, a.k.a., someone will get fired) might be needed by leadership. That could take the shape of a new project or change of team members.

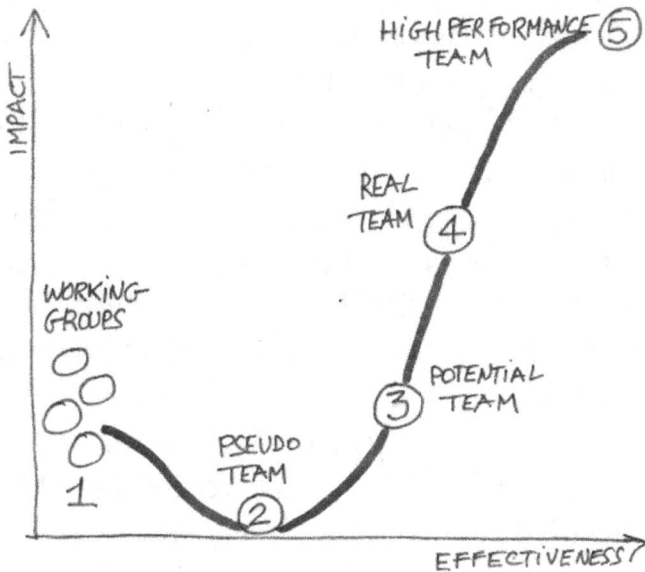

Figure 6   Katzenbach and Smith Team Curve

In my spare time I am a sailor. I sail boats up and down the U.S. Eastern coast and to and from Bermuda. I also did a little racing with sailboats, where my job was bow man–the guy (or the lady) that is at the front of the boat during the entire race and deals with the sails up front, particularly with the spinnaker. The spinnaker is that big puffy and colorful sail that boats have when they are pushed by the wind. Anyway, I also managed to coach at the U.S. Naval Academy (USNA) over the years. That's the Annapolis Naval Officer school that produces engineers, pilots, astronauts, submariners, Marines, and other fine people. I coached the summer offshore training program for several years and the Varsity team. We raced to Bermuda one year along with two other USNA boats and 20 others "civilian" boats. Our boats finished first, second, and third. I was coaching the third boat team. I am telling this story because most of what a manager has to do besides individual development is to manage the team of individuals. And a team is not just the sum of its members. Actually, in my experience, a team is often less, at first, than the sum of its people. It is a "pseudo-team". You have experienced that as well. Did you feel that within a team you could do things better, but because one team member was more vocal than you that you should let him or her talk? Did you feel that as a result your ideas were not heard, and your motivation slipped a little? What about when one team member is not pulling their weight? Are you not tired of stepping in and picking up where they left off?

My crew was made up of eight people. One was in charge. He was the Skipper and had a second in command called the XO. Others were assigned different positions and were staffed with experienced sailors, and somewhat less experienced ones. They all had trained during the spring semester, and we had been able to go out in the ocean already for practice. During that training around the DELMARVA (Delaware-Maryland-Virginia) peninsula one major event happened that would test leadership. One sailor clogged the toilet and broke off the arm mechanism that allows the pumping of the toilet bowl contents to get pushed to the holding tank (I know that is a little gross). That sailor said nothing, and the next sailor came on deck and said, "The toilet is broken, what should we do?" That is when leadership broke down. The Skipper and his XO should have assessed the situation; toilet (it's called a "head" on a boat) is broken and someone needs to fix it. On a boat each sailor has a title and a responsibility. One job is that of the First Lieutenant. His job is to make sure the entire ship is ready for sea and the crew has done what they needed to do per their job description. So, one thing the Skipper could have done is telling his XO to assign the First Lieutenant to fix the situation. It is called delegation. The job of the Skipper was to stay on deck and think about the strategy to win the race and direct the action. Except neither the XO nor the First Lieutenant were willing to do the job. Under the pretext that it was gross, they said no. What should the Skipper do now? Two choices were in front of him. He could take the XO aside and tell him, "Yes, it is gross, but that's the job", and as an XO he is in charge of executing the orders. After all it is a military organization. Or, the Skipper could have stepped in and say to the XO, "Ok, I understand it is gross, it is gross for me as well, but I guess the buck stops with me so I have to fix it." In other words, stepping in and doing it himself as possibly some form of leadership. He chose option two. I helped him on the technical side, as he had never dismantled a toilet before. But during that very gross repair job I told him that his choice was not the choice of a leader. It felt like leadership only because the crew was grateful to stay away from the task (you cannot dump your "business" overboard within three nautical miles offshore; thus, you have to hold it until the toilet is fixed).

Often you see that very reaction, particularly with managers that are green. What would my boss think of my operation if it is not fixed? What would the team say of my leadership if I do not step in? It is a trap. Leaders have to set the stage for the team to get motivated. Leaders have to find the informal leaders and get their buy-in. Leaders have to be directive when the situation calls for it. Leadership has to keep their eye on the ball, i.e., the mission and not be stuck in the gutter as it was the case. The toilet was fixed, we lost the race, and the Skipper had a tough time getting the team to follow him. On our race to Bermuda, again the Skipper was confronted with issues that instead of delegating or telling, or coaching the team through, he did himself. As a result, lots of frustration, and less learning, less efficacy as a team. Three team members including the XO quit the Varsity team after the Bermuda race. Maybe related, maybe not. One team member was promoted to a Skipper position the next semester. The skipper learned the lesson and is now a successful officer in the Marines. Go Navy!

Accounting

Accounting in its most basic definition is the method of counting the money that comes into the company and the money that leaves the company.

One principle in accounting guarantees the accuracy of the method, which is referred to as "debits equal credits." Simply put, accountants write down the money going out of the company (e.g., the payment of a bill) and at the same time they will show what the money was for by allocating the same amount of money to a special place in the books that reflects what was paid. For example, if the company buys office supplies for $100 in cash, then an entry is placed in the account title "cash," which shows the money coming out (called a credit), and $100 will be debited to the account as "office supplies." Thus, in the end the credit of $100 will equal the debit of $100.

There can be a lot of movement of money, therefore, many accounting debits and credits happen in any given month. At the end of the month, and most definitely at the end of the year, accountants will print the overall accounts in three summary tables that are called the income statement (or the profit and loss statement, P&L for short), the balance sheet, and the cash flow statement.

The P&L's most simple explanation is that it's a big subtraction (See Table 3). Yes, nothing more. Revenue (also called sales, also called gross income) minus expenses equals profit (if positive) or loss (if negative). That's it!

In a little more detail, revenue is made up of all sales to customers (each box of cereal times the price of the box). Expenses can be listed by type. For example, the P&L usually lists the cost of goods as the main expense directly related to the sales. For example, a box of cereal cost includes the cost of the actual cereal and what it takes to make them—cereal, sugar, and other stuff like vitamins and minerals. It is also the cost of the plastic bag and the cost of the box itself. It is important to know what these costs are variable costs. Cost of goods fluctuates each time we sell one box of cereal. If the price of the box is $3 and the cost of goods is $1, then we know that if we sell 1,000 boxes our revenue should be $3,000 (1,000 boxes times $3), and our cost of goods should be $1,000 (1,000 boxes times $1). Or expressed as a percentage the cost of goods of our cereal company is 33.3% ($1/$3).

When you talk about the cost of goods, you're also talking about inventory. Inventory is calculated by counting everything you have on hand that has not been sold yet and finding the value of that. It follows an accounting principle of First In, First Out (FIFO) versus Last In, First Out (LIFO). The method chosen will impact the way cost of goods are calculated on the P&L. A company that chooses a FIFO method of accounting for inventory is claiming that if they purchase sugar bags every month in order to produce their cereals, then they will use the oldest sugar bags purchased first when they need sugar in manufacturing. That is a question of how the cost of making the cereal will be accounted for. If the sugar purchased in January cost more than the sugar purchased in February, then the cost of goods of making cereal in February will be impacted with a higher cost for sugar in the recipe. If the company opted for a LIFO method, then the lower priced sugar purchased in February will be used first in the production (before the sugar purchased in January) and thus the cost of goods in February will be lower. While that seems counterintuitive, it is simply an accounting method. In reality, the manufacturer will always use the oldest sugar every time no matter the cost, otherwise, the sugar might go bad. Are you confused yet?

The margin left after we take away the direct cost of goods from the revenue is equal to $2 per box, or $2,000 if we sold 1,000 boxes. That margin is not a profit. It is simply what we have left to pay for all the other expenses. The P&L can get into details of all the expenses, more or less. For instance, we have to pay for payroll (workers' salaries) and benefits (health care costs, holiday party cost), administrative costs (supplies, printer ink), marketing costs (advertising, design, research), rent, reserve for equipment replacement (depreciation or capital expenditure reserves). That takes us to a new "margin" or result (See Table 3) called the operating income. This is what the "operation" or the business generates in terms of money after it pays for everything related to the sale of cereal boxes. Below that, we might also find financial charges, which could include interest on loans we might have with a bank, possibly for buying machinery that we could not pay for with cash. The results of operational income minus finance charges is called the income before tax and serves as a basis for our IRS declaration to pay our corporate income taxes. The income before taxes minus the actual taxes is called the net income or income after tax. That profit net of tax is what we can reinvest in the company by keeping it, or by spending it on new equipment (that is called capital investments or capital expenditures, CAPEX for short), or we could give whole or part of the net profit to the owners (as dividends) and the employees (as participation to profit sharing).

The balance sheet is the other main table or statement that accountants will produce. That is also a subtraction, but it is presented as a side by side (not always) table where on the left side are the assets, and on the right side are the liabilities. The assets are what the company owns: cash, inventory of cereal, future cash from customers that have not paid yet (account receivable), value of equipment purchased minus the depreciation of those equipment over time. The result is the "current" value or the book value of this equipment. For instance, if you buy a new car that's worth, say $20,000, one year later the market value of that car if you tried to sell it is maybe $15,000. In fact, as soon as you drive off the car lot, your brand-new car has instantly lost value [one trick car dealers and car makers do to consumers is that they decide that the year of your car, say 2019, ends in the middle of the 2019 summer. So, cars sold after the 2019 summer are now 2020 cars, and cars purchased after the summer that are brand new, but labeled 2019 models, are worth a lot less than the other 2020 similar model on the lot. Thus, they give consumers large discounts to buy a "brand new 2019" when in fact they want the inventory off their lot to make room for the "real new" 2020 cars. The great deal you made on the brand new 2019 you purchased in September 2019 turns out to be not such a great deal when you check the blue book value and see that it has depreciated more than if you had purchased a 2020 model]. So, the depreciation here might have been $5,000 because $20,000 - $5,000 = $15,000. Accountants have formulas to calculate depreciation. Notice here that the depreciation expense in the P&L is accumulated in the balance sheet, year after year, until the book value of the equipment is zero at which point if the company decides to sell the equipment for $1, they would make a profit of $1.

All these assets are "balanced" with all the liabilities on the other side of the statement (See Table 4). Liabilities are made of money the company owes to suppliers (the suppliers might give the company a credit of one month to pay for the cereal that has already been delivered), and the other liabilities are usually money we owe the banks, such as loans made for the land, the factory, the equipment, which all produce interests that we pay and show on the P&L. Finally, we owe money to the shareholders or owners of the company, and list that as well. The money we owe to the owners are called equity, or shares (one share times the price of the share times how many shares are left outstanding), and every year we also list the result or net income we just calculated in the P&L. This money can be positive meaning we made a profit, but it can also be negative if we had a loss. In which case, if it is negative the equity or the value we owe to the shareholders/owners is decreased by that loss. Assets all added up equal Liabilities plus equity added together.

Table 3: Profit & Loss Statement for the Cereal Business

Income statement (profit & loss)

	20XX
Revenue (sales)	3000
Cost of goods sold	1000
Gross margin	2000
Payroll	650
Benefits	260
Other expenses	
Marketing	420
General and administrative	140
Rent	200
Depreciation	120
	880
Operating income	210
Interests	115
Income before taxes	95
Taxes	33
Net income	62

Table 4: Balance Sheet for the Cereal Business

Balance Sheet

Assets	20XX	**Liabilities**	20XX
current assets		current liabilities	
cash	259	account payable	805
account receivable	300	notes payable	190
inventory	708		995
	1267		
fixed assets		long term debt	850
land	200		
plant and equipment	2000	Shareholder equity	
depreciation	-560	common stock	1000
	1640	retained earnings	62
			1062
	2907		2907

A Story of Accounts Payable

I was the General Manager at a boutique hotel in Washington, D.C. and one day a travel agent approached me and tells me that he has a group of Japanese lawyers coming to Washington, D.C. to visit and follow seminars with the Department of Justice and other legal firms. Would I want the business? What kind of rate (price) could I give him, etc. Fifty rooms for three days at $150 would $22,500 of revenue. Additionally, the business would be during a slow winter month, so, really, that was incremental business, business we did not have last year. We signed a contract, and as is the case, he gave me a check for the first night, or $7,500, and said that the remaining money would be paid at check in. I asked for a deposit because I did not know the travel agent and therefore did not have any credit history. In retrospect, I could tell something was off, but at the time all was well. The group checked in and the front desk was instructed to get the check before they gave out the keys. The travel agent was pretty slick as he managed to get the keys and distributed them quickly under the pretext that every lawyer was too tired to wait. Then, instead of giving the check, he said he'd come back. He did not, meaning I was potentially going to have to "eat" $15,000. Not cool. This was grounds for being fired on top of being professionally embarrassed. I called him, went to his place of business, no answer. Meanwhile, the lawyers came and went to their visits and training. No one spoke English. No one was in charge. The impact of that mistake was going to be important. First, the hotel was paying sales taxes on a revenue of $22,500. Second, the hotel was also paying for all expenses linked to the three-day business trip, i.e., cleaning, payroll etc., all of which was still happening, thus if the revenue was going to only be $7,500, the profitability of that business would have been cut in three, which would look bad on the P&L. So, like is done in these cases, we posted $7,500 to cash, and the remaining $15,000 to account receivable. So far, no problem, businesses do that all the time when clients owe you money. Except that this was a ticking bomb. If the travel agent did not pay within a month or two, the accountant would deem the debt bad, and would take what is called accruals against the debt in order to lower the debt on the books. These accruals would end up as expenses on the P&L! (remember the rule of debit equal credits). Could you imagine the look on the owner's face if one month I showed $15,000 of expenses that were, in fact, a recognition that a couple months ago we screwed up? I was simply buying time because I had an idea. Every time a guest checks into the hotel we ask for a credit card "just in case of incidentals" the front desk is trained to say. Incidentals are minibar charges and other charges that guests are individually purchasing and thus not part of the group deal. That meant we had credit card information for most of the guests in the group. And after checking my registration cards wording (the paper you sign when you get your key), it was clearly well written that you, the guest, would accept any and all charges related to your stay. Bingo! I could charge all these credit cards for the entire $15,000. And that's exactly what I did.

Long story short, the lawyers complained to the travel agent, the travel agent was very embarrassed because we told the lawyers he had stiffed us, the lawyers pressured the travel agent, he gave me a cashier's check (a cashier's check is a check that is as good as cash, so no funny business here), and after the check cleared, we reversed the credit card charges.

The cash flow statement is one that explains how the company uses cash. The company starts the year with a certain amount of cash and ends up with a certain amount of cash at the end of the year. The difference is explained in that statement including operating activities that used or got (created) cash, investing activities, and financial activities.

It is always a good idea to look at a comparison of the different statements between consecutive years in order to see if progress has been made by management. Sales should go up, expenses should go down or stay flat, thus, profit should go up as a result. And if money has been used wisely, cash flow should increase, and shareholders' equity should also increase.

Sometimes there is a delay between actions and results, and one must think that through when looking at statements for any company. For instance, a major change in packaging for a box of cereal, and the added marketing costs associated with the change might lower profit in the short term, but the results a few months later, which might be the next "fiscal year," might be more sales, thus more income, more profit.

Usually, these explanations are listed in the company's financial report. All public companies (companies owned by the public with shares listed on the stock market, think Dow Jones, NASDAQ, S&P 500) must publish these numbers and reports quarterly and yearly. The reports are accessible online on the company's website, usually in a section called "investors." The main document you want to read is called the 10k report. This is the yearly report to shareholders, and it has all three statements accountants created along with accountant explanations and management explanations.

This is not an easy read and it takes a little time to enjoy reading this report that is often a little obscure, particularly if the company has something to hide. More on that in Chapter 6.

To assess the health of a company, accountants like to analyze the statements by calculating some simple "ratios," or divisions, between some specific numbers on the balance sheet or the P&L statement.

Here are two examples:

A. The Acid test, or quick ratio, needs to be greater than 1 to signify good company health. It is calculated using the following division [cash + any stock the company owns + accounts receivable] / [accounts payable + short-term debts payable]. In our example of the cereal box business the acid ratio would be 0.56, which is below 1, thus the business does not generate enough cash short term that could cover the short-term debt. That could become an issue and might generate bank overdraft situation or a need for new injection of cash from the owners.

   If that ratio is greater than 1, it means that if the company has to pay its bills due today (accounts payable + short-term debts payable), then it has enough cash (after it collects it from people that owe the company money, and after it sells the stocks it might own).

B. Return on Equity (ROE) is calculated by dividing the net income to the shareholder equity. The result is a percentage that could be compared to the interests a bank would give. If shareholders would give their money to a bank instead of investing it in a company, would they get a higher interest from the bank than the company's return? In other words, if you are a person with money, do you put it to work with a bank and get an interest, or do you invest in a business as equity and get net income as your return? What's a good ROE? It depends, mainly on the risk level of being a company shareholder as opposed to simply investing in a lower risk savings account. In our example of the cereal box business the ROE is 5.8%. That seems to be low. If you think about the energy deployed to create a business with your own equity and you get 5.8% return at the end of the year, it feels that if you had placed the money on the stock market you could have gotten more return without all the trouble. That said there are other benefits to owning a business that we will see in Chapter 7.

Finance

Finance is different than accounting. Where accounting is counting the "beans," the movement of money coming in and out of the corporation, finance, is providing an assessment that the assets of the company are being used efficiently. Finance also uses the company's assets, more likely the cash, to invest it in the most efficient manner. Efficiency in finance is really the idea of making money with money. The essence of capitalism.

Finance also includes planning future investments for the company. In fact, it kind of act as the inside banker for the owners. Decisions in finance are often made based on increase in cash or interest on the money invested, otherwise known as the Return on Investment, or ROI for short. To know if the ROI is good or not one would need to compare it to some standard. Financial managers would compare the ROI to commonly accepted benchmarks. One benchmark is the cost of money or the interest banks charge for a loan. Say for example that a bank charges 3% interest for a loan, if an investment can get a return of 5%, then borrowing money from the bank to make it work and getting a 5% return, will give the company a 2% net return after it repays the bank (5% – 3%).

Financial managers are also working with the concept of the value of money over time. Every year prices increase. It is called inflation (sometimes it decreases, but very rarely as we know). Inflation means that something that costs $100 today might cost $105 next year. That would mean inflation is 5% (the increase of $5 divided by the original price of $100). So, the same $100 is buying less next year, thus, the money is decreasing in value over the year by inflation. And $100 today is worth, in our example, $95 or 95% of its value from the previous year. If we look at an investment (or a loan for that matter) over several years, then we have to think about what is called compounded interests. Compounded interests are interests on interests. For instance, if you invest $100 at 5%, then next year you will have $105 in your account. If you leave it there another year, then you will not have $110 but you will have 5% more than $105, or $110.50. The difference is important over time, and we'll dig into that in Chapter 4.

Financial managers also advise on stock (share) issues, such as should the company use some of the net income and distribute it to the shareholders at the end of the year or reinvest it all into the company (keeping it in cash or actually using it to buy new stuff)? If it is decided that a part of the net income is distributed to shareholders, then that would be called a dividend. Sometimes companies use their net income and cash to buy back their own stock! Yes, really. Why? Because that way there are fewer outstanding shares on the public market, so less people will be able to buy and sell and make the share price fluctuate. It also means the corporation has to give less dividend, since there are less shareholders.

Information Technology

The topic of Information Technology (IT) goes beyond understanding what the basic components of a computer are (although that is a start), or what the Internet is. It is also thinking about how IT can help your business strategically.

Let's start with the basic components of a computer (See Figure 7). Believe it or not it is an interview question for Amazon's Data Warehouse jobs. A computer has a Central Processing Unit (CPU) which is the "brain" of the computer. The motherboard is the card inside the computer that hosts many components that process commands in order to get the computer to do something for you (print, calculate, switch something on/off, keep things in memory etc.). On the motherboard you will also find the Random-Access Memory (RAM) that keeps all operations in short term memory. That memory, by its size, allows your computer to keep several windows open and several software to work at the same time. You know you don't have enough RAM when it takes a long time to open another app or another software. The issue with RAM is that if your computer crashes or you do not save your work, then as the computer switches off or restarts, you will lose all current work done since the last time you saved. When you save your work, you do not save it to the RAM, you save it to the hard drive (usually called "C:"), or to an external drive, or a thumb drive. There it is safe and will not get erased when you reboot your computer. There are several Input and Output devices plugged into your computer. For instance, input devices such as the keyboard, or the stylet, or the mouse allow you to tell the computer to do something—write, search, print etc. Output devices such as the screen, the printer, the speakers, allow you to get information back from the computer such as the text you are typing, or the video you are watching. Some devices function as both input and output such as a touch screen, a video camera, or a modem.

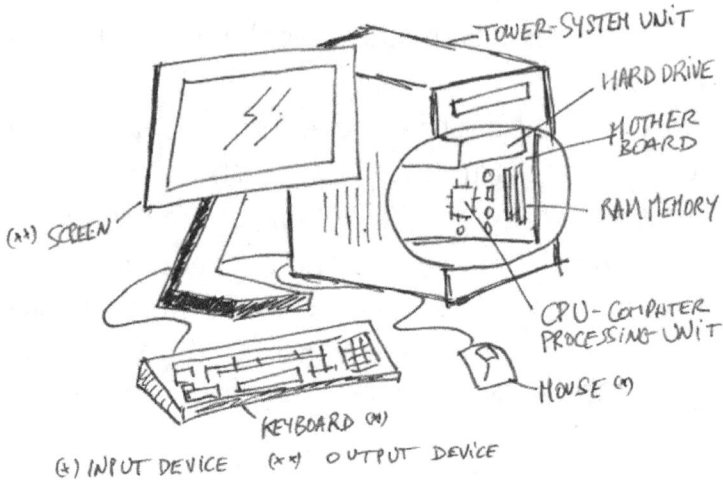

Figure 7   Basic Elements of a Computer

Today's computers are all part of the "web" or the "Internet." The Internet is the infrastructure of computers connected with others via a digital cable connected to your router/modem (that box on your desk with multiple flashing lights). These computers are all connected to bigger computers and servers that host the "World Wide Web" [note: that is where the "www" of any website address comes from], the "web" for short. Data, what you save not on your hard drive but "in the Cloud" might actually be on a web server somewhere in the world, or in a data warehouse. The "Cloud" is just that, a server on a rack somewhere in Virginia, or anywhere in the world, where your website is saved, allowing anyone with your website address to access and read your content.

The Internet of Things (IoT) is a rather new concept (watch TV series like *Black Mirror*) that connects all house appliances (fridge, TV, lights, air conditioning, locks, camera) with the Internet and allows you (or someone with access) to control your house appliances remotely (warm up the house in the winter as you are driving back from work) or collect and share information about your usage of appliances back to the Internet for someone (corporations, government) to make inferences about what you are doing (if the light is on, you're home) or learn what kind of consumer you are, your "persona" (if you are using the stove a lot, maybe you are a cook, and you get take out or go to restaurants less). Creepy, right?

Understanding the Moor's law is also quite important in understanding the speed at which innovation in the IT industry happens. Moor (an Intel scientist from the 60's) predicted correctly that every 18 months, due to innovation advances in miniaturization, the number of components (transistors) on a microchip would double. That means that every 18 months the speed of a computer can double, or the size of a computer can shrink in half, or the cost of the same computer can be cut in half. That means that soon enough computers will be so small we will be able to inject them in our blood stream (this actually already exists).

Some very important strategies are resting on computers' capabilities and access to the Internet. Almost no company can do business strictly offline. The end of the brick and mortar (name given to your physical stores) is here. Most, if not all, stores now have a website and are making business online as much, if not more, via the Internet. Consumers are talking to companies online via surveys or chats or comments. They are filling forms to the service departments, they are banking online, they are ordering online. Consumers are talking to each other (we call that the "voice of the customer") by posting comments and pictures online. An entire new industry is born out of consumers being able to organize themselves online with or without some intermediary platform. Look at Airbnb or Uber as examples of what is called the shared economy where consumers who own a house or a car want to make a little money on the side of their regular income by renting their assets to another consumer that found them online. Strategies are now also resting heavily on smart portable devices such as smart phones, tablets, smart watches, and soon smart eyeglasses or even implant microchips. Being online on your smart devices is not necessarily good for human interactions, but for a corporation, being able to attract your attention on any device is paramount to making a sale and making a profit. TV programs developed in the 50s for housewives (called Soap Operas) promoting house appliances, and cooking and cleaning products (soap), have evolved into the reality shows we follow today. Thousands of different shows are made by professionals or amateurs alike and target a smaller and smaller segment of the population. You can watch shows on digging gold in Alaska, surviving in the wilderness, picking the best antiques, or being a bachelor/bachelorette, and so on. New celebrities have emerged from these new medias, and today, bloggers, vloggers, and online influencers have almost the same weight on consumers' opinions and decisions than the more traditional celebrity push by the old networks or movie producing houses. In fact, the trend is so strong that traditional media houses have silently acquired new media and you might not know that less than ten corporations own 90% of all media in the U.S. Moreover, the Internet is a media as well and if you watch shows on YouTube for instance, you are contributing to Google's (the official name is now Alphabet corporation) strong hold on the Internet. Similarly, if you are using Instagram you are contributing to Facebook's success. The data created by companies, and mostly by us the consumers, is so large and so varied in form (videos, text, sound), and it is changing so rapidly, that a new term has been coined. Big Data is all the data in all its varied forms we can find on the web that we store and analyze in order to make decisions. Think about what can be guessed about you and your personality by looking at all the data you create, send, and receive on all your devices every minute of every day (Watch Netflix's *The Social Dilemma*).

Some IT related strategic issues are worth briefly discussing. For instance, Net Neutrality. Net Neutrality is the idea that internet service providers (cable providers, satellite providers, telephone providers, Wi-Fi providers, email and website hosting providers) should treat any flow of communication on their infrastructure equally regardless of whether or not it is coming or going to a competitor. So, for instance, if I use my computer to access the Internet via the router under my desk, which is connected through my cable company and I stream a movie I purchased on Netflix, then my cable company, which has a TV service and a streaming service, cannot prevent Netflix from sending the movie to me at the proper speed for my own enjoyment just because they would have preferred I use their services. Unfortunately, Net Neutrality is something that is politically charged as folks in favor of free markets are against it, while those in favor of some government control on the free market are for it.

The Internet economy has created a new way of doing business. Most consumers carry less and less cash on them. Slowly but surely even credit cards are replaced by electronic payments in the form of an app that holds your money, and that you "recharge" once the money is spent (albeit in most cases with a credit card). We are becoming a cashless society. That is taken to some extreme with the creation of cryptocurrency. Imagine that instead of moving money from your credit card or your bank account to your app to pay for your PSL (pumpkin spice latte), you would use a bank that would not be a bank. Some new currency that would be virtual. No bank, no bankers, no bank notes. An entire system created on the Internet and regulated by no one. The technology used by cryptocurrency companies (Bitcoin, Ether) to self-regulate and insure the validity of ownership rests on blockchain. Blockchain is a way for information (transfer of cryptocurrency but also other transactions like inventory management and purchases) to be secured while being read by the computer. Blockchain uses a coding and decoding mechanism that no one owns entirely. In essence, the software on one end talks to the software on the other end and agrees, or not, that a transaction can be done. This is done with small chunks of data (blocks) and allows anonymity if one block is corrupted, as one would need all blocks and all software keys to decrypt the message. Defenders of blockchain and cryptocurrency value the democratic decentralized approach. Others see the main issue with cryptocurrency in its anonymity and its lack of government control. This allows users of the dark web (a different world wide web made with less controls) to engage in illegal transactions. Thus, today cryptocurrencies have a bad reputation, and not many traditional corporations want to use them. But for how long?

A final strategic issue is Internet security, a.k.a. cybersecurity (sounds more like *the Terminator*, right?). You have more likely read that large companies like Experian or Target have suffered a data breach in recent history. That means that some hacker broke into their system and stole data (credit card, consumer names, etc.) and sold or published the information on the dark web. That is a Public Relations' nightmare and harms the customers that might switch to the competition thinking it is safer there. Companies, but also government (think about the 2016 U.S. presidential election), are weary of hackers for many different reasons spanning from leaking secret documents, to manipulation of information, to pure racket (See TV series *Mr. Robot* or Netflix's *Snowden* the movie).

Manufacturing

Manufacturing, sometimes called operation management, is the subject covering all aspects of product fabrication or service delivery, or both. Today's businesses are operating in what is called a service-dominant logic. That means that even if a company is producing a product, say for example a box of cereal, it is ultimately servicing customers as a way to differentiate itself from the competition. Thus, companies are making sure that the service aspect of the operation is pushed to the forefront. For a consumer-packaged-good (CPG) brand, being in the service business is a challenge, but if done well it might create increased value for the consumer. Think about Coca-Cola for instance. What are they selling? Is it more of a product or more of a service? The relationship that consumers have with the brand, and the creation of value that happens through the Internet, through the content created by customers, all make the service aspect more important than ever in the relationship that consumers have with any brand.

A few concepts related to manufacturing and production are worth reviewing here. The first one is the concept of quality. In the 70s and 80s total quality management was picking up as the best method for impacting the bottom line. If your production has zero-defect, in other words, if you produce boxes of cereal, all the boxes that leave the factory are perfect, they have the same taste, the same weight in each box, the same perfect box, etc., and they all took the same amount of time to be made from start to finish, from the source of the raw product (wheat farms, milk farms, wood and pulp factories for the boxes, etc.) to the distributor's (wholesaler, retail store) shelf for the consumer to purchase, the entire supply chain is hyper efficient. No money is wasted on bad products, delay of any sorts, inventory that sits somewhere without being used or sold, and customer complaints that result in discounts, refunds, or lost sales. From the 80s to the 90s we saw the emergence of quality programs that helped control all the supply chain. Noticeably, we have seen the six-sigma techniques and the certification that comes with it. Employees are trained on statistical methods that allow for the measurement of processes and outputs of manufacturing and service. These certified employees have earned different levels of expertise identified with a colored belt similar to the one you get in the Japanese martial arts system–yellow belt, black belt (note: the colored belt in judo or karate were invented to satisfy the westerners of achieving small incremental steps. In Japan you have a white belt until you have a black one). These total quality control processes have been created in Japan; thus, the colored belts system is a reminder of that.

Service blueprint and bottlenecks are also typical of processes encountered in the fabrication of a product or service. A service blueprint is the organization on paper of a sequence of events where the customer meets the employees in a service encounter–for example at the coffee shop, where management will measure the effectiveness of the quality of service, did the customer get his/her coffee on time? What is the optimum layout for the site? What is the optimum number of employees per time slots? And so on... Blueprints can also help identify bottle necks. Bottlenecks are processes that increase the time it takes for a product or service to be delivered to the customer. Think about a toll booth on the highway. Do you expect that it will slow you down? Yes, most likely. Because you cannot, legally or not, zip through it at the same speed than you have been doing prior to the booth. Thus, it is going to create a slowdown called a bottle neck, and the evidence of that will be that at peak hours or peak days you will be bumper to bumper waiting to get through. That is a bad service design (although it's a good design if the goal is to reduce accidents by reducing speed). The output of a kitchen in a restaurant can become a bottle neck (check out *Restaurant Impossible* or *Hell's Kitchen* shows). If only one cook can serve 20 orders in a "normal" time frame, but the restaurant can seat 50 people, what will happen when all 50 seats are taken? Restaurants often build bottle necks by design. Think about the bar area. You might come to the hostess booth and have no reservation and be told that will take 30 minutes to seat you. Meanwhile, you are not going to leave, you will stay and have a drink at the bar. That bar area might serve the purpose of optimizing the output of the kitchen throughout the evening, i.e., no down time, no delay, so more sales.

The 80/20 principle is a useful general principle (See Figure 8). The idea is that 80% of something creates or is related to 20% of something else. For example, 80% of a business's inventory (what is not yet sold but has been purchased by the company; think wines in a restaurant that is sitting in the cellar) represents 20% of the value of the inventory. If 80% of the inventory represents 20% the value, then it is also true that 20% of the inventory represents 80% of the value. That is actually more pertinent to the manager. You want to control that smaller batch of goods because they cost a lot more than the rest. Some bottles might cost $5, some might cost $100. That 80/20 principle says that if you check your inventory (the list of bottles in quantity and price) you will find that the most expensive bottles have the most value in your inventory, yet they are also the least in quantity. In accounting you can use that 80/20 rule as well to prioritize the work of accounts receivable (the money owed to the company). 80% of the accounts receivable will be made of 20% of invoices or clients. Thus, once identified, the accounts receivable person should focus on getting these invoices paid first because they represent 80% of all money owed.

We cannot talk about manufacturing without talking about Research and Development (R&D) and New Product Development (NPD). Not every company has an R&D department. High-tech companies like Microsoft, Google, Apple, etc., all have an R&D department.

So do Pharmaceutical companies (Pfizer, Johnson and Johnson), large consumer goods companies (Stanley Black and Decker, Procter and Gamble, 3Ms, Unilever), car companies, and so on. These companies are large or have large stakes in being the first ones to create a new product. The new product creation often follows a specific process called the NPD process. It often starts with brainstorming where many ideas are generated. Picture James Bond walking through Q's lab of new gadgets. Q's lab is the R&D of MI6. You can imagine that many of the original ideas and prototypes do not actually make it through the next steps in the NPD process. Each new invention has to be marketable; the consumers have to see value in the new product and should be willing to pay a price that will leave a margin or profit to the company. Some inventions are protected from being copied illegally by patents (think about drugs for instance). That allows the company to profit legally from a monopoly situation and make enough profit from sales to recoup all the R&D investment that was made to get that new product to the market. After the patent goes void the product can be copied because it is now in the public domain. Google, Apple, and others have been successful in getting patents for particular software. That allows them to control their competition or get royalties from the competition wanting to use their software. Brands, logos, books, and songs are also protected from being used without the agreement of the creator by a copyright. Food recipes are not protected. Thus, recipes for Coca-Cola, or the KFC batter are locked in a safe (or at least that is what we are told), because they could be copied. In fact, we know a lot of copycats in the restaurant business. Even Starbucks is easy to copy. Why are McDonald's, KFC, and Starbucks dominating the market without a patent or copyright creation? It has to do with the size of the network of stores they have, and the perception of constant new menu items they nurture with the public through marketing. Taking down one particular McDonald's by creating a better fast food across from it might be possible, but you could not get the equipment at the same cost as McDonald's or the raw product (fries, burgers) at the same price because you are just one restaurant and they have 38,000. What can you do? You have to create a different concept that is unique yet serves a segment of clients that are not quite happy with McDonald's today (Five Guys, Shake Shack).

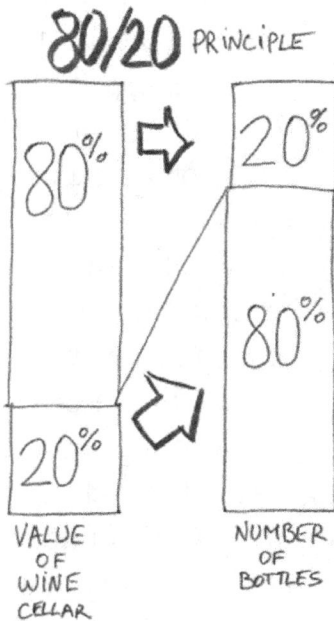

Figure 8   The Pareto 80/20 Principle

Marketing

Marketing is my subject. I teach marketing and I have practiced marketing at different levels in different countries for many years. To me marketing is in every aspect of human relations. There is a saying that "marketing is everything and everything is marketing." I believe that. When you try to convince your partner that you need to buy a new car, it is marketing. When you sell yourself on LinkedIn to future employers, it is marketing. When you think about new ways to save the planet at your level, like recycling, doing a compost, then you are improving your quality of life while potentially reducing costs; it is marketing. You get the idea.

Two fundamental concepts in marketing are segmentation and differentiation. Segmentation is the answer to the idea that mass marketing your product or services is no longer advisable nor profitable. If you think you can create a product that will be purchased by the entire planet, you're in for a disappointment. It took 100 years for the flush toilet to get into 80% of households. Actually, I remember my great grandmother's house, or my grandparents' summer cottage equipped with a shed behind the house that had a wooden plank with a hole placed over a bigger hole in the ground–yeah, tell me about it.

It took 20 years for the refrigerator to get into 80% of households, 15 years for color TV, 7 for the microwave, 12 for social media usage (in part because of the fact that you needed a smart phone and good reception). You get the point. We are adopting at a faster rate, yet products are not penetrating the market overnight. So, in the meantime, a company needs to segment its market into groups of customers that more likely need the same thing, or see value in something, and are able and willing to buy its product or services at a price that would leave a profit on the table.

There is an infinite way to segment a market. One can segment a market by demographic attributes. Men clothing versus women clothing are two different segmentation schemes that two different companies could take, or the same company could take. Another way to segment a market is by a psychographic approach. Psychographic has to do with the consumer's personality. Is the consumer willing to take a risk with a new product that will require them to switch from what they are purchasing today? Geographic locations are also quite easy to use for segmentation. If my side of town does not have a restaurant, then maybe that is where I would want a restaurant. Finally, I can also segment the market by looking at consumer behavior. For instance, I noticed that people tend to exit the metro on the sidewalk where their company building is located; they tend to not cross the street. Thus, I might want to locate my coffee shop on that side of the street and capture the traffic from the metro. The best segmentation schemes use a little of all of these methods. That confuses the competition and gets more "granular," or closer to customer needs.

Differentiation could be seen as the flip side of segmentation. Segmentation is about the consumer; differentiation is about the product or service offered to the consumer. The idea is that your product or service should be different in the eyes of the consumer in order for the consumer to get confused (sleezy marketers) when they compare your product to the competition. If the products are the same, the consumer will tend to compare only the price, and that could create a price war, which is a negative spiral for your company and for the competition. Take a look at the soda companies, burger companies, oil companies, and so on. You will see that when the product is the same, price war rages, which is good for the consumer not good for the business. Alternatively, when the product is different, then prices are more stable and fluctuate based on punctual marketing campaigns (discount, promotions) or even increase when inflation calls for it. A different product might only be different in the consumer's perception.

Perception is reality. Is the McDonald's burger really different from the Burger King burger? Is the chicken at KFC really different from the chicken at Chick-fil-A? Is a Ford four door sedan really different from a General Motor four door sedan? Is a room at the Marriott really different form a room at a Hilton? The answer is no. Actually, Audi is owned by VW, and a lot of what makes a VW car is the same in an Audi. The Audi, because of its perceived brand, costs more. The Chrysler voyager minivan was sold under the Dodge brand and the Plymouth brand with just a different sticker name.

So much rests on the power of brands in marketing that sometimes when we take away the brands, as in generic products (think generic drugs, or grocery retailers store brands), the price is expected to be lower. The proof of the value in a good brand is that sometimes a bankrupt company will still be able to sell its brand name to another company but not its factory or inventory. Look at the Twinkies story. Google it.

Differentiation and segmentation lead the marketer into what is called targeting. Targeting is simply a wise choice of a segment, usually the segment that really needs or wants your product, and that you feel you will be able to reach and convince to buy your product. Your targeted segment is often depicted by the marketer in the form of a person that has specific features, particular demographic attributes, and so on. This is called a persona. It is not someone in particular; it only gives an "average" representation of your targeted segment. That helps teams focus on the right customer with the right arguments.

Often marketing is described as advertising or sales. Advertising is part of marketing, so is sales. Marketing covers a much bigger area of business and includes input into NPD and particularly differentiation, branding, segmentation, and targeting as we have seen. It also includes all the decisions that stem from these choices such as pricing, promotions, distributions (where your product will be sold), communication to the consumers such as advertising, but also digital advertising, websites, online customer engagements, public relations offline and online, sales to the distributors or intermediaries, sales to the consumers, and keeping that customer relationship alive using the Customer Relationship Management (CRM).

Communication is of course targeted to the segment you have chosen and want to reach. Today ads are not made for mass communications, even if sometimes many segments have seen the ad (think about a $4 million ad during the Superbowl that is viewed by 100 million people). Companies create ads that resonate with the targeted audience and that are served on the proper channels that the targeted consumer most likely watches. Today that is no longer cable TV, or magazines, or billboards, but more often than not, multi-channel communications that leverage repeat occasions where the consumer will see the ad. It can be online on a social media platform, within a search engine, on TV via cable or a streaming service, and so on. Companies have to adapt to the way consumers consume information. And since companies have limited resources, i.e., limited money to spend on marketing; then marketing departments have to make choices on where to spend their budget in order to get the highest return on investment. Communication is what shapes the picture of what your brand has to offer in the mind of the consumer. This is called positioning. The goal of positioning is to create a unique, different, image of your brand's unique value in the mind of the consumer. That position is important because when the consumer has the need for your product, then they will recall from memory first, a set of brands, ideally a set that includes your brand, that they could choose from. Think about your lunch. What comes to mind as a possibility? That is the set of brands you can pick from. Now think about how you make your choice. Are you in the mood for tacos or burgers? If tacos, are you in for "fresh and responsible," or "low price and fast delivery"? That is positioning.

In my spare time I am part of an organization called SCORE. SCORE stands for Service Corps of Retired Executives. It is an outpost of the Small Business Administration (SBA). The goal of SCORE and its mentors is to help, for free, entrepreneurs in the community launching and growing their business. In my capacity at SCORE. I see at least one entrepreneur per week that needs some insight into their idea or proposal. More often than not, they want advice in terms of branding, legal organization, accounting, and so on. My first question to them after I introduce myself as a marketing expert is all about the marketability of their idea. Forget whether you need an LLC or a C-Corp, whether you should get Turbo Tax or ACT, whether you should have a logo and print business cards. What is important is their idea's capacity to get consumers excited enough to want to buy the product.

Marketing is the first thing that any businessperson should talk about and be concerned about, in my opinion. Marketing is the reason why you will sell your newly invented computer made from your parents' garage to more people than just your family. Marketing will create revenue. It is because you generate revenue that you will have money that then can be managed or invested and accounted for. Not the other way around.

Yet, marketing is the first thing to go when the business gets tough. You would think that when a company loses market share, they would double down on marketing and fire the accountants, but it is pretty much always the opposite that happens. I was Vice President of Marketing and Sales for a start-up in North America that was selling hi-tech equipment to the hotel industry. When the 9/11 terrorist attacks happened all capital expenditures (CAPEX) were placed on hold. Every hotel in the U.S. was empty, traveling stopped, and there was a loss of business that needed to be offset in the short-term. That need of cash to relaunch the hotels post-9/11 was taken from the reserves that are usually used to keep up with the equipment and the building (CAPEX). In other words, hotels would hold off on refurbishing and purchasing equipment for a year, or two, or three. Not good for the start-up that was selling hi-tech equipment to them.

Imagine you are the CEO of that start-up and you see your projection of revenue disappear. What do you do? You are under tremendous pressure from the board of directors to do something and protect their investment. You usually fire the marketing department. Why? The marketing department is often, wrongly, seen as an expense rather than an investment. So, cancel all ads, all shows, all Public Relations efforts, all sales meetings. That has an immediate effect on the bleeding of cash. And since all American companies do that, then it makes sense to do it as well. In my eyes it is short sighted, but I am biased. As I was walking out the door with my box of personal items, I was thinking about the use of accountants when there is no revenue, or installation teams, or R&D. I was thinking that sales were important to foster relationships; I was thinking that ads in the magazines were going to be very cheap since no one would advertise, thus making it cheaper to position the business in a better light than the competition. But I did not win; I was fired and moved on to my next gig.

Strategic Thinking

Most MBA programs, if not all, have a strategic angle, or a strategic component. Some actually try to be all strategic. It is a branding issue, but it is also a reality. Why would you not be strategic in your leadership? Your Human Resources policies? Your marketing? Your finances?

What is strategy? Most of the time we associate strategy with war, or the military in general. Sometimes we also associate strategy with games or sports. It is intellectually easy to understand that in order to win a game of chess you have to be better than your opponent. Being better means that you have to counter their moves in a way that will lead you to success. But if your opponent can think about all possibilities of what you can play several moves in advance and you only think about one move at a time, you might fall into a trap and lose in two or five moves. Similarly, war is a terrible chess game where people die and one opponent will eventually win and get the other side's possessions, land, and even people.

Business strategy is similar in essence to military or game strategy, and in some other ways different. One major concept in strategy is the concept of zero-sum game. A zero-sum game is a game, or a business or military situation, where there will be a winner and a loser. If someone wins say $10 and the other person loses $10, then the sum of what has changed is zero. It simply changed hands, but it is the same amount of money. When an army wins over the opposing army, it is a zero-sum game. When a chess player wins, the other loses, a zero-sum sum game. Most, if not all, strategies whether military, games, or business are zero-sum games. Think about market shares, or the proportion of revenue you have by getting consumers to buy your box of cereal compared to what all consumers spend on cereal. If your market share is 20% and you find a smart way to increase that market share next year to 30%, then what happened? More than likely, you stole the market share from another company or a set of companies. Yes, true, maybe the population increased, and you captured all that market without stealing it from others. When I say stealing, I mean it in the most "chivalric" way, of course. Business is ruthless. It is like a war. Even if you see business leaders smiling at each other and talking nicely to each other, one thing is always on their mind—stealing the other company's market share. Watch movies like *Wall Street*, or series like *Silicon Valley*. Better yet, read some autobiographies like "Steve Jobs" by Walter Isaacson.

The alternative situation to a zero-sum game is what is called a non-zero-sum game, or more often a "win-win" strategy. A win-win strategy is when two companies both win. In reality, a true win-win situation is improbable, although mathematically it is possible. For two companies to gain market shares, one or many others have to lose. You can make an argument that consumers might have disposable incomes they spent on these two companies' product, thus, no other company lost revenue as a result, but where was that disposable income? Maybe it was tucked away in a savings account, which means the bank loses; maybe it was kept under the mattress for a rainy day, which means that the money for an emergency in the future would be lost. I am aware that I might be suffering from what is called zero-sum bias. It is a cognitive bias where you only see the world as a zero-sum game. One example of a non-zero-sum game in the context of business strategy often given is when a company creates an entire new market that did not exist before. It is often called the blue ocean strategy because as the blue ocean it is infinite, and there is no other competitor (read the book "Blue Ocean Strategy"). Think about, for instance, the way Cirque du Soleil has created a completely new genre of circus that has very little to do with a circus and is patronized by consumers that would not have gone to the circus before but are going to see a Cirque du Soleil show.

A business strategy often starts with an analysis of a situation. It includes the internal situation of the company. The good, called strengths, and the bad, called the weaknesses, by product lines or by brands, or by business units (retail stores, company divisions). It also includes the competition analysis, which is critical. It needs to be done with the company in mind, the targeted segment in mind, and the brand positioning. For instance, in analyzing the car industry for Tesla one would want to limit itself to companies that can compete on the same fully electric market as Tesla, and in the same price range or that are targeting the same consumers. No need to analyze the truck market for example as it would dilute the analysis. Stay focused on the core market and core competition.

Tools have been created to help managers analyze their situations. One of these tools is the SWOT analysis. SWOT stands for Strengths, Weaknesses, Opportunities, and Threats. Strengths and Weaknesses help analyze the company, whereby Opportunities and Threats help analyze the market, the competitors, the industry, the trends, anything outside of the company's control that might affect the future.

In the digital era we live in many online tools are now available that help managers stay informed on a minute-by-minute basis about the key indicators that pertain to their business. These big tables are called dashboards or scorecards. They can get constant input of data via the Internet and let the managers look at metrics (key indicators) just as a fighter jet pilot would in order to make timely decisions. Data visualization software, more likely cloud-based, permits any manager anywhere to get instant information. That includes algorithm-generated metrics such as consumer sentiment, to be able to react appropriately and keep course.

In strategy one needs to think that any action a company will take in order to increase its power will result in a reaction from the market, a reaction from the consumers that could be good (they purchase the product) or bad (they refuse or even rebel against a change; Google the Coke Classic flop), and a reaction from the competitors that could be bad (the competitors defend themselves well and attack in return) or good (the competitors fold and let you win market share).

Strategies are also very present in large companies, especially companies that have many business lines and brands. Think about General Electric, General Mills, Procter and Gamble, LVMH, and so on. These companies are conglomerates of several companies. Each of these companies might have several brands, as well. All these lines of businesses constitute a portfolio. The portfolio needs to be analyzed in the context of the market at large. Decisions need to be made to allocate resources and create a market superiority maybe by developing and launching a new product. But since resources are limited, they should be taken from another line of business and reallocated into the line of business that is most in need of funds in order to survive and conquer. This is where the Boston Consulting Group (BCG) and the McKinsey Consulting Group have helped companies by developing a different, yet similar tool, for portfolio strategy.

The BCG matrix is a 2x2 matrix that has on the horizontal axis the relative market share of each of the company's business lines or brands, and on the vertical axis the growth rate of the market each of these business lines have. The matrix shows four boxes, each delimited by the average growth of all businesses (alternatively, that could also be determined by management arbitrarily) and the average market share. See Figure 9.

For each of the boxes a name is given, and brands or business lines that fall into these boxes have one strategy or more that are suggested. A high market share but low growth business line will be a "cash cow" and will be able to reallocate resources to help other business lines. A low market share in a high growth market will be a "question mark" that will need to be helped by using resources from the "cash cow" in order to penetrate (gain market share) the market. If that business line after being helped loses ground and subsequently moves below the average growth line, then that business line will be deemed a "dog" and might become a candidate to be divested, stopped, or dismantled. The thinking is that if several attempts to gain market shares are not successful and growth rates diminish at the same time, then the rewards (profits) are not worth the effort (investments). In other words, the corporation should cut its losses. Finally, if the question mark business line gains sufficient market shares, then it becomes a star. A "star" will generally have a future as a "cash cow" brand. It will penetrate the market more and more and the market saturation (when close to 100% of the population buys the product from all brands available) will create a lower growth rate overall. If everyone has a color TV, then color TVs will sell less rapidly. So, the portfolio strategy here is to create or acquire new business lines that will be supported by the "cash cow", often the legacy business brand, and will become a "star", before becoming a "cash cow"; and to be quick at divesting "question marks" that can become "dogs" in order to free up resources and limit those losses.

Figure 9   The BCG matrix

McKinsey has a similar approach and matrix, although the matrix is a 3x3 matrix, but essentially the use of the matrix is the same. Know what business lines to grow or nurture, which ones to harvest, and which ones to divest.

This is where Mergers and Acquisitions (M&A) are important. When a company feels that it needs to launch a new line of business, what is the most strategic move; is it to create the new business from scratch? Or is it to acquire an existing business that does what you want to do, and that you can afford to purchase? This is the question of M&A. Watch movies like *Wall Street* or *Pretty Woman.* McDonald's has always tried to capture different segments of the market by developing its own new business lines. For instance, McDonald's launched pizzas in the 90s, then stopped because it did not pass the test (maybe they had a BCG matrix type of analysis). They have been successful at launching chicken items, fish items, or coffee items lately, but pizza or fajitas have not been successful. Maybe they concluded that they did not have the skill set to launch these lines. In fact, McDonald's launched and discontinued 100s of new product lines. At any rate, in 1998 McDonald's invested in Chipotle Mexican Restaurant, and eventually helped the chain grow from 12 units to more than 500 units. McDonald's invested $360 million in the venture over eight years, before Chipotle went public where its IPO (Initial Public Offering) was one of the most successful at the time. McDonald's sold their shares, divested the business line, and took home $1.5 billion (not a bad profit). So, what happened here? Seems that Chipotle was a "star" with a good market share in the growing market of fast-casual dining. However, as it is often the case in mergers and acquisitions, the culture of McDonald's and that of Chipotle clashed somehow over the demand of McDonald's executives. For instance, McDonald's wanted to introduce breakfast menus and drive throughs at Chipotle, and Chipotle management resisted the idea. Thus, they were both cultural and strategic differences.

In the end, McDonald's shareholders pressured McDonald's to concentrate on their core business and divest non-core businesses like Chipotle.

You might be asking yourself "Why do I have to know that stuff?" The answer, at least from my perspective, is that we all have to know basic business concepts because business is what is all around us. We interact with businesses every day, we buy business shares for our retirement plans, we work for a business, or organization that works like a business more often than not, or we might want to create a small business of our own to supplement our income or simply because we have a good idea. At any rate, I tried to keep it to the point without becoming overwhelming.

The MBA program takes 18 months of course work in most cases, and a lot of reading. So, if you want to know more, you need to read, or watch movies and shows, or even sign up for an MBA!

That's it! You've got your (5 minute) MBA!

That wasn't too hard was it?

CHAPTER 4

Know How to
Get Stuff

*"If you don't have what you want, you
are not committed to it 100%"*

You've got a Bachelor's, you've got a job, more than likely paying around $35-$45K (depends on many factors like your industry or your residence), you are thinking about a Master's, but in the meantime, you need stuff. You need to get a car because the car your parents bought you 5 years ago is not the one you really want, you need professional clothes, you need furniture for your new apartment, and so on.

There are two ways to get stuff. You either pay cash or you pay over time where someone gives you the money up front, and you pay them back with interest over an agreed upon period of time. Of course, you can get an interest-free loan from family or find money on the street, but for the most part when you need to buy stuff, you choose to either pay in cash or over time. That is whether you have the capacity to pay cash or not.

I remember at least two instances where I needed stuff and did not have the money to pay for it in cash. If my grandfather were still here, he would say: "Save the money until you can buy the stuff." He was not found of interests and loans. But, in our "modern" economy we are almost required to buy stuff now (marketing and social pressure "forces" us to get the same flat screen TV our neighbor just got, as evidenced by the large cardboard box left on the street curb for everyone to see. Cheap manufacturing, that leads to low prices, also forces us to replace the broken product we bought not too long ago instead of trying to repair it). Thus, we have to find a bank to lend us the money to buy "cash," yet be indebted to our lenders to repay the amount, plus interest over time. We have to get a loan.

Many things are just so expensive to the average person that we cannot even think to pay cash for them. Think about a car costing around $9,000, or a bed with a mattress costing $900. If you are making $40,000 a year, can you afford to pay for the car or the bed with cash? And if you can, the question becomes, should you?

I arrived in the U.S. in 1989. I needed a car. I quickly found out that I really needed a car. The first day I woke up in the Chicago O'Hare hotel I was working at I wanted to go to McDonald's. For me, part of the American dream was having a "real" hamburger at McDonald's (crazy, right?). So, I asked the front desk person to tell me where the closest McDonald's was. "Easy," she said, "Exit the hotel and go straight; it is past the highway on the other side; you can't miss it." Perfect! I thought. I exited the hotel and went on foot in the direction that the front desk agent indicated. Of course, I got stopped by the highway. At which point I said to myself, you are not going to be afraid of a road. I crossed the highway. Traffic was not crazy as it was a summer day, but it was still a little scary, and illegal. I understood at that moment that you need a car in the U.S. to do a lot of things, maybe everything? Next on my list was to get a car. I searched the yellow pages (this was pre-Internet) and the nearest car dealership was on Golf Road. I took a bus. I went to the wrong address; in Chicago addresses can go North or South, East or West, so 19010 East Golf road is really far from 19010 West Golf road. But eventually I made it to the dealer. The car salesman was your typical pre-CarMax type of guy. Think Steve Buscemi in *Fargo*. He saw from miles that I was a very fresh-off-the-boat French man. He showed me a used Renault (French brand) that cost $6,000. As a recent immigrant (I was actually on a work visa) I had "no credit" in the U.S., no bank account, no credit card. After a talk with his manager, which is what salespeople would say and which some still do, in order to make the customer wait and think about the possibility of being rejected. After ten minutes the salesperson re-appeared and said: "Good news, my manager approved you for credit!" I was so thrilled that I barely looked at the contract. All I wanted was to pay no more than $250 per month, and that's what I was going to do. What else was there to worry about? Nothing, right? Wrong!

My interest rate was 21%. 21%!!! And the term was for three years. Thus, my monthly payment was $226.05. I was happy. I ended up understanding that after three years of paying $226 per month I would have paid back $8,137 for a car that cost $6,000. $2,137 of interest. Or put another way, 35.6% (2,137/6,000) more than the cash price over three years. How stupid was I? Very. But, hey, I was fresh-off-the-boat, remember?

Another instance of fresh-off-the-boat economics happened in October of that same year. In Chicago, October gets a little cold, and everyone warned us that it was going to get really cold in the windy city come winter. We were coming from Marseille (south of France), where it was sunny and hot ten months out of the year. We needed some winter parkas. Something super warm. So, we went to the mall and tried to buy three parkas. One for myself, one for my wife, and one for my baby daughter. The cost of the three parkas was $500. No problem, I had that much (but not really more) in our bank account. I started to write a check and the cashier said: "I will need a second form of ID, like a credit card." The reason I was asked for a second form of ID was that first, my checks did not have my name and address printed on them (they were still the starter checks you get when you open an account) and second, most businesses wanted a way to charge your credit card in case your check bounced. Some guarantee of payment. I had no credit card (remember fresh-off-the-boat?), so I was caught in the middle of either freezing to death (exaggeration) or finding cash. I came back with $500 cash and got the merch. Humiliating, but at the same time a lesson for the future.

The moral of these two stories is that credit is good because it gets you out of having to carry cash or access more cash than you have in your bank account. But you need to be aware of the way you can be eaten by the sharks. Once you are aware of each option, cash or credit, and their impact on your finances, then the decision is yours.

Impact on your finances? What do I mean? Read on.

Buying Now or Later

Gen Z POV: "When I started at [my first job] full time, you know, it was completely different. I was paying my own bills for the first time. The way they start you is you start making $12 an hour, then you have to hit certain goals, then you're bumped up to your $50k salary. So, you know, when I was an intern, I was making $12 an hour but my parents were paying for my rent, and my car, and my insurance, all that stuff. So, it did not seem like a big deal. But moving here and paying all my bills making $12 an hour was, like, impossible."

Think of yourself as a company. You make an income, that's your salary. Some people do not have a salary but have income from independent contracting jobs. That's different, and we'll touch base on that later. But for now, let's assume we all get a salary.

With that income you pay the different bills you have to pay every month. These are your expenses. What is left is either money you could save for later, or you spent more than what you made, and you need money to pay the bills, so you'll ask for credit from someone, be it the bank, a friend, family, or the vendor (the one selling you the stuff you want).

The key to being able to buy stuff, whether with credit or cash, is to not live beyond your means. What I mean is that you need to make a budget and know exactly how much you have to spend on each of the things you need or want every month. The worst budgeting practice besides not having a budgeting practice, is to use credit every month to buy what you want or need without knowing if you can pay it back. That obviously will not get you very far, as you'll have to repay the credit plus interest.

> *Gen Z POV: "I remember when I opened my first paycheck I almost started crying in the bathroom, 'cause that was like $300 and something, so I was like, three of these aren't gonna pay my rent. I don't understand how I'm supposed to do this. So, I was like, ok, I can at least make overtime, so then I'd be working 50 to 60 hours a week."*

Let's try to do a budget for a young graduate with a job paying $40,000 per year.

The first thing to do is to talk about the net pay you will get. Payroll in your company is more likely done every two weeks. Thus, when you get a job, you have to wait one or two weeks before you get your first paycheck. Once you get your paycheck it might have an actual check with it, or it might just be a "stub," a document indicating how much was transferred to your bank account, called a direct deposit. Choose direct deposit because you will get the money faster than with a check. Remember what we said about bank days in Chapter 2? Also, you might get your check at work on a Thursday, by the time you bring it to your bank (or "picture deposit" it), it might be Thursday after bank hours (usually early afternoon) so it won't be taken by the bank until Friday, then if you are not paying attention that Friday might be a bank holiday, plus the weekend, your pay might make it to your account only on Monday.

Net pay is what you will eventually get in your bank account. The difference between your "gross pay," the $40,000, divided by 26 bi-weekly pay that is $1,538.46, and your net pay are all the deductions you will see listed on your pay stub.

Deductions are your federal and state income taxes, your federal insurances (listed as FICA on your stub), your medical insurance cost, and other deductions depending on your company's benefits (401k retirement funds, life insurance, parking, meals, etc.).

Federal taxes are only an estimate based on your declaration of status (married or not, dependents or not) you make when you start your job (usually done your first week at work) on the W-4 form. You can re-do that form every time you have a major change (get married, have kids, etc.) by going to see your accountant or Human Resources person. If you declare more deductions, your federal tax deductions will be less than they should be, and you will have more money to spend until you file your taxes in April the year after. Don't do that. If your federal taxes withdrawn directly from your paycheck are less than what you owe by 10%, you might get fined by the IRS. The opposite is often done without negative repercussions, where you claim less deductions than you could so that your federal taxes taken out of your paycheck are more than what they should be. In that case the IRS collects more than they should, and they will give you a refund after you file your taxes the year after. People do that as a form of savings, although the major drawback is that you collect no interest on that money.

For a single person making $40,000 per year the federal income tax will be around $3,180 or $122.31 for each paycheck. That is about 8% of your gross income. Income tax is not simply a percentage of your income, it is gradual. You pay a certain percent on each "brackets". For instance, in 2019 you would pay 10% on the first $9,875 you make, then 12% on the money you make between $9,876 and $40,125. If your salary is $40,000 then your income tax will be $987 on the first bracket plus $3,615 on the second bracket ($40,000-$9,875) for a total of $4,602 or 11.5%. In fact, you will pay less than that given that your taxable income is going to be less than your salary after making some deductions allowed by the IRS. For example, in 2019 the basic deduction for a single person was $12,200. So, your $40,000 salary would be reduced to $40,000 – $12,200 = $27,800. That would be called your taxable income. That means that your second bracket income tax will now be 12% of $17,925 ($27,800-$9,875) or $2,151 for a total of $2,151 + $987 = $3,138. That comes to 7.85% of your $40,000 salary. The highest tax rate based on your salary, 12% in our example, is called your marginal tax rate. You hear people complaining about the highest tax rate being 37% and a deterrent to making more money, but in fact this is only a marginal tax rate for income over $518,400 per year which affects less than 10% of the population. The rate you will be taxed on average after all deduction will be a little less than 8% in our example. That is called your effective tax rate.

State income taxes vary by state. Some states do not have taxes, like Florida, while others have varying percentages. Let's say that your state has a 2% effective rate, meaning you will contribute $556 per year or $21.38 per paycheck to your state income tax ($27,800 x 2%).

Income taxes are a very complex topic and can vary widely from person to person even with the same gross salary. When you do your tax filing in April (or before) you will have many potential deductions you can use to lower your taxable income. For example, donations to non-profits might be deductible. Your income tax will then be calculated on that lower taxable income. So, in essence, even if you make a perfect W-4 declaration, you might (emphasis added) get a refund. Don't count on it too much, though.

There are two kinds of deductions under the Federal Insurance Contribution Act (FICA) that will be taken out of your pay as well. First is the social security deduction of 6.2%. That pays for the retirement of your grandparents, and the people that will be employed when you retire will pay for your retirement. The second deduction is Medicare at the rate of 1.45%. That pays for the medical insurance of the retired people.

These FICA deductions add up to 7.65% of your gross income. In dollars it totals $3,060 a year, or $117.69 per paycheck.

Thus, at this point your net pay is only 90.4% of $40,000 ($40,000 - $3,138 - $556 - $117.69) or $36,188 yearly (See Table 5).

Medical insurance cost is a deduction that you will incur if your company provides health insurance as a benefit and you choose to take the benefit (you don't have to if say for instance your parents still can cover you, or your significant other has a better/cheaper benefit coverage you can participate in). If your company offers health coverage, it will often pay for a part of the cost and you will pay for the other part. Some companies offer the coverage for free to employees (they pay 100% of cost), some split it 80/20 or any other way. That cost is also function of what you choose for a health plan. Companies can offer different choices of health plans–a cheap one, a medium one, and the Cadillac plan. Each one covers health costs, more or less. It is a little "à la carte." It is a jungle, so you'll need to ask Human Resources to explain the different advantages and cost for each option. If your company does not offer that benefit, and you are lucky enough to be in good health, you will have to make a choice. You either don't get insurance and save the money, or you get private or subsidized insurance (i.e., Obamacare a.k.a. the Affordable Care Act insurance) on your own. Private insurance or "Obama care" can cost you $200 (in some states more) per month. This is a very difficult decision for you to make because if you fall sick and you don't have insurance, you will have to pay the full cost of medical visits and treatment. If that happens to be appendicitis, for instance, it could cost you upwards of $30,000 for the surgery. 1 in 1,000 people aged 20 something gets appendicitis. That is a chance (probability) for you to get it of 0.1%. To put it in perspective it is almost twice as much chance than to get syphilis (a sexually transmittable disease).

The good news is that, for some of you, at the time of reading this book you still have until you are 26 years old to stay on your parent's health coverage. So, if that is the case, do it and save the insurance cost. Otherwise, the cost of health insurance and dental (yes, it is separate, makes no sense, but that often is the case) will be, as an example, maybe something like $60 per paycheck.

> Gen Z POV: "I played the card, like, I'm too poor so don't cut me off until I'm 26. And my parents were cool with that. But now I am on the company HMO plan that is 100% covered by the company."

Your company might offer retirement benefits like a 401k plan. Usually, it is a good idea to sign up because the company often matches your contribution up to a certain amount. That money the company is giving you is free money, and you'll get that money later when you retire. So why not take it, right? Say, for instance, the company matches your contribution up to 3% of your gross income, so if you put 3% of your gross income, $1,200 yearly ($46.15 per paycheck) in our example, you will get $1,200 from your company in your 401k account for free! Combined, the $2,400 will grow in value based on the stock market choices you make. More on that later. One catch though is that you cannot touch that money until you are ready to retire. So, make sure that you do not save too much and then have to use credit to buy food. That would be a bad choice. One immediate good news about participating in a 401k is that you will pay less income tax. In our example you put $1,200 toward your retirement account per year, thus your taxable income is now $26,600. Your federal and state income tax will be reduced by $168 (12% of $1,200 for the federal income tax and 2% of $1,200 for the state).

Your company might give you more benefits that cost you a very little amount of money but is still taken directly out of your paycheck. Things like parking, the cafeteria, or even life insurance can cost you some money. All these are most likely benefits that make sense to you, but you can pick and choose the ones you want and pay for them.

What is your net pay after all these deductions?

Simple. $40,000 minus the income tax and FICA is $33,414. Per paycheck that is $1,285.15 to which we need to subtract the medical cost of $60 per paycheck, so your net is $1,225.15. If you choose to save in a 401k, say $46 per paycheck, then your net will be $1,179.15.

Now that we know what we will have in our bank account every two weeks, it is time to budget our expenses (See Table 5).

> *Gen Z POV: "One of the adjustments I had to make was to take a serious look at my budget and deductions coming out of your paycheck. What my parents instilled in me is the need for a rainy day fund. So, while it would be great to go out and get an arcade 1Up retro game, which I did eventually get, you're supposed to leave, you know, a little cushion for yourself."*

The big expenses are rent, food, car related expenses, clothing, utilities (electricity, gas, water), cable/Internet, and phone. All these expenses recur every month and are fairly difficult to avoid.

Renting an apartment can run you somewhere between $400 to $1,200 per month or even twice that if you live somewhere like San Francisco or New York City. Strategies to lower the rent are often similar to what you experienced in college, like having a roommate or two. That can bring some challenges in terms of privacy, responsibilities, noise, shared spaced, but it definitely cuts your rent down.

Landlords like to look at your income (gross pay) and evaluate how much they think you can afford in terms of rent before they sign a lease with you. Usually, they want no more than 30% of your income going to rent. So, for a $40,000 income you can get a $1,000 a month apartment (30% x $40,000 is $12,000 for a year rent or spread over 12 month $1,000 per month).

When I was renting, and single, that ratio was the norm as well. But I know, as you know, that sometimes it just does not work. And more often than not people end up living in a place that costs them 50% of their income without a major problem. I did that when I worked in Paris. There were no apartments cheap enough. I didn't have a roommate. I found a way to get a landlord that would accept me even though my rent was 50% of my income. In those cases, you might have to get a co-signer on the lease. A co-signer is someone that pledges for you that if you do not pay your rent they will pay. Thus, it is someone with an income, and good credit rating (See below for credit rating talk). Usually that person ends up being one of your parents. For now, let's assume you find an apartment that costs you $1,000 a month. To that you need to add renter's insurance of $30 a month. That is mandatory and covers the landlord for your mistakes (i.e., you flooded the apartment) and covers some of your belongings if damaged.

Utilities, as in electricity, gas, and water might cost you another $40 per month depending on the efficiency of the systems and how much you crank the heat or air conditioning. Your mom will silently laugh when you complain to her of your electrical bill, since you are the one that always complained that the house was too hot in the summer. Now you get it.

Groceries are another big cost. It includes food, drinks, and other cleaning supplies such as soap, toilet paper, detergent, etc., and these things are not cheap. Count $100 per person per week for all that, including the supplies you'll need less frequently. Now if you eat only spaghetti, the budget will go down, and your health as well. But if you eat shrimp every day, then the budget will go up, and your health might or might not be better. Depends on how you are going to cook those shrimp (See Chapter 9 for a good recipe). If you choose to go out and have food or drinks at a restaurant or bar, or if you eat lunch at a fast food or take out, that will be a different budget. You might save $50 on your grocery bill a week, but that $50 will not take you far in dining out. Thus, you might want to figure out a "dining-out" budget separate from the groceries budget. Say, for instance, groceries are $50 per week and dine-out budget of $100 per month (after all you are probably single and need to hit these bars, right?). Respectively groceries will be $217 and dine-out $100 per month.

Cable/Internet in the apartment might cost you $40 per month (that is without any streaming services), to which you might add the streaming apps at a cost of maybe $5 per month per app. So, your total budget here might be $50 (I counted two apps since your phone provider might give you access to a third one included with your phone plan).

Your phone will cost you $30 per month for the phone (you know that you are stuck into paying for a new phone each month for the rest of your life unless you can face your friends with an older version phone that is paid for. In marketing we call the effect that fashion has on consumers, perceived obsolescence. That means that the product is out of fashion and one must upgrade to follow the fashion trend).

Clothing might be a monthly expense if we think about clothes and what goes into hygiene maintenance like haircuts, manicures, makeup, lotions, etc. So, if you are a woman that cost might be more, but maybe not. Some sneakers cost way more than stilettos and make up combined. Let's budget $30 per month.

Final big expense is transportation. You might have a car, you might have a monthly car payment to make, you might have to use your car to go to work, or you might use public transportation like the bus or the metro. Let's budget a car payment of $200 per month. A cost for insurance of $100 (you are still considered a young driver, meaning a risky driver by insurance companies. More on this later). Cost of gas might vary, but let's say $40 per week. Costs of oil changes and repairs might be $50 per month (based on a $50 oil change twice a year depending on the type of oil and your mileage, and a mechanical issue costing $500 once per year. If your car does not need a mechanic's help, you will have given yourself a $500 bonus to spend on New Year's Eve!). Car related expense total $350 plus gas.

Where do we stand now? See Table 5.

> *Gen Z POV: "So now I know how to budget, and as soon I get paid, I know how to put aside for loans and everything is fine, but it is a struggle at first."*

Your net pay is $30,360.20/12=$2,530 per month. Minus all expenses you are left with $2,530 -$2,020 = $510.

Not bad, right?

What will you do with that $535 of disposable income every month? Wait a minute, do you have student loans to pay? 69% of students took loans in 2019 to the tune of $30,000 on average in balance. So, you might be in that situation. Thus, the $535 is going to serve these loans before you can spend the money on any other thing. For instance, a $30,000 loan balance at 7% interest, spread over 10 years is going to cost you $348 per month. Now the play money is down to $187.

What should you do with that money? There are many things you can do. Some are very bad decisions, like gambling it or spending it on booze. Some are very responsible, like paying off your debts faster. Giving all $535 a month to pay the student debt will save you $5,301 and the loan will be repaid in 64 months instead of 120 months.

It will probably be something in between. I suggest you pay the $348 per month for a year or two until you know how stable you are on the budget. If you happen to have some money at the end of the year, or after you get a refund from the IRS, then payoff some of that debt. But what if you have a big issue with your car? Your health? Or what if you want to take a vacation far away? All that will cost you. Think about gifts for the holidays, birthdays, Mother's Day, etc. Maybe you need a new laptop, maybe you need sports equipment. Maybe you want to play the stock market. For all those reasons get stable in your budgeting habits, and then think about what you want to do. Notice that it does not take much for that "left over money" to melt in the sun.

For example, if your gross income is not $40,000 but $35,000 now your disposable income is down from $535 per month to $208 per month. That is not enough to repay your loans, thus you'll have to spend less on food or entertainment to find an additional $140 needed to pay your student loans.

So now comes the question about that big expense. Say you want to buy a pair of Gucci shoes (or a trip to Costa Rica, or a new surfboard) at the cost of $600. Should you wait 4 months so that you can save enough for it, or should you buy it now with store credit (a credit card branded with the store you are buying the TV from that you can only use at that store), or your regular credit card (a card issued by a bank you can use anywhere)?

Before you can even think about whether you want to pay cash or credit, you need to know about credit scores, or credit ratings. Do your own budget with the worksheet at the end of the chapter.

> *Gen Z POV: "It's really, like, understanding how to budget and save your money. 'Cause I know a lot of people who get paid bi-weekly, but here we are paid monthly, so it's a lot harder. It was a lot more difficult for me to budget at first. I think it is really important to make your own budget like on excel to figure out how much you have in the end and how much you can put into savings."*

Building Credit to Get Credit

Your credit worth is based on whether you can repay a loan in the agreed upon manner. If you don't repay your loan in the agreed upon terms, you partially pay the loan amount, or you just don't pay, there are consequences for that. Of course, this is not *The Sopranos* (great series to watch), and no one will have their knees busted with a baseball bat. But the consequences are that you could be forced to pay through a lawsuit settlement, possibly directly out of your paycheck, or by forcing you to sell some of your assets (e.g., car, home).

Table 5: Example Budget

Gross Pay	$	40,000
per paycheck	$	1,538
Paychecks deductions		
Federal and State Tax Withholdings & FICA	$	253
Medical and Dental	$	60
401k Contributions	$	46
Net Pay (take home every two weeks)	$	1,179
Pay per month	$	2,530
Rent	$	1,000
Insurance	$	30
Utilities (electricity, gas and water)	$	40
Groceries	$	217
Eating Out	$	100
Cable/Internet	$	50
Phone	$	30
Clothing	$	30
Car related expenses	$	350
Gas	$	173
Total expenses	$	2,020
Left Amount	$	535

In case of goods like cars or homes, banks will repossess the car or the home, and because the value of the car or home might be different (think lower) than what you still owe plus interest and legal costs, you might (will) still have to pay the remainder from your paycheck. Not a good situation to be in. At the same time that you are trying to not pay your loan back for whatever reason, the bank is going to inform the credit bureaus of the fact that you are delinquent, meaning you are not paying on time or not in full. In the U.S. there are three credit bureaus: Equifax, TransUnion, and Experian. They each have a slightly different way to use the information from the bank, but basically, they calculate what is called a credit score. The credit score (commonly called FICO score) ranges from 300 (you are the worst at paying back debts) to 850 (you are the best at paying back debts). The FICO score calculation is a secret sauce. But over the years, people have figured how it works a little bit, and some credit habits will significantly move your credit score from low to high (and of course, in the opposite direction).

Why would you want a high credit score? The higher the credit score the better loan options you will have. So, for instance you see that car loan at 3% advertised but if your credit score is not near 700 you have zero chance of getting it. You might get a car loan, but it might be at an interest rate of 5% or 7% instead, or 21% in my case. And if your score is below 550, you will probably not get any loans.

Bottom line, your credit score is critical. It drives loan rates down and the amount of credit you can get. It allows you to get a credit card. It will be used by landlords to evaluate if they should rent you an apartment. It will be used at the cash register where you are trying to buy that flat screen TV (Gucci shoes or surfboard) on store credit.

Gen Z POV: "I did not know anything about FICO scores or credit at school and I was a finance major. I did not learn about personal finance. I miss that. I had to learn on my own, and having to budget, and having to pay back my student loans, and having to try to have passive income, whether that's with stocks or something else. And now being with an investment bank seeing people investing their money, I'm like dang here I am being a peasant."

You are entitled to one free credit report per year (if you ask for it). Just check out www.annualcreditreport.com. All credit bureaus have an app that let you check your score more often. If you have a credit card it might actually let you look at your score every month for free. Banks, when they issue a loan, have to let you know what your score is. So, there are plenty of ways for you to know what your score is and to assess where you stand on the totem pole of credit worthiness.

The median FICO score was 711 in 2011 (50% of the population was below that number and 50% above). A FICO score lower than 580 is deemed very poor, between 580 and 669 is deemed fair, between 670 and 739 is deemed good, between 740 and 799 is very good, and between 800 and 850 is exceptional.

As a student, given that you have student loans, but also that you have a Bachelor's Degree (finally some good news), your score might actually be a little greater than 600, which is a fair score. If you plan on getting credit, then you want to aim for a minimum score of 660. And if you'd rather have a lower interest rate and a larger amount to borrow, then you want to be near 750.

How do you change your credit score? Your FICO score is more likely impacted by these big areas related to your credit habits: your payment history (do you pay on time?) makes up 35% of the change in the score; the amount you owe makes up 30%; if you had new credit inquiries recently, that makes up 10%; the length of your credit history makes up 15%; and, the types of credit you currently use (store credit, credit cards from a bank, mortgage, students loans) makes up 10%.

Let's look at an example. You are fresh out of college, and you have the financial situation we described above–that is to say a $40,000 income, a car loan and a $30,000 student loan balance.

Just like accountants and financial analysts (See Chapter 3) use ratios to evaluate the financial health of a company, bankers do the same to evaluate your financial health. The debt-to-income ratio (DTI) for instance is the ratio of your debts (in our example, we owe $200 per month for the car loan and $348 for the student loans) to our monthly income. In our case, it comes to 16.44%. Bankers and credit bureaus like to see less than 36% here. So, you are in a good place. In other words, you could technically incur another $652 of loan payments per month. That is because 36% of your $3,333 income per month is $1,200 and you are already in the hole for $548. The astute will notice that given your budget there no way you could afford another $652 of credit repayment per month. This is where people often fail. Thinking that because a bank gives you credit you can afford it and repay it is short sighted. You need to make that decision for yourself looking at your budget.

Another ratio to understand is the debt-to-credit ratio. The amount of credit you have been given on a credit card for example, versus the amount that you have used, or that you owe on the credit card. So, if you have been given a $5,000 credit limit on a credit card but you owe only a balance of $1,000, then your debt-to-credit ratio is 20% ($1,000/$5,000). The goal here is to stay under 30%. So, for instance if you have one credit card with a limit at $5,000, you can charge and owe $1,500 without impacting your credit score negatively. What if you need another $2,250? You could very well charge the same credit card since your limit is $5,000 and you only owe $1,000 currently, but that will increase your ratio from 20% to 65%. Instead, you could apply for another credit card and be given another $5,000 limit, and charge $500 to the first card, and $1,750 to the second card. Combined that would give you a ratio of 32.5%, which is less impactful on your credit score. Crazy, right? Welcome to the world of living on credit.

> *Gen Z POV: "Credit cards, oh my gosh. I think like I have $5,000 on a credit card right now. Just because it's so easy, you know. Just swipe it and forget it. It was great for my credit score for the first two years I had it, but I think like my credit score after a year was like 790 something, it was pretty good, and then at some point it was like 560, now it's back to the low 700."*

One of my employees at the restaurant I worked at when I first arrived in the U.S. was very proud to show me his credit cards. He had a wallet with transparent pockets, one for each credit card, and the pockets were all attached together, so that when he would let them fall down the credit cards would hang from his arm holding the wallet down to the floor! He probably had 50 credit cards! That, of course, is borderline compulsive. But the moral of that story is that it took me one year to get a pre-paid $500 credit card, a card for which I had to convince my banker that if I gave him $500 cash to put on a special account as guarantee then he could give me a credit card with a limit of $500, which he did after a lot of negotiation! My employee had probably $30,000 in credit lines combined.

Your first credit card will be difficult to get. Although I have seen banks on campuses giving credit cards away based on the fact that college graduates have a better chance of earning a good salary than others, it might still be difficult to get a first credit card. So, if that's the case, you can go to a store–a clothing store, electronic store, pretty much any large national brand store–and ask for a store credit card. That limits where you can buy things, so stores tend to like it and might be more lenient to give you a card, albeit often at a higher interest rate. You, getting a store card will show the credit bureaus that some other corporation trusts you. Buy something you need. Wait for the bill to come in. And pay it in full and collect points or cash back. Then leave that card in the drawer. Now you have a good payment history and a low debt-to-credit ratio, thus your FICO score will increase. Ask for a second credit card. Try to get a bank credit card (Visa or Mastercard depending on the bank), then only use it for purchases you would have paid cash and pay the balance in full at the end of the month. That way you do not pay interest, and you can increase your credit score. Call the credit card folks and ask for a small limit increase because you want to buy a flat screen TV. They will give you an increase, but you don't have to use it. And just like that you have decreased your debt-to-credit ratio and more likely increased your FICO score!

How Much Credit is too Much Credit?

If you listen to the banks, then 36% of your income is the threshold, some even suggest 35%. You will be tempted. You will go to a store, and plan to pay cash, or with your regular credit card, and the cashier will say: "If you charge that on our store card, which I can open in one minute, you will get an extra 10% off." You bite, and now you feel as if your regular credit card limit is still fully available and you buy more on that card. Thus, at the end of the month you are now over the threshold. Control on paying with plastic is difficult. This is why it was invented. It is to get folks in debt so that the banking system can make a profit (half of the banks revenues are made with interests; half are coming from fees. Think about it, the bank charges you a credit card fee, then you go use the card, they charge you interest, then you fail to pay on time, and you are charged more interest and an overdraft fees...it is all a win for the bank). Wait, if I am too much in debt and I can't pay, why would it be good for the bank? Good question. You are in debt, you will pay something every month, and that money will mostly go towards interest. In other words, the bank pays itself first. Then, if the loan is attached to tangible goods, like a car, the car can be repossessed and sold, or in the case of pure credit card debt, the bank can and will threaten to ruin your credit score, and if that is not enough, then they will threaten to sue you for the balance and possibly garnish your wages (have your employer send the payment to the bank by taking it directly from your paycheck before you see anything). Also, think about large numbers. There are millions of credit card holders in the U.S. Some will pay, with interests, some will not. But overall, the bank knows that more people will pay than won't pay. Thus, even if you, personally, are a credit risk for the bank, many other clients will largely compensate for your short comings. This is also one of the reasons the credit card interest rate is more in the neighborhood of 12% to 20% rather than below 10%.

How Should You Manage High Interest Rate Credit Cards?

Most credit cards charge high interest rates. An interest rate of 12% on a credit card balance of $1,000 will take you 3 and a half years to pay off if you only pay the minimum payment of $30 each month. In total, your $1,000 will have cost you $1,222, or 22.2% more.

In general, start paying more towards your most expensive credit card, meaning the one with the highest interest rate. While you do this, you need to continue paying the minimum payments on any other credit cards you may have. What I mean is that you should always pay what you owe given the regular terms, and if you can pay extra, then put that extra money on the most expensive card. For example:

Say you have two cards—one has a 12% interest rate, the other a 20% interest rate. On the first one you owe $1,000, and on the second one you owe $500. When you get the statements the first card says your minimum payment is $35 and the second card says your minimum payment is $20. What should you do if you only have $600 to pay toward both balances?

The first thing we need to do is understand how much interest we will have to pay next month if we leave a balance on any of these cards. For that we divide the annual interest rate by 360 days (some banks use 360, some 365, read your contract) and then multiply by the number of days until the next payment. Let's say 30 days. So, for the first card you have an interest of 1% on the balance ([12%/360] x 30 days), and for the second card an interest of 1.67% ([20%/360] x 30 days). Suppose now that we pay equally each card with our $600, meaning $300 for each card. Then what happens? Our fist card balance will now be down to $700 and accumulate 1% interest until the next statement, or $7. Our second card balance will be down to $200 accumulating $3.34 in interests. The total interests will be $10.34.

What if we put more money on the second card with the higher interest rate? Say we pay it off and pay only $100 on the first card. The balance of the first card is now $900, and the interests owed in 30 days will be $9. Thus, by putting more money on the most expensive card we lower our interests by $1.34 ($10.34 – $9), or 12.96% less interests. Always pay more if you can on the most expensive card first (that goes with student loans as well).

One more point here is the notion of compound interests. Compound interest is the idea that if next month you owe the balance of your credit card plus the $9 interests, but you still do not pay off the whole amount, the interests the month after will be calculated on the balance plus the interests of last month. In other words, the bank is charging you interests on the interests! Fantastic concept. Should you care? Yes.

$1,000 with a compound interest at 12% yearly will become $1,126.83 by the end of the year. If the interests were not compounded, then the $1,000 would have become $1,120 ($1,000 + 12% interest). The difference is $6.83 of interests on top of the interests. Almost one full percentage point.

The much better behavior with credit cards is to pay them off every month. No interest at all. But sometimes it is not possible.

[**Note on APR**: APR is short for Average Percentage Rate. It is what you will pay in interests on a loan, on average, over a year. The average here refers to the fact that often the interest rate is variable. That means that the interest rate is based on some index that can go up or down every month. Often banks guarantee the APR will not fluctuate for a period of several months. When comparing different loan offerings, use the APR. APR differs from the "interest rate" advertised in that the APR includes all fees in the calculation of what you owe and what interest you will have to pay, where the interest rate does not, thus APR does not present a better marketable picture for the lender, but that's what you should focus on as a consumer.]

How Should You Manage Credit Card Checks You are Receiving in the Mail?

Almost all credit cards allow you to take "cash advances" at a higher interest rate than regular purchases on credit. So, if your interest rate is usually 12%, then maybe the cash advance rate is 18%. You can call the credit card company to request a cash advance, but usually they will send you checks in the mail that you just have to write to yourself. You write the check for $1,000; you deposit it in your bank account, and bingo you got a cash advance. Now that $1,000 is going to show on your credit card statement under a special heading of cash advances with a special interest rate of 18%. The marketing offer might even be that your first six months are interests free, or that balance transfers (other credit card balances you would pay off with your checks) would be at a low rate, or even a zero rate for a while. Be careful here. The zero payment is hiding that first, the credit card company might charge you a transfer fee no matter what, and that second, if you transfer a large sum, then the interest rate will be 18% after you benefited from the initial zero interest period.

So, do the math. Say your balance on credit card one is $10,000 (you bought a car "cash" with your credit card, which is a very bad idea) at a 15% interest rate. Your second card has an interest rate of 12% and offers you a balance transfer for free, no fees, and six months of no interest, before it goes up to 18%. Should you do it?

Here, the second card rate of 12% is irrelevant to us since we are going to make a cash advance or balance transfer. The rate we need to use is 18%, knowing we will have zero interests for six months. If we do nothing the first card will charge 15% on a $10,000 balance, or $125 for 30 days, then compound the interest every month. Compare that to the other card and the 18% interest rate that will cost you $150 for 30 days. It seems that the balance should stay on the first card. Except that the second card has six months of no interest. So, over the course of the next six months on the first card you would pay $774 of compounded interests that you would save if you transferred the balance to the new card. On the second card you will have to pay $935 of compounded interests for the next six months (assuming you do not pay any money to lower the balance, and you are looking at a one-year comparison). So, in the end if you do not transfer the balance, you will be paying $1,608 of interest for the next 12 months, and only $935 if you transfer the balance. In that case you save $673.

Of course, if you keep the balance longer than one year the saving starts to dissipate because the interests of the second card with the cash advance is 3% higher. So, you have to "strategize" when you are making these moves. Watch out for the attraction of points or cash back as these advantages might hide the reality of the inevitable interest hike coming up. So, if you use that new card to benefit from the zero-interest period and collect the points great. But don't forget the deadline to avoid the interest reset date.

If you are planning on significantly lowering the balance by paying it down, say because you are expecting an IRS refund, then maybe the balance transfer is great because by the time the interest starts to kick off, you will be ready to pay off most of the balance. But if you are just trying to take advantage of the free six months of no interest, then you do not see the forest for the trees. You will be stuck soon enough with a more expensive card.

How Should You Manage Credit Consolidation?

Debt (credit) consolidation is the idea that instead of having multiple credit card balances you would benefit from having just one credit card balance with one lower (key word here) interest rate rather than the combined average interests of the current credit lines or credit cards. Let's look at an example. You have two credit cards–the first one has a balance of $10,000 with a 15% interest (that bad car purchase is following you), the second one has a balance of $5,000 with an interest rate of 20%. Question: what is your average combined interest rate? Answer 16.67%. Add up your balances, which would be $15,000. Find out the proportion of the first loan to the total combined balance. $10,000/$15,000 = 66.67%. And do the same for the second balance: $5,000/$15,000 = 33.33% (notice the two proportions added equal 100%). Now multiply the proportions by the interest rate of each respective card and add up the two results together. [15% x 66.67%] + [20% x 33.33%] = 16.67%. That combined rate is what you need to compare offers of credit or debt consolidation with. Along with your FICO score (which as we have seen will increase or lower the interest rate and terms the new bank or financial institution is ready to offer you) you go shopping for a better rate than 16.67% with an amount of $15,000 of credit. Unfortunately, it is not quite that easy to compare options. First, you might get an offer that suggests a very low rate of 7%, but the terms might be long like 15 years. This is usually what a bank would suggest if you owned a house and have equity in the house (See Chapter 5) with a loan called HELOC, short for Home Equity Line of Credit. The low rate will lower your monthly payment, but the long term might have you pay more altogether.

For example, if you borrow (or consolidate) $15,000 at a 7% fixed rate over 15 years, then you will pay $135 per month for 15 years. That will total $24,268.

On the other hand, if you borrow the same $15,000 at a 10% fixed rate, but over a period of 10 years, then you will pay a higher monthly payment of $198, but you will only be paying a total of $23,787. That is a savings of $481 and you are done 5 years earlier.

It is in the eye of the beholder (you). If you think you can pay $198, then by all means do it. If you can only pay $135 per month, then be ready to pay a little more overall.

The math is not that important here, what you need to really understand is that a low rate is good, but a low rate over a long term might not be that good, unless you have made the calculation and you truly understand what you are getting into.

In general, fixed rates are better than variable rates (See Chapter 5); short terms or long terms depend on the rates and payment schedule. But if you have your pick, choose a low monthly payment if you are short on cash, or if you can choose a short term, which means a higher monthly payment, so that you can pay off the loan faster.

Getting Out from Under Too Much Debt

Have you watched *Back in the Game* on CNBC with Alex Rodriguez? The reality show (that only ran for 4 episodes) features the former Major League Baseball superstar as a host who helps celebrities like Evander Holyfield or Ryan Lochte go from bust to back on track. If you find yourself crawling under debt, then there are a few lessons you need to learn from that show and apply them to your particular case.

1. Know what your numbers are. You have to know what money is coming in and what money is going out. So, take an hour and write down all of that using your bank statements so you do not forget anything. If you are under too much debt, it is probably because you're spending more than you earn. Use the budget worksheet at the end of this chapter.
2. Cut your expenses drastically. Live under your means. For a while be ready to just pay for your apartment, phone,

insurance, and groceries. No more expensive restaurants or take out. No more just released video games. No more shopping sprees. If you live in a place that is too expensive for you (more than 30% of your income), then move to a cheaper place. Move to a one-bedroom place, rent a room at your friend's house (if they accept you), or move back in with family. Get your Wi-Fi from a coffee shop.

3. Pay the most expensive debt first. And write down your progress. Have a chart or spreadsheet and see your progress as you pay off debt. That means a commitment to pay more than the minimum due every month.

4. Increase or stabilize your income. If you have a good job, don't change it. Make sure it is secure. Be indispensable. Always say yes to new tasks or projects. Seek that promotion or that overtime. If the job is not really good, then look for a better one. Do not leave your current place, though, without having another job lined up. That could backfire as you will lose benefit coverage, and employers tend to see unemployed people as less qualified than employed ones (a wrong perception, but a reality).

5. Once your debt is under control and your income is secured, start resuming a fun life, but be very careful with any splurging. Go very slow at spending any disposable income on non-essentials.

Gen Z POV: "Save 1k in cash for an emergency like a car issue or something unexpected. Then focus all of your excess money into paying off loans n' debt."

Chapter 4 Appendices

Make Your Own Budget Worksheet

Gross Pay

per paycheck

Paychecks deductions

Federal and State Tax Withholdings & FICA

Medical and Dental

401k Contributions

Net Pay (take home every two weeks)

Pay per month

Rent

Insurance

Utilities (electricity, gas, and water)

Groceries

Eating Out

Cable/Internet

Phone

Clothing

Car related expenses

Gas

Total expenses

Left Amount

Students Loans

Amount left for savings (disposable income)

[Bonus: how to write a check]

① John Doe		⑥ Date 12/30/2020
3400 golf road		
Chicago, IL, 60666		
⑦ Pay to the order of __Chicago Rental Properties__	$ 1,000	⑧
__One Thousand__ ———————————— Dollars ⑨		
② Bank of Chicago		
Memo __rent january__ ⑩	_signature_	⑪
③ 123446879	④ 1001001239	⑤ 0125

A. Elements of a check:
 1) Your name and address.
 2) Your bank.
 3) Your bank routing number (you might need that when doing a fund transfer).
 4) Your account number.
 5) The check number.
B. What you will have to write on your check:
 6) The day you are writing the check.
 7) Who you are writing that check to (if you don't know, ask the person what the correct name should be: Who should I make this check to? For instance, a business might give you their formal business name as in Chicago Rental Properties, LLC. Some might give you the more common name they're known by, often called the "doing business as" or d.b.a.; that name could anything. The name they give you is the name their bank account is registered under. Be a little skeptical if a complex

apartment manager gives you his personal name to write the check to. Best to check on your invoice or contract for what the correct name should be.)

8) The amount in numbers. Notice the little dash after the last digit? This is to prevent someone from adding more zeros after.

9) The amount in letters spelled out. It is customary, given the limited space, to write cents in numbers even though this is the spelled-out line as in, "one thousand dollars and 55 cents." Also, notice the line linking the last letter to the word "dollars" to prevent fraudulent changes.

10) The memo space is for your own use. You don't have to write anything, but it is a good practice to write what the check is for, so you remember later. If you are paying a supplier, this is where you could write the invoice number to help them, as well as figure out what you are paying.

11) Your signature. I see a lot of young people struggling here. Coming up with a signature that is unique and that can be replicated by you many times is a work of art. Check out Obama's signature, or Trump's.

12) Not shown here is the fact that most check books allow you to keep track of your cash on hand. You start the month with a certain amount of money from your bank account. Each check is deducted from that amount at the time you are writing the check, thus you know exactly where you stand. Remember that the balance in your checking is not the cash you have on hand (See Chapter 2)

CHAPTER 5

Get a House

"The biggest risk in life is not risking"

Part of the American dream is to be a homeowner. I admit that it took me a while to understand what the advantages of being a homeowner were compared to just simply renting. Everyone I was talking to that was a renter would say that owning a home was a restriction on your freedom. You have a house, and now you are stuck. What if your job requires you to move? What if you can't sell your house fast enough? Or at the right price? Also, what about the repairs and maintenance on a house, or the taxes you have to pay when you are the owner? Homeowners' friends, on the other hand, were bashing the renters, of course. Renting is money thrown out the window, when a mortgage is like saving your money that you'll get back upon retirement when you sell the house and move to a more affordable housing.

I was too busy working for my next job at that point and I could see myself moving every three years or so, so I figured that renting was the right thing for me. Some of my friends were higher up in the organization and would get help from the company when they moved, but I wouldn't get that. When you are an executive in most large corporations your moving expenses are covered, and sometimes you even get help selling your house, and possibly even a sign-on bonus that covers any loss you might incur as you are moving. I was not going to get that, yet.

> *Gen Z POV: "I have my own IRA. It's not particularly aggressive since I have it in ETFs. I have a house now, so I am getting financially stable. I am a proud property owner here, living the American dream."*

Rent or Buy? Why?

So, the first question you need to ask yourself is whether to rent or buy. What are the advantages of renting and what are the disadvantages? What are the advantages of buying and what are the disadvantages? If your career is important to you, as it was to me when I was at the beginning of my professional life, you want to be ultra-flexible. If my boss wanted me to get on a train or plane to go help a hotel to open or one to become more profitable, I was the guy. I was a fixer, a change agent. Drop everything, pack a suitcase, and go. Flexibility when renting is not always as flexible as one thinks, though. You have a lease with the landlord and might be able to get released from your commitment if the landlord is nice. "Breaking a lease" is not really something that is done unless you have a clause (a paragraph in the contract) in the lease that allows you to do it. So, what happens? You are responsible to pay the entire lease. So, for example if you have a one-year lease for $1,000 per month, and six months into the lease you have to move for your job, then you still owe six months at $1,000, or $6,000! You might still get your security deposit back, though. What about renting your place to someone else until your lease is finished? If it's ok in the lease, then sure; if not, then you can't sub-lease. The landlord (notice the name "land-lord") wants to protect his/her investment and judgment in your capacity to keep the place in good standing and continue paying rent. A person that you chose who wasn't vetted (reviewed and accepted) by the landlord might present more risk to the landlord than to you. When you sign a lease, you sign a legal contract that binds you and the landlord in doing certain things. You commit to pay a rent every month, keep up with the usual cleaning and upkeep of the place, let the landlord know if something is going wrong so that they can fix it on time, to have an insurance that would cover the repair of the apartment in case you do something stupid (BBQ inside the apartment and start a fire) or just make a mistake (leave the faucet on and flood the place). You also commit to being a good neighbor and not making too much noise (no loud music; no parties). You commit to leaving the apartment in the same state you got it, and if you don't, the landlord will take your security deposit and will fix the place after you leave.

In exchange for your rent, the landlord will also commit to a number of things. They will give you the place and will not bother you (visit while you are there or not) without your consent, or at least your knowledge. They will come fix problems that are beyond your responsibilities, such as heating, ventilation, and air conditioning (HVAC) issues, plumbing, and so on. Now if you have ant or cockroach issues, you will have to discuss that with your landlord as to who is responsible. Were they there before you moved in? If so, it's up to the landlord to rectify the problem. If they showed up after you moved in, it will be deemed your issue to solve. Of course, that is a typical legal issue that creates a possible exit from the lease for you if you can prove that the landlord knew or should have done something. In a word, the landlord is in breach of the contract. Breach of contract gives both parties (you and the landlord) the opportunity to leave or evict. That wording will also be on the contract. You might have to go to small claims court and sue your landlord, which is a lot of fun (not).

Landlords have seen it all and have had time and resources to craft (isn't that a nice way to put it?) the perfect lease. Meaning the perfect lease for them. Yes, when you get the lease you have to read it, and you have to ask questions, and suggest modifications before you sign. But let's get real, if you are just a regular renter, you will have no say on how the lease is written. You have to decide whether to sign it or not. That's all.

I have seen a lot of issues with renters and landlords. Some I was the renter, some I was the co-signer, some I was simply a witness. Every time I see a pile of clothes and some dismantled furniture on the front lawn of a house or apartment it breaks my heart. I know what happened; I don't know whose fault it was, but I know that the landlord got the right to evict the renter and did so without much remorse. You do not want to be the renter who was evicted.

For instance, three girls were co-tenants in a leased apartment. One decided to leave the apartment during the last week of the last month of the lease with her portion of the lease paid. No problem here. Except that when the landlord did the inspection, a microwave glass plate was missing, so the landlord wanted to hold the security deposit from all the tenants to pay for the missing dish. Since the girl that left a week earlier did not do a walk through with the landlord, and thus did not get a formal clearance that everything was in good order, then she was also responsible for the missing dish. You have to learn to get your ducks in a row when dealing with the law. Another renter was giving notice to the management office of a large apartment complex that he would vacate the apartment at the end of the lease. The lease otherwise would automatically renew for another year. The office manager took possession of the letter but did not give any proof of having received the notice on time or ever even receiving the notice from the renter. When it was time to move out, the renter was told that no notice had been received, and that the lease was automatically renewed. Maybe it was simply incompetence on the part of the office, or maybe it was done on purpose. So many young renters do not know what to do to protect or defend themselves that in that case the renter would have easily given up his security deposit as a way to get out of the automatic renewal. But rather than doing that he sent a well-crafted letter, this time via certified mail (in order to get proof of delivery) to the management office explaining in detail the situation, staying courteous yet firm in his arguments that he was acting in good faith and that the office had made a mistake. I want to emphasize that details are important when contesting something. First, details allow you to explain the course of events in a sequential and logical manner. Second, details allow you to increase the credibility of your claim. It is very different to say, "I called your business, and I did not get what I wanted," than to say, "On Monday July 5th at 10:30am I called your service department at 800-234-3434 (fictitious number). John answered the call and I explained that..." Eventually the landlord did not go through with his threat and the renter got his deposit back. But so many renters probably don't fight back. Don't be the one who doesn't fight.

We were renting an apartment in a tall tower that had a pool on the top level. I was playing with my kids in the pool on Sunday, and we were otherwise alone. Nevertheless, the building security guard came up from her desk in the lobby, where she could see us on the CCTV system, to let me know that jumping in the pool was not permitted. One of my children, or maybe all of them, were doing that I admit. But what was the harm? No one else was in the pool, and what's a pool if you cannot get a little playful right? Well, that was against the rental agreement rules (a question of liability in case of accident). On Monday, taped to my apartment door, I had a notice of eviction! WTF (pardon my French)? Can you imagine being evicted because your kids jumped in the pool in your arms while being the only family in the pool at that time? I went to see the management and asked for an explanation; it seemed that the security guard did not like the way I talked back to her. Knowing me, I knew that I might have been sarcastic and even maybe a little inquisitive, or rude. In one word, French. I was boiling inside. But I kept my cool and apologized (which took a lot out of me) and tried to negotiate my way out of that predicament. I was successful in the end and all was back in order. We just did not go to the pool ever again. Laws regarding leases vary by state. So, look at your state's website for more information on what you can and must do regarding leases.

So, do you still want to rent? Maybe if you knew a little more about buying, you would be able to make a more informed decision. So, let's look at that.

> *Gen Z POV: "So, for me I am thinking, "Oh great, I am renting for another 5 years. 5 years of a $1,000 a month rent is a lot. Especially when there is no equity in there for me."*

Equity, Leverage, and Risk Aversion

Buying a home is a lengthy process including a ton of paperwork, which will last at least a couple of months, not including searching and visiting open houses. But buying a house is similar to buying a car, or a flat screen TV. You search for the house you can afford and that you like, you make an offer, you sign the check, you get the keys. Of course, it is perceived as a riskier purchase than a TV, or a more involved purchase in terms of making the decision, because of the time you will spend thinking about it, the sums of money involved, the amount of mortgage papers and other closing documents that are all here to reinforce that perception.

What steps should you follow to purchase a house?

> Gen Z POV: "It would have been a stretch to afford my house on my own, I would have had to stretch my budget, so I found a friend to be my roommate, too, so what he pays is a nice little help out to the mortgage each month."

First, figure out what you can afford. Given your salary and the amount of money you can put down in cash, the bank, which will lend you the rest of the money needed in a form of a mortgage, will want to make sure they get paid back. For that they will look at your capacity to repay, often assessed with the debt-to-income (DTI) ratio. Remember that from Chapter 4? Your bank or lender will more likely not give you a mortgage that creates payments greater than 28% of your gross income/pay, including expenses related to the mortgage such as property taxes, house insurance, homeowners' association fees, and mortgage insurance, all together your "housing costs" or "Principal, Interests, Taxes, and Insurance (PITI)" costs. Additionally, your PITI costs plus your other debts (student loans payments, credit cards payments, car payments) should not make up more than 36% of your gross income/pay. This is called the 28/36 rule.

In our example from Chapter 4, your gross income was $40,000 a year, or $3,333 per month. You could afford a PITI of $933.33 per month. Your debt was $548 (student loans plus your car) per month, so your "back end" ratio is 44.4% ([$933 + $548]/$3,333), which is greater than 36%. Bottom line: you do not qualify. You need to increase your income, or reduce your debt, or both. This is not the end of the world. In a good economy where the housing market is booming, house values are increasing year after year, inflation is controlled at a single digit level, unemployment is below 3% or 4%, lenders will look at you in a much more positive way than if you try to buy a house with out-of-whack ratios in a bad economy. After all, lenders, realtors, legal firms, insurance brokers, and sellers are all here ready to make a deal. Some underwriters (the officer you'll never see or know, who will look at your case and will decide for the lender if you are good for the loan) might look at the risk level for your case in a more favorable light than looking strictly at the ratios. For instance, they might use what is called the residual approach. Under the residual approach a list of all your "hard" expenses (backed up by your most recent bank statement) is made, and your remaining income is what can be used for PITI. With this method some of your expenses might be lowered based on specific regional averages allowing you to afford a house that otherwise you could not afford or qualify for. This method is used for Veteran's Affair (VA) loans for instance. VA loans also qualify for a zero-down payment in most cases.

> *Gen Z POV: "I did a lot of research on the area, was part of the neighborhood association, met a realtor and had friend realtors to give me advice, as well as other friends in my network. I had to calculate my budget and see what I could afford."*

What happens if you work gigs, are self-employed, or a free-lancer, also known as a "1099" worker. 1099 refers to the IRS form that the employer of the free-lancer will produce at the end of year to report the income paid to the free-lancer. Free-lancers are self-employed and, thus need to pay both the employee and the employer part of payroll taxes (mainly the FICA taxes) to the tune of 12.4% instead of the 7.65% an employee would pay (the rest being paid by the company). So, if you are a "1099," you do not get constant income. By definition your income is variable and unpredictable, and you must have several clients. That is a problem for the mortgage originator. How do you justify your claimed income in order to qualify for a mortgage? Most of the time the mortgage originator will ask you to demonstrate several years of income using your bank statements and IRS declarations. Then based on that, an estimation of what the average income is will be made to calculate the amount of mortgage you could qualify for. Be ready to show a very detailed account of your business dealings.

When you are ready to buy a home, you will also need to think about the down payment. The down payment is the amount that you will bring in cash. So, for instance if the house costs $100,000, and you bring a down payment of $10,000, then you will have to borrow "only" $90,000 from the bank. The down payment for first-time home buyers is sometimes limited to 3% in certain states, even down to nothing in some cases. Check out your own regulations. What if you don't even have the 3% required? Can you borrow from your family? Yes, but that will be scrutinized. Usually, any money that is not explained by your income or your savings and appeared on your bank account in the past two months will be deemed to be some kind of family loan, or gift (now if you had the money on your bank account for more than two months, it might not raise a flag). You will have to show where the money came from, in part because it could be from illegal sources, but more important because the lender wants you to have "skin" in the deal. They want you to suffer personally if you lose the house because you defaulted on your payment. If you borrow everything, you will not be the one suffering, unless of course you borrowed from the Sopranos!

The second thing to think about after the down payment is what is called LTV for Loan-to-Value ratio. This is the amount you will borrow from the bank/lender divided by the cost or value of the house. That will need to stay at 80% for two reasons. First, if you borrow 80% of the value of the house, that means that you have a 20% down payment. Underwriters like that because it presents less of a risk for them. Second, to ensure that they will get their money back if you do not pay, and if you have less than 20% skin in the game, they will force you to take a Private Mortgage Insurance (PMI) on top of all other costs. That PMI might cost you another $30 per month for a $100,000 loan. The good news is that when the LTV ratio goes back down below 80% you can ask to stop paying the PMI, albeit with paperwork. That can happen because you paid your mortgage for quite a while and the balance is now $80,000. Or the value of the house has increased and is say worth $140,000 and even if you owe $95,000 the LTV will be down to 70% ($95,000/$140,000). To show that the value of the house has increased you will need to pay for a new home appraisal that can cost you $400, so think twice about it.

Once you know what house value you can afford, and what amount you will need to borrow, you need to think about what kind of mortgage you want or can get, or more accurately you "can" get. There are many different types of mortgages. They can be categorized into two groups: fixed rate mortgages and variable rate mortgages. A fixed rate mortgage is a loan that will have a consistent agreed upon interest rate for the life of the entire loan. So, for example a 30-year fixed mortgage with an interest rate of 3% is never going to change. All your monthly payments will be the same for 30 years. You will pay $421 per month of principal (the balance of the $100,00 loan you still owe) plus interest. This is possible because the lender will calculate what is called an amortization table (See table 6) with consistent monthly payments. Since you pay a little bit of the principal every month your principal balance decreases every month and your interests are calculated on that balance, thus at the beginning of your repayment you pay more interest than at the end. The bank pays itself first. Cool, right?

Table 6: 3% Interest, 30 years Fixed Mortgage Amortization Table (first and last year's only)

DATE	PAYMENT	PRINCIPAL	INTEREST	BALANCE
Aug. 15, 2020	$421.00	$171.00	$250.00	$99,829.00
Sep. 15, 2020	$421.00	$171.43	$249.57	$99,657.57
Oct. 15, 2020	$421.00	$171.86	$249.14	$99,485.71
Nov. 15, 2020	$421.00	$172.29	$248.71	$99,313.42
Dec. 15, 2020	$421.00	$172.72	$248.28	$99,140.70
Jan. 15, 2050	$421.00	$412.84	$8.16	$2,850.81
Feb. 15, 2050	$421.00	$413.87	$7.13	$2,436.94
Mar. 15, 2050	$421.00	$414.91	$6.09	$2,022.03
Apr. 15, 2050	$421.00	$415.94	$5.06	$1,606.09
May. 15, 2050	$421.00	$416.98	$4.02	$1,189.11
Jun. 15, 2050	$421.00	$418.03	$2.97	$771.08
Jul. 15, 2050	$773.01	$771.08	$1.93	$0.00
Total (as of 2050)	**$151,912.01**	**$100,000.00**	**$51,912.01**	**$0.00**

The second type of mortgage you can get is a variable rate mortgage. The main difference is in the name; the interest rate is variable.

Meaning it varies every month based on the financial market. In fact, it is linked to the treasury bill, or an index like the London Interbank Offered Rate (LIBOR), thus not a stock, and doesn't fluctuate like a stock, yet the LIBOR has fluctuated in the past 10 years up and down 2 points from 1% to 3%, and back down to 1%. That means that if you have a variable interest rate at LIBOR plus 1.5%, then you might get a total interest rate of 2.5% at the lowest end to up to 4.5% at the highest in that 10-year period. Meanwhile, the fix mortgage rate is still 3%. So, sometimes you are doing better, sometimes you are doing worse. Take a variable rate mortgage if you can stomach the risk and the potential anxiety levels. The beauty of most Adjustable Rate Mortgages (ARM) is that the initial period within the first 5 or 10 years of the mortgage repayment are at a set rate lower than the comparable fixed rate mortgage, and the next period is at a variable rate greater than the fixed rate in order to make up the difference. For example, you could have the first five years of your ARM (note: a 5-year fixed that then changes to an adjustable mortgage is called a "5/1 ARM") costing you $300 per month for five years, and then varying with a rate of LIBOR plus 1.5% (note: there is a legal cap on the maximum rate an ARM can get to). For the first five years compared to the 30-year fixed mortgage rate at 3% that costs you $421 a month, you save a total of $7,260! The catch is that after that you will pay an amount greater than $421 for 25 years. So, in the end it can cost you more, but it can cost you less if the LIBOR goes down substantially for a long period of time. How does the LIBOR fluctuate? In general, it fluctuates based on the economy. If the economy is not doing well, the government and the banks want to lower interest rates including the LIBOR in order to stimulate the economy. If the economy is doing well, then interest rates are set higher, including the LIBOR.

Why would you buy an ARM? There are two reasons that might make you choose an ARM over a 30-year fixed mortgage rate. First, you are not planning to stay in the house more than five years. So, in that case you will benefit from the low payments and the savings, and then will sell the house and move to another location. That works if the house maintains its value or if the value goes up. If the market goes down and the value of the house is below what you owe on your mortgage balance, then when you sell the house you will have to actually bring money to the table! This type of strategy and issue is in part what led to the mortgage crisis in 2008. The second reason you might want to get an ARM is that you want to stay for the long term, but you are confident that in five years you will be able to refinance your mortgage into a new ARM, or a 25-year fixed rate. Your confidence is a bet on the future of the economy and is as good as many people's. You are a risk taker, good for you. If you are right, then again you will save the $7,260 and will refinance into a new ARM that might restart the cycle for you. Again, several variables need to line up perfectly. The market has to be better in five years than it is now, the interest rates similar, the value of the house the same or better, your situation also needs to be the same or better. Nevertheless, it will cost you money to refinance. And that cost will be out of pocket or financed inside the new mortgage.

How Much Does It Cost to Get a Mortgage?

This is a weird question. You would think that the interest rates are what the mortgage costs you, but no. Buying a mortgage is going to cost more than the interest! It is a little bit like getting a credit card that has a yearly fee. Except that the fee is much greater! What you will borrow from the lender is not only the difference between the price of the house and your down payment, but also what are called the closing costs. Closing costs can run from 2% to 5% of the mortgage value and are made of appraisal costs, home inspection costs, real estate agents' commissions, fees (application fees, loan origination fees, prepaid interests, mortgage broker fees, PMI, title fees, title insurance, real estate taxes, home insurance, and discount points). That is a lot. A few of those fees you want to watch closely. The mortgage broker fee can fluctuate from 0.5% to 3% (maximum depends on state law). So, on a mortgage of $100,000 your mortgage broker can make either a $500 commission or a $3,000 commission.

Within three days of giving all your information (income, debts, credit check authorizations, IRS information to verify income) to him/her your mortgage broker should give you a standardized form called the Good Faith Estimate (GFE). Once you are signing documents later on in the process, that GFE will be a way for you to check if the official documents, particularly the HUD-1 form, correspond to what was sold to you. The HUD-1 form is the formal form that lists all costs and should match the GFE.

Let's say you pick a 30-year fixed rate at 3% and you borrow $97,000 for a house that costs $130,000. Your down payment is $33,000 of seasoned money (you had savings, and a gift from your parents was on your account for more than two months). Your closing costs total $3,000. So, you will seek $100,000 (97,000 + 3,000) from the lender. Your mortgage payment on $100,000 will be $421 per month, and to that you have to add property taxes ($100 per month) and homeowner's insurance ($30 per month) for a total housing cost of $551 per month. Your LTV is 76.92% (100,000/130,000), below 80%. Your front-end DTI is 16.53% (551/3,333), which is below the 28% recommended ratio, and finally your back-end DTI is 32.97% ([551 + 548 of other debts]/3,333), which is also below the recommended 36%. You are good to go ahead to closing!

Closing is the process by which you review and sign all the documents needed to transfer and register the property from the seller to you. It takes a little bit of time due to the amount of paperwork. You will have to go to a title company where a notary will make sure it is you signing the papers. The realtor and the mortgage broker might be there to explain things and make sure you sign (they have a vested interest). Don't expect the sellers to be there, but maybe the realtors will be to represent the sellers. A day before the settlement you will be able to read the documents (things change until the last minute because of interest changes, and other things, but mainly because the system is a little slow). Do not go to a store the day before settlement and get a store credit card. That might change your credit worthiness and the deal might go sour. Once the documents are signed and notarized, then you are the owner of the house, you get the keys, and you can move in. Congratulations!

I don't intend to tell you everything about mortgages here, but beyond the main principles you have to be aware of other issues and traps that people will set for you. Here are the main ones.

> Gen Z POV: "It would have been a stretch to afford my house on my own, I would have had to stretch my budget, so I found a friend to be my roommate, too, so what he pays is a nice little help out to the mortgage each month."

Discount points

Discount points are pre-paid interest charges you pay within your closing costs so that your interest rate is lowered. This decision should be made based on the differences between the short term and long term, so it's best to ask for a quote (the good-faith-estimate, or GFE), both with the pre-paid interest charges and without, so that you can see the difference.

Sub-prime loans

Beware subprime borrowers, those with FICO scores of 600-630 or below depending on the lender's policy. You could be paying 10% rates when someone else could be offered a 4% rate, even for the same house with the same salary. Is that legal? Yes. You might remember the "subprime crisis of 2008." In those crazy years prior to the crisis all sorts of "wild" types of mortgages were offered particularly to the subprime folks. Why? Because legally a lender can cover the higher risk (potentially higher risk) by increasing its interest rate. The government sees a way for folks with less than perfect credit to access home ownership, the lenders get a client, the buyers achieve the American dream, and the seller moves on. Everyone is happy. Except that from the late 90s to the early 2000s, houses on average had increased in value more than 100%. In other words, if you had purchased a $100,000 home in 1997, it would be worth $200,000 in 2007. Doubling the value of your home in 20 years is not bad. That's an average, but in Nevada for instance, it took three years in the early 2000s to triple your home's value! Mortgage brokers during that period helped the entire system behind them, from the credit rating houses, to the lenders, the realtors, targeted subprime borrowers to sell ARM mortgages that required no income verification (people could lie on their income no problem), and presented a very low five-year fixed payment (See above explanation). Then, not only would the rate reset to a very high subprime variables rates, but also would accrue negative amortization interests. Negative amortization interest is the interest on the mortgage that you do not pay in the first five years of fixed payments (kind of the equivalent of the minimum payment on a credit card), which are then added to the principal you owe, and will be the new base for your mortgage interest. The entire sales pitch was something like: "instead of paying $421 per month in a 30-year-fixed today, you will pay $100 per month for five years, and you can now invest the difference in the stock market!" The financial market was packaging these shady loans together and was selling them to investors on the financial market. Why would the market buy these bad loans? Because the credit rating agencies said the loans were not this risky. So, banks and others trusted the credit rating firm, and purchased the loans. Then came the time where the first batch of these 5/1 ARMs had to reset at variable-rate full repayments. And folks that were paying $100 per month for five years and had settled into a lifestyle where they were spending the difference had nothing left to pay $1,000 a month on a LIBOR plus 4.5%! Many went bust and filed for bankruptcy, and the rest is history (Watch the movie *The Big Short*).

No cost mortgages

Some mortgage brokers will try to sell you a "no cost mortgage." The catch is that the interest rate will be higher by 0.125% or more. You see a 0.125% interest increase as not much, but on a 30-year-fixed $100,000 mortgage the difference overall is $2,391.60. So, if your cost would be more than that, take the deal. In a similar fashion some brokers will sell you higher interest rates instead of charging a PMI. Again, if you compare with and without cost overall you should be able to decide what is best for you.

Balloon payment

A balloon payment is the idea that after a time of say 20 years on a mortgage or loan, instead of continuing to pay monthly until the loan is repaid, you owe the entire balance as a lump sum. It would be unusual to have a primary (first) mortgage with a balloon payment. The idea is usually used in commercial mortgages or second mortgages. Here the payments are low, lower than usual, sometimes even just the interest is paid, and at the end of a 10-year or 20-year period, the entire balance is owed. This is not for you unless you intend to refinance or sell the house before the balloon is due.

Yield-spread premium

Beware of what is called the yield-spread commission or yield-spread premium (YSP). Mortgage brokers are financially rewarded by the lenders for selling the borrower what the lenders would prefer them to sell. Sometimes a borrower accepts a mortgage rate that is above what they could get based on their credit worthiness and income. For instance, someone might qualify for a 30-year fixed loan at 3% but is proposed a 30-year fixed at 3.5%. Close enough right? The 0.5% difference creates more money for the bank, and to motivate mortgage brokers to sell this they give the broker what is called a yield-spread commission on top of the mortgage broker commission. Difficult for the borrower to see that commission on the GFE, but it should be there. Think of it as the opposite of the discount point. If your mortgage broker makes a 3% commission plus a 3-point YSP they will make $6,000 on your $100,000 loan.

Appraisal fee

You should not have to pay upfront fees before you sign the mortgage. The only fee that you might have to pay upfront is the appraisal fee. Appraisers during the subprime crisis got a bad reputation as well because they were not even visiting the homes to appraise them, thus, some homes that were in the middle of construction got loans based on newly finished house values. Today expect the appraiser to measure each room and do a good comparison with similar homes that recently sold in the neighborhood. An appraisal will cost you around $400 depending on several factors. You can shop around for an appraiser as long as the mortgage broker/underwriter is ok with your choice.

Pre-payment penalty

You do not want any pre-payment penalty for you paying your 30-year mortgage in 25 years. Most mortgages have language in the documents that stipulate that but ask the broker and ask to be shown where in the two-inch thick closing documents it is buried. If you have extra disposable income every month, then it might be a good idea to pay more than your mortgage payment. The overage will go towards principal, thus lowering your next interest. Actually, lenders will have to recalculate the entire amortization schedule, and they might not do that right away. But just make sure your extra payment was taken into consideration.

First-time home buyers

Some states offer help in the form of a grant to first-time home buyers, so check it out because it's free money.

Should you get a 30-year fixed mortgage, or a 25-year fixed one?

You will have to make the calculations. First of all, the lender might not give you that option because it might not fit within the 28/36 rule. A 30-year fixed will cost you $421 per month and a 25-year fixed will cost you $478. For only $57 more per month, you will save $9,514 and will be mortgage free five years earlier. If you can do it, do it.

Prequalified or preapproved

When you will hunt for the home of your dreams you could be prequalified for a loan or preapproved for a loan. Prequalified is not very strong. The mortgage broker talks to you, and roughly calculates what mortgage you could get, thus, what size home you could hunt for, but there is no guarantee you'll get that mortgage in the end. A preapproved borrower, on the other hand, has gone through most of the process with the mortgage broker and the lender will get the loan if nothing else changes in the borrower's situation. Thus, when the market is hot (the market is favorable to the seller when more than one buyer is competing for the same house, which is called a seller's market) then a preapproved buyer can be viewed more favorably by the seller and get their offer accepted even if a slightly better one (always contingent on bank approval) is on the table.

Is it better if there are two of you buying a house?

Of course, it is! Everything we've discussed here is much better if there are two of you. Why? Because you have twice the income, but not twice the expenses. Thus, your buying power is much greater, and you probably can afford a bigger house, or qualify for that $100,000 house easier. For instance, two incomes totaling $80,000 or $6,666 per month, your $421 mortgage plus other related costs might total $620, making your DTI ratio 9.3%, which is way below the 28% test. Compare that to 18.6% DTI for a single income borrower.

Advantages and Disadvantages of Being a Homeowner

So, in the end, now that you understand what it takes to buy a home, are there real advantages to owning a house?

After all, we can list several disadvantages. We have seen some already, like the property taxes you have to pay, and the repairs you will have to do in order to maintain the house value. Changing an HVAC system can cost you $8,000 easy. Redoing a roof can cost

$15,000. Cutting a dead tree in your yard that seems dead will run you $3,000 minimum.

First, think of the house as an investment. Check what you paid for the house on websites like Zillow. See what other similar houses are sold for in the neighborhood. If your house value is increasing say by 3% and you pay $130,000 for the house, next year it should be worth $133,900. That extra $3,900 in value is good news. It covers $3,000 of the closing costs you are paying as part of your mortgage (although not the interest). Give yourself a target of closing costs (say in your case 3%), plus realtor commission (usually 6%) or a total of 9% before you can think about selling the house and recouping your down payment. Say, after three years, the house value is $141,700 and you get an offer for that amount; as the seller you will get $133,198 after you pay the $8,502 realtor commission at 6%. If you still owe the lender $93,844 (the original amount of $100,000 minus the amount of principal you paid off in three years), then you will get a check of $39,354 at closing. Remember that you put down $33,000 three years ago, so you netted a profit of $6,354 or about a 6% return on average. Better than a savings account.

Second, and even if it feels that you are paying more expenses as a house owner than as a renter, do the math. A renter pays $1,000 for the same house (you can check renting estimates for similar places than yours, or as a rule of thumb think about the price of a home divided by ten as annual rent. So, in your case the price is $130,000, which when divided by ten is an annual rent of $13,000, or $1,083 a month). Compare the $1,030 rent and insurance to the $551 PITI. Then add any annual costs to the maintenance of the home–gardening and landscaping, changing the rug, hiring the plumber once a year, maintenance of the furnace and HVAC, and the occasional big expense like a tree cutting, or a new roof. Say that amount is about 5% of the house value per year. That is $6,500 or another $542 per month. The total cost of being a homeowner is $1,093 versus renting, which is $1,030. The advantage of being a homeowner, though, is in tax savings, even though that diminishes every year thanks to government legislation. On your income tax return, you will be able to claim the total interests paid during the year. If you paid $3,000 of interest in one year, then your savings will be roughly $360 in income taxes, or 12% of $3,000 (that is if you are in the 12% marginal income tax bracket).

Here you have it, being a homeowner saves you taxes and makes your down payment grow. What is there not to like? Of course, the value of your house might plunge (house values in Nevada during the subprime crisis went down 60% almost overnight. But again, do your homework.) Look at the value of your house and the housing market trend in your zip code over a period equivalent to the period you intend to stay in the house. The risk is always there, and it is best to be aware of what could happen.

Refi or Not to Refi

Refi is short for refinancing. As soon you settle on your house, your mortgage broker will send you emails and flyers about refi opportunities. Should you do it? What's the catch?

What is refi?

Refinancing is paying off your original mortgage and getting a new one at the same time. The advantage of refinancing is often in the savings you get. It could be a saving of time and money, like refinancing a 30-year fixed mortgage into a 15-year fixed mortgage, or a refinancing a 30-year fixed mortgage with a 30-year mortgage at a lower interest rate. It never works exactly like that, as your original 30-year mortgage is probably already in its first five years of repayment. But you get the idea. So, it is best to compare the before and after picture in order to be able to make the proper decision. Mortgage brokers get paid on a refi, so their interest is not really in your favor. However, and particularly recently after the subprime crisis mortgage, brokers have to show a substantial saving for their clients refinancing so that the underwriter accepts the deal.

Should you refi?

The question of whether you should refi or not is a difficult question because it depends on your situation and of course on the interest rates and products (mortgages) available to you. In general, and if your situation has not changed for the worst, that means if your house has appreciated normally and if your credit is good, then a refi is a good idea when interest rates fall half a percent or more from the rate you have on your current mortgage. Refinancing too early after you get your fresh new mortgage is not recommended because these conditions might not be ideal. Either you have not yet built enough equity in the house, or the house has not appreciated much since the original mortgage. Waiting too long into a mortgage is not a good idea either, because the way amortization schedules are you pay the interests up front, the bank pays itself first before you pay the principal, thus, your principal balance will be high even if you are 20 years into a 30-year mortgage. For instance, 20 years into a 30-year mortgage represents 2/3 of the life of the repayment, in other words you should still have 33% of the payments due. Yet, due to the interests being front loaded, the balance on the principal will still be 45% of the original amount and not 33%.

Refinancing is an opportunity that you need to evaluate on a case-by-case basis. Just be ready and make your move when the occasion arises. Let's look at an example. Your original mortgage is a 30-year fixed rate at 3% and you have been paying it for three years. Today's 30-year rate is 2.5%. Should you refi?

On your original mortgage your principal balance is $93,567, so that is what you have to refinance. Add to that closing costs of 3% and you need to borrow $96,374. Your house value was originally $130,000. Three years later it is $141,700 (your estimation based on looking at comparable houses on Zillow). If you get a new 30-year fixed mortgage at 2.5%, your monthly payment will go from $421 to $380 per month. Your property taxes and insurance will not change. So, your monthly savings will be $41. Over twelve months that is $492 of savings. Not a big saving, and you probably have caught this already, but your original mortgage "only" had 27 years left, and now you are getting a new 30-year mortgage, thus, you will be paying three more years.

If you look at the time it will take for you to recoup your new closing costs of $2,807 (3% of loan) with the savings, you will find it will take 69 months, almost six years to recoup those costs [note: that's a rough "back of the envelop" calculation as there are also tax implications]. If the interest rate is 2% instead of 2.5%, then your monthly savings will be $65, or $780 yearly, and it will take less than four years to get your money back. A much, much better deal. Always look for a less than five-year return of your investment.

Second Mortgage HELOC

You can get a second mortgage at the same time you get your first mortgage. Sometimes, this helps to get underwriters to approve your loan and the ratios to work. But most of the time you get a second mortgage later and it is called a Home Equity Line of Credit (HELOC).

You've likely heard the term "second mortgage" before. People say, "I had to take a second mortgage out to pay for my education!" Or something like that. That means that a homeowner that typically has a mortgage and also has equity in the house can buy a second mortgage on their house. When they buy the second mortgage, they get money as a loan, equivalent to a cash advance on a credit card. The main difference is that this loan is guaranteed by the house. Just like the first mortgage, if you don't pay the second mortgage back, the bank can take your house from you. Credit card companies don't have that option. They can only give you a bad credit score. That is what is called a secured debt (mortgage) versus an unsecured debt (credit card). Usually, this second mortgage has a slightly higher interest rate than your typical 30-year fixed; they might be a 15-year term instead of 30 years; they might be interests only with a balloon payment at the end; they might be a lot of different beasts. So, watch out.

If you get a HELOC it will not be 100% of the equity you have in the house. More likely, and it depends on the lender, it will be 80% or 90% of the equity. In the hay days of housing bubbles (before the subprime crisis), some banks would give 110% of equity HELOC. Why? Because the housing market was growing constantly at a good rate, so by the time you get that HELOC your home value was already up and your HELOC was already back down to 100% or 95% of your equity. Crazy times, which might come back. It is cyclical, and you should be cautious.

Let's look at an example again. Your original mortgage is a 30-year fixed at 3% and you have been paying it for three years. On your original mortgage your principal balance is $93,567, like in the example we used earlier. Your house value is now $141,700. That means that your equity in the house is $48,133. If the bank is ready to sell you a HELOC for 90% of your equity at a rate of 3.5% fixed over 15 years, do you take it?

What are the advantages? Well, you could use that money to pay off your student loans (your balance is $25,000 now), or you could pay your credit card debt (your balance is still $10,000), or you could buy a car in cash! So much you could do with that money. Some banks will be really quick to suggest putting that money to work in some mutual funds they manage.

As with most investments, you have to do the math in order to compare and decide what is best for your situation.

One advantage of HELOCs is that typically they are not designed to give you the whole amount as a lump sum, although it is possible. The idea is that you use the line of credit as you need it. That complicates things a little because each portion of the line you use has a different repayment schedule.

For the sake of an example, say you want to use the line of equity to pay off your debts and get a new car. So, you need $25,000 + $10,000 = $35,000 for the debt, and the rest you will spend on a car. The HELOC amount will be $43,320 ($48,133 x 90%). After you pay your debt you will have $8,320 to spend on a car ($43,320 – $35,000). Does this make sense?

Let's do the math.

The first indication that it could be in your favor is the difference in interest rates. Just like when you pay a high interest credit card first, it is a good idea to transfer a debt at 7% into a debt at 3.5%. Your student loans are at 7% and you pay $348 per month; your credit card's average rate is 12% and you pay more than the minimum every month, say $100. Your car is paid off, hence, you need a new one. A new five-year car loan might have an interest rate of 5% and a payment of $151 per month.

So, today your debt is costing (or will cost you when you get that new car) [$348 + $100 + 151] $599 per month.

Borrowing $43,320 at 3.5% over 15 years will cost you $309 per month. Thus, you save $290 per month in the short term. If you do the math over the life of each debt (The student loans, the credit cards and the car) versus the 15 years of the HELOC, then maybe the savings disappear. This is because, for the car for example, instead of paying it off in five years, you now will pay it off in 15. 10 more years of payments! Here, what you have to weigh is the short-term advantages versus the long-term costs. Do you need the cash flow now? Can you refinance later? Some of the disadvantages of getting a HELOC to pay off debt is that now that your credit cards are paid off it is very tempting to use them again. Watch that.

Refi Strategies

In general, if you can pay more today for any type of loan, then pay more. That means that if you can afford to refi a 30-year fixed into a 15-year fixed, your monthly payment will increase, but overall, you will pay less interest, and you will save a lot. For example, the difference between a 30-year and a 15-year loan interest paid on $100,000 is a savings of $27,580! So, if you can muster the $690 per month instead of the $421, take it.

CHAPTER 6

Learn to Beat Wall Street

"You can only have two things in life, reasons and results. Reasons don't count"

We all want to beat Wall Street. Since I have seen Wall Street the movie (the first one with Michael Douglas as Gordon Gekko) I have always thought that if I had a couple million dollars, I'd do very well in the financial market. Well, needless to say I never had a million dollars to play with, but over the years I built a little portfolio that I play with online. I tripled my money over the years, and I beat Wall Street every day (mostly). You can do the same.

What does it mean to beat Wall Street? The idea is that if you can do better in terms of return on your investments than the financial market in general, then you are better than the financial market and you should keep doing it. If you can't beat Wall Street, then maybe you should put your money with the professionals, i.e., the fund managers, the financial advisors. They will take a commission for managing your money, but you won't have to do anything. You're probably asking yourself: will the professionals beat Wall Street? There's no guarantee that they will. In fact, you can look up all these historical returns before you buy a mutual fund or give your money to a professional to manage. History tends to repeat itself, but sometimes it doesn't. Did I give you enough doubt? That's the point. The financial market is volatile. That means it can fly one way one minute and the other way the next. That volatility is difficult, if not impossible to predict. Thus, no one can really say for sure that the market today is going to close at this level, or that a particular stock will be worth this much.

> Gen Z POV: "I have my own IRA as well and put some money there. And then after that I can honestly say I forget I have that money."

Some basic understanding of what we are talking about when we say: "Wall Street," or the financial market is interesting to learn first.

Stock Market 101

Wall Street is the street in Manhattan, New York, where the traditional and historical financial market is located. The New York Stock Exchange (NYSE) is the place you have seen in movies where traders buy and sell stocks (See the movie *Trading Places*) where people are screaming at each other, computers are flashing red and green, papers are on the floor, other people on the balcony are ringing a bell and slamming a gavel. Most trading today happens electronically and the traders we see on TV are almost always there for show. Today's traders are sitting in their open space offices just like in the series *Billions*. There are many different types of stock exchanges. Besides the NYSE, you have the NASDAQ, which is also in Manhattan, and many others in the U.S. and throughout the world, including Paris, London,

Tokyo, Shanghai, and so on. This allows traders to trade 24/7 around the world. Individual markets like the NYSE typically open at 9:30am and close at 4:00pm, Monday to Friday. Each of the stock exchanges trade unique company stocks, which are sold and purchased only at that exchange. For instance, Facebook is traded on the NASDAQ and General Electric (GE) is traded on the NYSE.

We have seen in Chapter 3 that a company has equity on its balance sheet. That equity is made of shares that have a unit value, a price. For instance, a company might have 10,000 shares at $30 each, thus, an equity of $300,000. Shares are listed on the market under a unique set of letters called a "ticker." For instance, Apple ticker is AAPL, Budweiser is BUD, Harley Davidson is HOG, Southwest Airlines is LUV, IBM is IBM. There are slightly different kinds of shares, but for the most part a share gives the shareholder the right to vote at general assemblies (See the movie *Wall Street*) where the new CEO presents his/her results for the past year and future plans. Being a shareholder entitles you to get dividends when the company makes a profit and decides to distribute some of that profit to the shareholders. Some shareholders have so much money in shares of a company that distribute dividends that they live solely off of that; it becomes their income. It is the epitome of a "capitalist," you know that guy with the mustache and the top hat from Monopoly. It's not a bad idea since dividends qualify for a capital gain level of income tax of around 15%, compared to the regular marginal income tax that could be 22% or 35%.

Stocks or shares are titles of ownership in the company. When you own a share, you are the owner of that company. Pretty cool to be an (part) owner of Google or Facebook.

Companies have a limited number of shares in the market. You can see that on the balance sheets and annual reports (called "10-K") these companies must publish (look for the investor side of the company website, scroll all the way down on the website, or "Google" it). Unlike the private companies, that have shares as well but don't sell them to the public, public companies have to report their results quarterly, and have many more requirements, all to prevent manipulation of the markets and potential market crashes like the one in 1929. Regulations come and go with different governments and sometimes a mini crash happens because of what is called a "bubble." A bubble is the inflation of a stock beyond its "real" value to a point that when shareholders realize that the stock is overvalued, they will dump it in mass and the price will go down very rapidly. That can happen on one stock or many, or even an entire industry like the Internet bubble of the late 90s, or the real estate subprime crisis of 2008.

The market acts as an intermediary between the buyer of stocks and the seller of stocks. Initially, the company will sell a number of shares during the initial public offering (IPO). The buyers, banks, financial institutions like retirement plans, and people like you and me (although individuals that have access to IPO shares are not you and me; they have been vetted by the financial folks to be high wealth people who can afford to lose their money) will buy the shares from the company and then when the share has increased in value, will sell the share to someone else that wants it and pocket the profit. On that profit the person will pay capital gains income tax.

If the shares are in demand and there are less people selling than people wanting to buy, then the price will go up until some equilibrium happens, meaning there are as many people wanting to buy at that new price as there are people wanting to sell. Similarly, if there are more sellers than buyers, the price will go down. Prices can go up because the company is doing well or is introducing new products that consumers will want to buy, or because the company is merging with another company. Prices go down for similar reasons, but reversed–the company didn't have good results, they have issues with the quality of its product, or a lawsuit is going to cost the company a lot of money in the future.

Regulations decided by governments and international trade can also influence industries and directly impact public companies and their stock price. For instance, a tariff imposed on imports (a tax added to the price) of aluminum into the U.S. could favor U.S. companies selling aluminum to U.S. companies that need it for their manufacturing. So, the companies making the aluminum will see their sales, profits, and stock go up. The companies having to purchase the aluminum from the U.S. companies might have to buy it at a higher price due to the tariffs imposed in what is usually cheaper importers, thus these companies' profits might go down because their cost of goods have increased, which means their profitability might go down, and their stock price might go down. Of course, they can protect their margins and profit and charge consumers higher prices to compensate the issue of tariffs and cost of goods. That would work only if the consumers can still buy the same amount of goods at the new increased price.

Stocks might be purchased by fund managers and be part of a portfolio (an account with different shares from different companies). That portfolio is then divided into parts, think shares, that are not tied to a specific company but are a weighted average (just like your GPA, a weighted average is calculated by adding all the shares multiplied by their price and divided by the sum of shares the funds want to sell) of all the stock owned by the fund. Funds are "packaged" in a way that give the consumer an idea of what they are buying. For example, some funds are more tech oriented, or financial sector oriented, or pharmaceutical oriented, and so on. Some funds are riskier than others. Some funds have more international stocks. You get the idea. It is pretty much infinite.

Stocks are not the only financial product sold on the market. Bonds are another type of "securities" you can buy. A bond is a debt that one company or one city (called municipal bonds) will issue. They will get the money from the people buying the bond and will promise to repay the bond plus interest in the future. Bonds are safer than stocks but do not appreciate as much as stocks. A bond does not give you ownership of the company or the city's assets.

Money markets are basically savings accounts, but instead of being available on your bank account, they are frozen for a period of time and you'll get access to the money in the future with an interest. Some of these money market instruments are CDs or certificate of deposits. The return on these financial instruments is usually higher than a typical savings, but lower than a bond or a stock.

You can also invest in what is called an index or an exchange-traded fund (ETF). Think about a portfolio made of stocks that has the same proportion as the market they are trading in. For instance, the NASDAQ. You could buy shares from the 3,500 plus companies listed there and basically mirror the NASDAQ results every day. When you watch TV and see the NASDAQ went up 3% then you know your portfolio went up 3%. But that would require a lot of money. So, instead you can buy a NASDAQ index ETF. The shares of that index are a sample of shares that make up the market (or sometimes an industry). They are a kind of mutual funds. The advantage is that by buying these ETFs, you mirror the market, so if the market goes up, your portfolio goes up. And vice versa. They often are free of fees.

You can also buy commodities like sugar, wheat, oil, or even gold on the market. The available products are almost limitless. Only the financial market imagination and the regulator like the Security Exchange Commission (SEC) can limit what you can trade.

It's a good idea to start small in the financial market before going big and more complex. But in general, be diversified in the way you invest to protect yourself from market fluctuations you have no way of seeing coming or controlling.

> Gen Z POV: "I had interest in stocks and investing and stuff like that, so then I feel it has become more popular. There are podcasts on stock, a lot of younger people are talking about it now, or they have new apps that talk about it. The resource is just there."

Financial advisors usually have to assess the level of risk that each investor is willing to take before they can sell you securities (i.e., shares, bonds, etc.). They conduct an interview and at the end you are deemed to be a conservative, moderate, or aggressive investor. Hence, you will be presented with portfolios of mutual funds that are created to be conservative, moderate, or aggressive. For instance, a conservative mutual funds will have more bonds than stocks, more national stocks than international stocks, less new companies fresh off an IPO, more cash or gold, and so on. Similarly, if you are the one managing your investments, you should consider building a portfolio that mirrors your risk level. Except that you might want to have a little more fun than just getting mutual funds. For instance, if you love Apple, you might want to get a share of Apple.

> Gen Z POV: "It's also social media, or You Tube, you have You Tube videos you can just watch on how to invest starting with $10. That's something that catches your eye, you say, "Oh, I can do this."

I remember that when I was in Paris and had my slightly higher than minimum wage job, I was also buying stocks. Ok, I was buying one stock of one company, and held on to it for six months. I was more so imagining what I could do than really playing the market. I was reading the financial paper during the metro ride. Just the act of picking a company, studying it, buying the stock, following the market every day, deciding to sell the stock, and pocketing the whopping $10 profit was worth it. It taught me the basics, and I risked less than $100. Start small. Buy one stock of one company that you love.

How do you pick a company's share to purchase? After all, you might be a consumer of a brand and love it, but that brand might not be doing very well on the stock market. Should you just read the magazines or watch the financial folks on TV and pick what they tell you to pick?

Finding the Gem

In Chapter 3 we looked at accounting statements like the balance sheet, the P&L, and the cash flow statement. We also looked at ratios that are used by accountants and financial people to assess the financial health of a company. In the world of Wall Street there are plenty of financial analysts that spend their days studying companies, usually focusing on a particular industry. For instance, an analyst might be a specialist in the car industry, or the travel industry. These people look at public companies' accounts every day, and they make recommendations for the traders that are then also published in the media for others to report on and follow. Each analyst works for a particular financial company, whether it's a bank, an investment company, an insurance company, a retirement fund etc. So, technically you have several analysts from different companies studying the same industry, the same set of companies, the same particular company every day, but their opinions differ. Why? They are looking at the same information, and follow the media, which gives them intuition about the context, the economy, the international relations, all of which they think will influence the stock of a particular company in one way or another in the near future. Then, you read these people's analyses where one says to buy the stock, the other to hold the stock, and the last one to sell the stock. What should you do?

That's when you thank your (accounting, finance, economy) professor and start digging into the financials of the company you want to buy. It can get very complex very fast. So, the idea is to keep it simple. There are some fundamentals in reviewing a company. I have 10 commandments in making a decision on whether to buy.

> *Gen Z POV: "I manage a Roth IRA outside of my 401k. I did not understand the advantage, but my friends said to do that, and I did it, but I did not really understand why, but now I really understand the advantage of doing that. It is good for me to know at this point in my career; I invest in ETF and stocks. At first, I invested in stocks, but I had some issues with what the company was doing, and someone said, "Do you believe this much in that company that you would put so much of your money into it?" That is a serious bet, so you need to really believe in them. Over the years I worked out a strategy that works for me and the ETF balanced it out."*

1. Love: Do I like the company or the industry? I rarely buy something I don't like even if I heard or read that it could be a good buy. In that sense I am not a typical investor. I don't diversify with respect to my taste. I like tech companies, so I buy Apple, Google (Alphabet), Microsoft (yes, I know why buy Apple then? Diversification), Facebook, Twitter, Netflix, etc. I like the restaurant business, so I'll buy Chipotle, Starbucks,

McDonald's. Some people, sustainable investors, also invest with the belief of doing good rather than making money. They will not invest in a company that hurts the environment or is associated with the defense industry. I tend to follow that ethical line, but I also diverge from time to time. Your portfolio is going to be your nest egg come retirement. Keep that in mind, as well.

2. Sales: As stated earlier, without sales there's nothing to count, no money to spend. So, sales are the main metric to study. Is the company growing? Are the sales in each of its stores growing year after year (which we call same store sales, or "SSS"); in other words, if one particular Starbucks store at the corner of my street is growing by 3% every year, then I can assume that they did that by increasing their prices (not the best because consumers see that and might not want to buy as much), or by getting more customers (that's good), or by selling more to the same customer, such as a hot drink in the morning and a cool one in the afternoon (the best). If the SSS are not good, for instance, if they are up 1% when inflation (one country's total price increase) has increased 3%, then I am skeptical, because prices should have increased at least as much as the inflation, and stores should have gotten more sales from each customer, and/or more customers. Maybe there is a strategic reason. The company might not want to increase prices systematically every year and might wait every two years to increase a full 50 cents on a latte, or they might wait until news of higher coffee prices from South America are known by consumers who will understand Starbucks has to increase prices. Some companies will try to hide that issue with reporting growth overall in the 10-k and

playing down SSS. Growth can come from new store open-
ings. So, if I started the year with 100 stores and opened 50
new ones, then my growth is double digit, as in 50%, without
even considering the SSS growth. And if my SSS is negative
10%, meaning I lost business in my existing stores compared
to the same time last year, then my overall growth will still
show positive double digit at 35% (See Table 7). So, watch
what is behind the reported numbers. More reasons to love
the company you invest in because you know them well
from a consumer point of view, and you might have learned
quite a bit about their operation along the way.

Table 7: Impact of Same Store Sales and Store Opening on Total Growth

	Last Year	This Year	Growth
Number of Stores	100	150	50%
Sales per store (SSS)	500,000	450,000	-10%
Total Sales	50,000,000	67,500,000	35%

3. Margins: You want to look for margins as a percentage to be
   either constant (the same) or increasing year after year, which
   means costs are decreasing as a percentage of sales when your
   margin is increasing. For example, if Starbucks' (ticker: SBUX)
   margin is going up, then the cost of goods, coffee, milk, is decreasing in relation to sales either because the price of coffee
   or milk is decreasing, or SBUX is doing a good job at sourcing
   and purchasing raw goods, or SBUX is doing a better job at getting consumers to see value in drinks that are more expensive,

have less costly ingredients, or have less ingredients. Either way, if margins are up, then profits are up.

4. Profits: Margins can be up or down. Margins down is usually bad news, but not always. Maybe the company is investing in marketing to "buy market share." Buying market share is when a company acquires new customers through some successful marketing operation. "We will give you a watch and a tote bag if you subscribe to our magazine." Or seen on a billboard: "buy a new truck, get a new gun". Study the P&L and look for increases line by line compared to the previous years and read the company's explanations. Profits in the financial circles are called earnings. And the metric used by the analysts to assess companies by profit is called the earning per share, or EPS (total earnings divided by the number of shares).

5. Cash: Companies might reinvest profits into the business, or give some back to shareholders, but if they don't do any of that, or a little bit of that, then the money stays inside the company and the company has lots of cash on hand. Having lots of cash is not always good in the eyes of financial analysts because they want that money to work, be used to develop the business, buy new companies to merge with, develop new products. But a company with lots of cash is also in a good position to protect and defend its interest in case of a recession, an attack from the competition, or a potential acquisition. So, for me cash is good.

6. Receivables: A company that has too much money in receivables, depending on its industry, is less of a good pick. Remember my story of the Japanese lawyers' group in Chapter 2? Receivables that are not paid by the client will become expenses and will diminish the profit. SBUX should not have many receivables because we all pay cash or use the SBUX

phone App. They should actually have lots of money pre-paid. Boeing might have a lot of receivables and that might be ok in the aerospace industry because airlines companies or countries buying airplanes are a fairly safe bet in terms of credit (although not always). In comparison a lot of receivable in the restaurant industry is not good because customers credits might not be as good as Lufthansa or South Africa. Compare the metrics or ratios of one company to those of the competition or industry at large. Pick the one stock with better metrics.

7. Payables: If you don't pay your suppliers, your accounts will show that you have more cash in the bank than you really have. If your suppliers are nice enough to give you two months to pay your invoices, and your clients are paying cash, then you have created a nice cash cushion. But eventually if you make a point to not pay your supplier, it might be because you don't have enough cash to pay them, or maybe it's because your customers owe you too much money, so you can't pay your suppliers. That is bad news. Again, know your industry; compare the metrics to other competitors.

8. Research and Development (R&D): If I am investing in a tech company, I will expect that R&D expenses will be high. Similarly, defense, pharma, cars all will have substantial R&D budgets. Compare this to the industry practice. Try to make sense of a company that spends more than the industry average on R&D. Are they particularly good at R&D and thus, the expenses in excess will yield great results, or are they not and are they spending money on things that don't really materialize as star products?

9. Competition: Companies do not operate in a bubble. They compete on the open market. If you invest in one company, you need to understand how they compete and with whom

they compete. So, studying the competition is as important as studying the company you want to buy shares from. Sometimes, public companies compete with private companies. It is difficult to study a private company, but with the help of Google (or Bing) you might find enough information to make an assessment.

10. Environment: This is a little bit of everything else. The economy, the actual environment in terms of political climate, cities, and neighborhoods the company operates in, the global climate, the world in one word. Depending on the company, any or all of these environmental aspects could positively or negatively impact the company's stock you are trying to purchase. Think, for instance, of South American political climate, and import-export legislation that can impact export of coffee beans to the U.S. for SBUX. The actual climate change and the potential impact of the harvest and price of coffee beans. The local political unrest or pandemic that could stifle business throughout the U.S. for most SBUX stores. A new minimum wage federal law imposed by a new government. So many of these local, national, or global effects can have an impact on the SBUX share price.

Take a little booklet and start studying your potential companies. Read what there is to read. Write down the metrics and follow their evolution throughout a period of time, maybe three months. Then you are ready to make your move.

What does it cost to buy stocks? The competition is fierce in the financial market. Companies that let you open an investment account where you can trade, buy, sell stocks or bonds, ETFs, or mutual funds, are advertising in the media for commission free accounts, no opening fees, a certain amount of commission free trades, etc. In general, there is a fee to open an account, which disappears when you open with a large amount of money. Something like $25,000 would get you a fee-free account no problem, but you'll have the same flexibility, and so fun game-like experience using Apps like Robinhood that let you open an account with nothing and will even give you a free share. What is there to hate? Well, do you research. Robinhood is the Google of investing. Meaning they resale your online behavior to financial companies. You become the product. But, if you can bear that, then Robinhood is a good choice for a first timer. You can always transfer your stocks to another firm later.

Gen Z POV: "I had maybe in my last year of college, a family friend that said, "Hey, you should start thinking about retirement, as early as possible," and I was like, "Ok, I am not exactly growing with money as a college student," and he said, "Just like open up this account, and I can kinda, like, tell you a few things to invest in, just to get started." And I did not follow their advice like immediately, but, like, did not really know what I was doing or, like, kinda, like, let that fall to the wayside, for a few years."

Each time you trade stocks, or ETFs, or bonds you will pay a commission, both when you purchase, and when you sell the security unless your firm has a free-trade policy. Mutual funds will have management fees as a percentage, often something like 0.25%, that can be a one-time entry fee, or can also be taken when you sell the mutual funds. Do your research. If you have to pay a fee or commission, then you need to add that amount to the price of the stock in order to calculate when to sell the stock at a profit. For example, if the stock costs you $100 and has a commission of $2 to buy or sell, then when the stock value reaches $104 (a 4% increase) you can think about selling.

When is a good time to buy or sell? People say: "buy low, sell high."

That is a nice concept. In reality, you don't know enough about the market, the company, and the environment to be able to do that consistently. What you can do is buy and hold for a reasonable amount of time, just like a house. Because over a period of ten or twenty years (I know, it's long), stocks and the market in general, tend to be positive. For instance, in Table 9 you see that the NASDAQ returns were 14.79% on average per year in the past 10 years, but only 3.2% in the past 20. Gold returned 2.68% in the past 10 years, but 7.54% in the past 20. Moreover, all indicators seem positive in the last 10, 20, or 30 years. While this does not mean it will be positive in the future, it gives an idea of what it can be on average.

Give yourself time to make a profit and give yourself a limit before you cut your losses. If you invest in stocks, ETFs, bonds, or mutual funds, you will not lose more than you have invested. Other products like options (see the movie *Margin Calls* or the series *Billions*. Also take a look at the *Reddit GameStop story of early 2021*) will let you leverage your money invested and buy or sell more than you can afford for a multiplicative potential profit, or loss. In case of a loss, you are committed in buying or selling all the stocks you said you wanted when you purchased the right to the options. You don't want a margin call, which requires you to cover the difference between what you already paid and what the value of all the stocks you are committed for is going to be. Stay away from options.

> *Gen Z POV: "I definitely gravitate towards videos to find information on credit or investing; I am a visual learner. You Tube videos are great, podcasts I can do. You'll find a lot of information on the internet that may be true, but also might come from an angle, especially in the financial world."*

You might want to tell yourself that your investment in the stock of a company you like very much is going to stay there until you are ready to retire, if and only if the company does not do something stupid (like poison its customers) or if the market in general is healthy. For instance, and I saw it too late, when the COVID-19 pandemic hit in late January 2020 I waited until the end of March to sell my positions. I lost 25% from the value I had in January. After I sold everything, my account contained only cash, and I was protected from any other negative impacts until we were out of the woods. If I had known better, like the politicians who were in the room with the decision makers and the data, I would have done that earlier, like they did. By the way, when you trade information that you can only know because of your position in the government or in the company, it is call insider trading, which is illegal. Also, fun math: since I lost 25%, it will take a gain of 33% to get back to the same level I was before the pandemic (see appendix). More efforts to go up hill. The market high in 2020 was February 29th when the Dow Jones Industrial Average (a key index made of a set of 30 large companies) was at 29,438. One month later on March 23rd it plummeted down to 18,591, a decrease of 36.65%. So, people that had done nothing to their portfolio lost about 37%. I sold in the middle of the debacle and lost "only" 25%. It is always easy to judge what should have been done when you know what happed (hindsight is 20/20). Experts would say do not sell in a panic; it is the worst time to sell when the market is going down. And they are right in hindsight. But on the other hand, their advice is based on the fact that in the long-run markets rebound, and what comes down will go up, so don't look at your portfolio and wait. For my part and given the context of the pandemic where no one could really say what was going on and when things would come back to normal, I assessed that it would be best to sell and keep the cash than wait for some stability in the market before coming back. What I meant by stability is also a little subjective, but I was looking for an end to the pandemic in terms of either a low number of new cases and death, and/or a vaccine. At that point, businesses would reopen, and things would go back to normal, until the next event.

During the pandemic I used the cash to play the market a little with some success. For instance, one day the U.S. government announced that hydroxychloroquine usually used to treat malaria could be used for the coronavirus. If the government, in a pandemic that had everyone on edge, was pushing a particular drug, then the makers and distributors of that drug would see a sharp increase in sales. So, I searched for who was making the drug, found two labs that both were traded in the U.S. and purchased a significant amount of their stocks, all while I was on my phone at the gas station. It took me 5 minutes tops. Teva Pharmaceutical Industries (NYSE: TEVA) and Mylan (NASDAQ: MYL) were the two companies I found involved with hydroxychloroquine. I was a little late to the market as their stocks had already increased on opening day due to high demand, but that also confirmed that I was correct in identifying the companies. I bought TEVA at $7.77 and MYL at $15.94 on March 20th, 2020. I watched all the news reports and followed both stocks very closely several times a day. I saw that MYL was not increasing much, and actually started to dip below my purchased price. I sold it at $15.20 on April 14th. I took a loss there but gained more on TEVA that I sold at $10.46. By that time, the news reports were more negative about the drug and its claimed effects on the virus, and that not much was known about it, so I needed to get out while ahead. I lost 4.6% on MYL and gained 34.6% on TEVA in less than a month. I felt like a day trader. A day trader is someone that trades stocks at a very rapid pace, someone who buys and sells large quantities within a short period of time, sometimes a day, sometimes an hour, and makes little profits on each trade, but multiplied by the quantity of trades ends up positive every day, making a living out that. I did the same kind of trade on the testing kits. President Trump was claiming that certain test kits were better than others and actually posed in the rose garden with test kits manufactured by Abbott Labs (NYSE: ABT). I immediately jumped on the stock and snatched a few at $81.88 and sold them five weeks later at $94.28 for a 15% profit. This is to show you the importance of context and reactivity. When the government pushes or approves something, especially pharma related, but also telecom or defense related, the market listens. As a small investor you will always be behind the eight ball. Plenty of people in the know are already there. But you can make a little profit. This was more opportunistic than strategic and is not reflective of my overall advice. It is exciting to get a little profit fast, and to play big trader boy, but it is risky. BTW, I finished 2020 30% up from where I started even with the COVID-19 market drop. Silver lining.

There are different ways to buy or sell a stock. The most basic type of purchase order you can give to your bank, broker, or online software is the market order. Here you will buy or sell at the market price at the time the order is processed, which will be as soon as you push the button on the computer, or when your broker or bank will do the same on their side (here is one advantage of you controlling the order timing). The other most popular type is the limit order. Here you set a limit for a price for you to buy or sell, and the order will be executed at that price or better (i.e., in your favor). Think about it as a protection you set for yourself, and an option to get a better price at the same time. This order may take more time than a market order because the price has to be at the limit or better for you to get the stock. For example, say you want to buy Google (NASDAQ: GOOGL) and it is valued as of today at $1,187.56. You could set a market order and snatch it at whatever price it would be at the moment you push the button, or you could set a limit order at no more than $1,200, which will let you buy it at $1,200 or less depending on where the trend is going to take the stock. If the stock goes up to $1,230, you will not buy; if it goes up to $1,190 only, you will buy; if it goes down to $1,100, you will also buy. There are other types of orders but let's keep it simple for now. See Example below.

I'll give you an example of a portfolio (See Table 8). In this example I picked 10 stocks that I like and that are well known companies with strong fundamentals (my earlier 10 points). The example looks at a 10-year period between June 2010 and June 2020. During that period some of the stocks took a beating due to the COVID-19 crisis more than others. For instance, Marriott was hit pretty bad, GE as well, but also for other reasons. Marriott is intimately linked to the travel and tourism industry, which stopped completely at the beginning of 2020. GE is also linked to the travel industry via its aviation unit but had lost its innovative R&D and marketing punch in past years. Other companies fared well during the COVID-19 crisis like Netflix, Google, and Tesla and largely offset GE and Marriott's bad returns. The portfolio performed very well over the 10 years and yielded an average return of 25%. $10,000 invested in June 2010 would be worth $92,964 10 years later. Compare that to what the overall market would have yielded to see if we beat Wall Street. I picked three indices ETFs that mirror the Dow Jones, the S&P 500, and the NASDAQ (See Table 9). $10,000 invested evenly amongst these three ETFs would have yielded $33,946, or an average return of 13% yearly. 13% isn't bad compared to a savings account, but 25% is better right?

Table 8: Example Portfolio

Stocks	Exchange	Ticker	QTY	June 30 2010		June 30 2020			
				Purchase price	Value	Sold price	Value	Profit	CAGR
Netflix	NASDAQ	NFLX	20	17.93	358.6	527.39	10547.8	10189.2	40.2%
Crocs	NASDAQ	CROX	20	12.48	249.6	36.47	729.4	479.8	11.3%
Google (Alphabet)	NASDAQ	GOOGL	20	225.23	4504.6	1514.92	30298.4	25793.8	21.0%
Chipotle Mexican Grill	NYSE	CMG	10	150.83	1508.3	1129.51	11295.1	9786.8	22.3%
Mc Donald's	NYSE	MCD	15	73.06	1095.9	190.92	2863.8	1767.9	10.1%
Nike	NYSE	NKE	30	17.6	528	97.26	2917.8	2389.8	18.6%
Tesla	NASDAQ	TSLA	21	20.5	430.5	1500.64	31513.44	31082.94	53.6%
Marriott	NASDAQ	MAR	20	30.14	602.8	93.11	1862.2	1259.4	11.9%
General Electric	NYSE	GE	26	13.92	361.92	7.05	183.3	-178.62	-6.6%
Pfizer	NYSE	PFE	20	15.91	318.2	35.6	712	393.8	8.4%
					9958.42		92923.24	82964.82	25.0%
Cash					41.58		41.58	0	
Portfolio Value					10000		92964.82	82964.82	25.0%

Table 9: Example of a Portfolio Invested in Indices Mirroring the Market

| Indices | Ticker | June 30 2010 | | | June 30 2020 | | | |
		QTY	Purchase price	Value	Sold price	Value	Profit	CAGR
DJI	DIA	40	100.2	4008	267.47	10698.8	6690.8	10.3%
S&P 500	SPY	40	105.31	4212.4	320.79	12831.6	8619.2	11.8%
NASDAQ ETF	QQQ	40	43.28	1731.2	259.19	10367.6	8636.4	19.6%
				9951.6		33898	23946.4	13.0%
Cash				48.4		48.4	0	
Portfolio				10000		33946.4	23946.4	13.0%

Using Your Retirement Plan to Play the Market

You are probably not too familiar with retirement plans because at your age you do not care too much about retirement, but you should. You should be thinking at least about what will happen to you in 40 years. My dad was an insurance salesman and he had signed me up for a life insurance policy that doubled as a savings account. That is called a whole life or a permanent life insurance. I did not care too much until one day some 20 years later, I cashed the insurance and took a $2,000 check to the bank. It did not feel like I had saved much along the way, but that made my day and financed a vacation for my family.

> *Gen Z POV: "I think it is a little weird to think about retirement when you are fresh out of college, but I had people say, "Hey, don't skip out on a 401k." I kinda knew blindly that message but did not know the whys, so, like, when I got my job I set up my 401k, and, like, outside of what my company offers, I had started to invest because people I respected told me to, but I did not know why I picked what I am picking and why it matters, and now it's really cool."*

The common life insurance is sometimes called the death insurance and is the one that you see advertised a lot. It is very cheap. You can get a $250,000 life insurance as a 20-year-old for $15 per month (cheaper for women, cheaper if you don't smoke, cheaper in some states). The only problem is that it is wasted money unless you feel that you want to cover your students loans that your co-signers (your parents more likely) will have to pay if (and I don't wish that to you, of course) you pass away. After you pay $15 a month for 10 or 20 years ($1,800 over ten years), and provided you did not die, the insurance disappears, and you are left with nothing. It is beneficial to cover those you love that will survive you in case of your death, and more importantly that will have to pay for your debts. So, if you have student loans, a mortgage, or other debts, that might be a smart move.

[**Note:** Why is it that if you pay $1,800 over ten years you can get $250,000 if you die? That is the beauty of the pool. The pool is the number of people that sign up for a life insurance policy and who never cash in because they do not die. They pay for the few that die within these ten years. How many does it take to finance the one that dies? That is the probability that actuarial accountants use. If the probability of dying within the next ten years at 20 years old is 1%, then out of 100 people 1 will die and 99 will not. So, if you sell insurance to 100 people, you pocket $1,800 x 100, or $180,000, but you have to pay $250,000 to the family of the one that died. Not a good business. However, the probability of dying in less than 10 years is much smaller for the 20-year-old. So, if you have young people signed up for your insurance who are 20 years old (and 21, 22, 23, etc.), the average probability is much less than 1%, say 0.5%. That means that on average out of 200 people from ages 20 to 30, 1 will die. If you get 200 x $1,800 in revenue that will be $360,000, of which you will pay out $250,000 and pocket the difference of $110,000. Now, that is a better deal.]

The other kind of life insurance, called a whole life insurance has a death benefit; it pays a sum if you die, but more importantly it also has a savings component that grows with interest and can be invested in many mutual funds, or securities (that was what my dad had signed me up for). Each month you pay a certain amount of money, and a portion of that money pays for the management fees, the death insurance, and the rest is invested. After 10 or 20 or 30 years you can decide to cash out the insurance; you lose the death benefit, but you get your invested money back plus interest. This is a basic instrument to save; it is better than a savings account, and it can be less risky than the stock market since most plans will have a guaranteed return no matter what happens to the fund and the market, but of course it is also costly in fees, and will not grow as fast or as high (potentially) than a stock portfolio.

Most reputable companies will offer a 401k. A 401k is a retirement account that the company sets up for their employees. The employees participate on a voluntarily basis, and save money directly from their paycheck, up to a maximum amount of their income per year (see IRS rules). The company will match up to a certain amount of what the employees will save. For example, a company might match up to 3%. So, if you save 3% of your salary, the company gives you an additional 3% for free! If your salary is $40,000 per year and you save $1,200, the company matches you by giving you another $1,200, so at the end of the year you have $2,400 of savings in your 401k account. There are rules for you to access that money. First, it is supposed to be there until you retire. Actually, you can get it out starting at 59 ½ years old. But if you touch it before then, you will have to pay penalties of 10% on top of paying the income tax. Yes, you pay income tax on that money when you withdraw the money. Why? Because you are saving it into the 401k plan before your income tax is calculated as we have seen in Chapter 4. In other words, your income tax will be calculated in our example not on $40,000, but on $38,800 ($40,000 - $1,200). Thus, you will pay less taxes now, and defer these taxes when you withdraw the money. The idea is that when you are retired you will not have a salary anymore, so your income will be mainly these 401k withdrawals, and will substitute as your income.

> *Gen Z POV: "I did not start thinking about a retirement plan with the company I work for until maybe two or three years after I started."*

The good news is that usually if you stay with the company for two or three years (depending on the company's policy), the money it gave you is yours. If you leave early, then you might only get a portion of that money. Companies use that benefit as a retainer mechanism to lower turnover.

Some of the disadvantages of 401k accounts is that you cannot really play the stock market. You are kind of stuck into picking mutual funds based on your risk profile. An advantage of the 401k is that you can borrow money from the account; for example, to make a down payment on a house. You will have to replenish the account, though.

> *Gen Z POV: "My previous company matched on 401 k, but at the time it did not mean anything. Now my new company, they match the first 5% at 100%, and anything after 5% they match 3%. So now that I am a little more educated on that stuff, you know, that's great."*

What if you want to leave the company? No problem, you will be able to transfer your 401k account to a company of your choice (Fidelity, Vanguard, TD Ameritrade. At the time of writing Robinhood was not set up for that) where you will open an individual retirement account (IRA). Now that you have transferred your money there you can start playing the stock market or buy mutual funds. The only disadvantage of the IRA is that you cannot borrow from it to make a down payment on a house.

Yes, you can have an IRA and a 401k with your company at the same time. Any time you can get free money, take it!

There are many different other forms of savings. But one that is interesting to talk about here is the ROTH IRA. That is a retirement account, but you fund it by putting money from your bank account, thus, money that has already been taxed. That is the main difference from the traditional IRA. That money grows, and when you are 59 ½ years old you can start taking it out tax free.

Maybe a good time to talk briefly about retirement?

I don't know at what age you plan to retire, and you might have some goal like, "I will retire at 40 years old." But, in reality, most of us will retire somewhere around 70, give or take. If you can do it earlier, more power to you. If you have to retire later because you do not have enough income, that is a problem. And that is why you should think about it now.

Say, for example, you plan to retire at 70 years old. And say that you are 22 years old now. That leaves you 48 years to build a nest egg that will allow you to live comfortably for the rest of your life. How long will you have to live past retirement? I gave myself a goal to make it to the average life expectancy. Unfortunately, in the U.S. it has gone down significantly in recent years. Today, an American is expected to live until around 78.7 years old on average; 80.3 years old is the age for the Organization for Economic Co-operation and Development, OECD in short, most developed countries. The U.S. is number 38 on the list of all countries, but enough comparisons. I think I will live until 85 anyways because I am in relatively good shape, I exercise, my dad is still alive, and he is 85 currently. So, my plan is to add a few years to that "target" of 85 and I'll need some form of income to sustain me until I am 90 years old.

Between 70 and 90 there are 20 years for which I need savings. I will have a base income with Social Security. Remember in Chapter 4 we are paying FICA taxes from our paychecks to finance retired people's income, so I plan to have that happen to me as well.

Social security benefits are at their maximum when you retire at 70 years old. You can estimate the maximum benefit you will get form the Social Security website, which depends on your age and salary before you retire. But you could get $3,600 per month every month of your retirement (these numbers vary based on your salary and retirement age. See here https://www.ssa.gov/OACT/quickcalc/). That amounts to $43,200 per year. You have to add the withdrawals you will make from each of your retirement and stock accounts to that Social Security amount. In this example let's say you figure that upon retirement you will not have a mortgage to pay anymore, but that everything else you pay for today you'll want to keep (usually it is a better plan to say that you would scale down on expenses upon retirement, and that is a goal that if achieved would give you a seamless transition into retirement. Equivalent of making the same salary without having to work).

> Gen Z POV: *"I did not start thinking about a retirement plan with the company I work for until maybe two or three years after I started."*

If your salary is $100,000 per year before you retire, and you get $43,200 from the social security then you need another $56,800 per year from your different savings. Is that possible? How will you achieve that?

Now we have to work in reverse. We have to ask ourselves the question: "What amount of money will give us $56,800 per year for 20 years?" The straight answer is simple. 20 years times $56,800 a year equals $1,136,000. If we have that much in our bank account upon retirement, we are good to go for 20 years.

There are a multitude of strategies to get there. Let's look at a few in the next chapter.

CHAPTER 7

Become a Millionaire

"The way to win is to make it ok to lose"

So, you want to become a millionaire? Actually, let me rephrase that. You need to become a millionaire by 70 or you will be working your entire life until you die. Did I catch your attention? I hope so. There's nothing wrong with working your entire life as long as you choose to work and you like the work, but there's nothing wrong either with retiring from the rat race and enjoying traveling, your family, your friends, life without having to report to a boss. At 70 you are cynical (I know I already am). These youngsters coming to your business and thinking they know it all. They come up with "ideas" you had 30 years ago. Ideas that never worked, and you know it, but hey, let's see if it'll work. Stop being a downer; be a team player! (did you like that rant?)

Back to the million-dollar idea.

Stocks Versus Real Estate

We have seen a few ways to grow money already. We have seen that we can own a house and grow equity in the house as we pay off our mortgage. That equity is ours. Ok, fine, but how do we get that money?

It is nice to live mortgage free, but that is not going to pay for the wine. There are two strategies here. First, you can downgrade your house needs and move to a smaller house that you could buy in cash with what you make off your existing house and keep the balance of cash for wine and more. That is doable.

Suppose that the house you have purchased for $130,000 in Chapter 5 is now worth $800,000 48 years later. That seems like a lot, but it is an average increase of 3.9% per year over those 48 years. How much do you get to pocket as savings that you could use to supplement your retirement income? Let's assume that you do not have a mortgage anymore, the house is 100% yours, it is "free and clear," as the lawyers say. The calculation has to include expenses you paid to improve the house and expenses you incurred when you purchased the house like real estate commissions, mortgage fees, etc.; and the expenses you are incurring as you are selling the house. Based on these expenses you calculate your profit to be the price you sold the house at, minus expenses, minus the price you paid the house, plus the expenses you incurred when buying it. In our very simple example: $800,000 – $130,000 – $20,000 (for expenses that need to be justified like replacing the roof and HVAC) = $650,000. If you are single and have lived in the house two years, then you can deduct $250,000 as a gift from the IRS. So, your basis for capital gain tax is $400,000. Your capital gain rate might be 15%, so you will pay $60,000 of taxes and you will pocket $340,000 (there are also state taxes in some states). [Note: the number work much better if you are a couple, since now the IRS gift is up to $500,000, therefore you will only pay $22,500 on your capital gain]

Should you get that smaller house with the proceeds? Yes, you could. But you could also purchase a secondary house at some point during the 48 years you are working that could be an investment property while you are working and living in the first house, and then once you retire, you take that small investment house over for you, and keep the proceeds to supplement your income (you will have some tax implication to convert a rental home into a primary residence, so consult a pro at that point). If you choose to do that and we assume that along the way you have been able to purchase a smaller house or apartment for say, $90,000 without a mortgage balance (you paid cash or paid overtime and it is free-and-clear), you have on your bank account after capital gain taxes $590,000 ($250,000 + $340,000). If you need $1,136,000 to retire (See Chapter 5), then you still need $546,000 in a retirement account of some sort.

> *Gen Z POV: "Honestly, I just started reading a book on personal finance, really. I just try to diversify my portfolio. So, get a 401k and then maybe, you know, start fooling around with some stocks a little bit."*

How much of your income should you put into a 401k or an IRA every year in order to get a balance of $546,000 after 48 years?

Let's be conservative and say that given your risk profile, and your investment choices, maybe you can only get a return of 10% on average each year over the 48 years that the money will grow (10% is conservative over a long period of time given the historical market returns (but remember that I am not a financial advisor, so check with a pro. See Table 9).

If you invest $570 per year over 48 years at a 10% return, you will get $547,298 at the end. $570 per year is less than $50 per month. That might seem like a lot today, and you might want to start smaller saving only $20 per month, and later increase that amount. But the example shows that it is possible if you start early to watch your money grow exponentially. In our example, you "only" have invested out of your paycheck a total of $27,360. The large majority of the money you have 48 years later is compounded interest. I say interest, but if you choose the stock market remember that it can also go down.

If your company gives you "free money" when you contribute to your 401k, then your own savings can be cut in half maybe, or you can invest more altogether. In our example you could invest half of the $570, or $285 of your money and the company would match with $285, or you could save the whole $570 yourself, and the company would still match $570 (up to their maximum). In the latter case you will get to your target of $546,000 sooner.

Buying into a Bigger House

Some people like to move into bigger houses as soon as they can financially. That is a strategy to save money in the long run. For instance, you have been in that $130,000 for four years, and now you want to move to a $250,000 house. Your current house is now valued at $160,000, and you have a balance on your mortgage of $91,300. If you sell your first house for $160,000 you will net $150,400 because of the realtor's commission. Minus what you owe the bank for the balance on the mortgage you will get a check of $59,100. Remember that three years ago you made a down payment of $33,000? (See Chapter 5)

Gen Z POV: "My house will not be a big house but like a starter house. And then have a rental property; move on to the next thing. However, now it's more like from now in five years I can think about maybe putting down 10 and who knows if a mortgage company will get me on the ground floor, so the plan is now to find a new job that pays more."

So now you can buy a house with a down payment of $59,100. If that down payment is 20% of the house price, then the house you can buy is worth $295,500. You can definitely get that $250,000 house and have enough money to pay the closing costs.

Why would you want to buy a bigger house? A bigger house has a bigger value (and a bigger mortgage), so if you can afford the mortgage payment, then your money is going to work better for you. We say that you have more "leverage", meaning that you can buy into a larger investment with a relatively smaller increase in your own out of pocket. The banks allow you to do that because of your good credit and good ratios. Let's take a look at the scenario of staying in your current house 10 more years or moving to that new house. After ten years here is the situation. After ten years, the first house will be worth $211,756 at an appreciation of 5%. If you sell it, pay the 6% commission to the realtor, and pay off your mortgage balance, then you pocket $122,946. If instead, you move to a larger house after four years in your first house, then that new house purchased at $250,000 (with a $50,000 down payment) will appreciate at 5% (just to keep the example comparable) to a value of $335,023. If you sell it, minus commissions, and minus the balance on the mortgage, you pocket $141,942, or $18,996 more than if you had stayed in the first house. That is without mentioning that when you sold your first house you reinvested in the new one only $50,000 and kept $9,100, which you could have put to work on your IRA.

The disadvantage of moving to a bigger house is that first, you will have a bigger mortgage, so you need to qualify and be able to afford it; second, you will have larger expenses, a bigger HVAC system, and bigger lawn, higher property taxes, more rooms to fill with furniture. And let's not forget more windows to clean! There might also be a psychological tax. If you have to move a family with children, you run the risk of being the bad guy for a while because they might lose their bearings and their friends. All that is not trivial. That is why instead of buying a larger house, some people prefer to buy a fixer upper or an investment property.

You have seen the TV shows *Flip That House* and other remodeling shows. It seems easy if you are a little handy. Can you do it? If you can, then do it, but be aware that if you are not lucky in calculating the cost of the remodel, or the way the housing market is growing in the location you are buying that fixer upper, then you might be in for a big disappointment. Some people have played that game and found the local market collapsed from under them, and their fixer upper, not yet fixed, was already under water. You are under water when what you owe to the bank, the mortgage balance, is more than the value of the house (for example your mortgage is $100,000 and you purchase your house for $130,000, but now the market value of your house is $90,000. So, if you sell the house, not even factoring the realtors' commissions, you owe the bank more than you will get at the sale. You are underwater. Some call that being in the "red" referring to the way accounting shows losses in red and profits in black). Needless to say, you have already lost your equity, but if you sold the house, you would have to be the one coming to the closing with a check to make up the difference between the house value, plus commissions, and the mortgage balance. Beware of the people trying to sell you fixer uppers, because more likely it will be sold "as is," meaning that a house inspection might not be done, or if it is, the seller will not do any of the work listed. Lighter fixer uppers might have major remodeling work to be done inside that are not structural (structural means anything major like the foundations, the main beams supporting the house, the roof beams, the plumbing systems, the electrical wiring), or major upgrades (roof, windows, paint, landscape, HVAC) that can be done fairly easily. Make your calculations, think about what you can do yourself, and what needs to be done by a pro. Think about permits, and whether you will be able to get them. Then think about the value once renovated and compare that to the market. If you flip the house fast enough, then you might be protected again a downturn, but if you take too long, there might be bad news on the horizon. One more point about a second home, whether it is a fixer upper or an investment property ready to move in, the lenders see more risk in these deals because you are not living in the house and you might care less about making your mortgage payment, so they will ask for a 30% down payment more often than not. Some states or some lenders are a little more understanding, but be ready for a more difficult access to mortgage.

Note: the rule of 72 is an approximation calculation that allows you to very easily figure out how many years it takes for an investment to double at a particular interest rate. For example, if you want to know how many years it would take for an investment to double at 5% you divide 72 by 5 to get 14.4. So, it will take any amount of money 14 and half years to double at 5%. Similarly, if the rate of return would be 10%, then it would double in just a little bit more than 7 years (72/10). Pretty cool, right? You can even figure out the impact of inflation on the value of money in the future with that trick. For instance, say the inflation on average is 2% and you want to know when your money will devalue by half. Put another way, when will $100 of today be worth only $50? Answer is 36 years (72/2). In 36 years with an inflation of 2% on average every year, your money will be worth half of what it is worth today. That means that if you want to maintain the standard of living you have today, if you need today's income of $40,000 per year, then in 36 years these $40,000 will be worth half, so you will need twice as much to live the same way because everything will have doubled in price. Put another way, in 36 years with an inflation at 2% you will keep todays standard of living if you make $80,000. Keep that in mind when you make your retirement calculation. Inflation takes some of the interest, or investment gains, away from you. An investment yielding gains of 2% with a 2% inflation rate is an investment that will get you 0% of return after inflation. Thus, if you really want 2% you need a savings account that yields 4%.

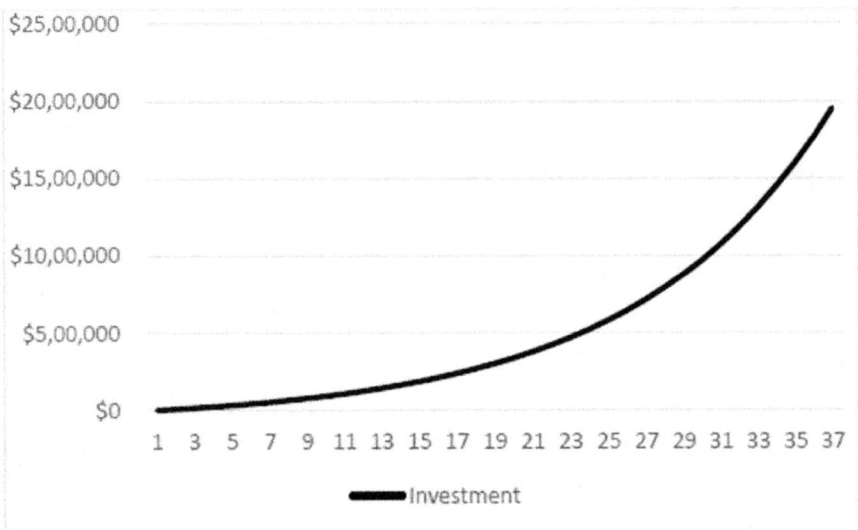

*Figure 10   Value of a $5,000 Initial Investment at a 10%
Return, adding $6,000 Per Year, Over 36 Years*

Bottom line: save 6% to 7% (don't forget to factor in inflation, so maybe 8% or 10% is a better number) of your salary into some savings account that yields 10% or better. That means not a regular bank savings account, not just buying gold, or CDs, but taking the measured risk of investing in the stock market via mutual funds, ETFs, or stocks. As an example, if you start with $5,000 and then you save $500 per month for 36 years at a return of 10%, you will get almost $2 million, $1,946,324 (See Figure 10). Quiz: What is the value in today's money of that $1,946,324 if the average inflation was 2%? (Answer: Rule of 72. 72/2=36 thus, 36 years to double the money at 2%, thus, the $1,946,324 is half of what it would be today, thus, in today's money it is worth $3,898,648. Give yourself a gold star, even you did not get it right, you participated!).

Becoming an Entrepreneur

Another way to become a millionaire is to become an entrepreneur. This is also the American dream. Anyone can be an entrepreneur. It is fairly easy to create a business and start making some money. Ok, is it this easy to become a successful entrepreneur? Let alone a millionaire entrepreneur? No, of course not. But most people believe they can become that entrepreneur. And maybe you are the one. In fact, I am pretty sure you are the one. What does it take?

I don't know about you, but I am a big fan of shows like *Shark Tank, The Profit, Restaurant Impossible*, and so on. Even if you don't like these shows, watch a few episodes and you will get the basic advice any entrepreneur should listen to as they are on their couch dreaming about their genius idea of a product or service. First is the business concept. Is your business concept capable of making money? Second, is there a strategy to get that idea into a product that sells, not just to friends and family but to a large market? Finally, it is about you as an entrepreneur and what you want to get out of that venture?

The Idea

I have an idea every minute. I am a little too creative sometimes. It can manifest itself into many projects that have been started but don't really move forward, or don't get anywhere. I am a victim of my hyperactive mind, and I control it with the hope that one day one of these ideas will be successful. I have hope in myself. I trust the creative process. Back to the idea we began with in Chapter 1 where you need to fail a lot in order to have a shot at that three-pointer or that hole-in-one, or that Grammy.

When my first child was 1 or 2, she would play with small toys that hurt my bare feet. That gave me the idea to create a toy vacuum cleaner for small toys (I know David Wallace from *The Office* stole the idea from me 'cause I had that idea in 1989). I figured parents would prefer a vacuum instead of having to pick up the toys every evening. It did no go very far for two main reasons. First, I was not in the toy business or the manufacturing business, I was in the hospitality business. Therefore, I had little idea on how to manufacture toys or vacuums at a low cost. I knew nothing of the business fundamentals. My expertise was that of a parent, a user, and that was it. Second, within a few months of me having that idea, the toy companies at the time actually launched a toy vacuum. I am certain that you have had that experience before. You think of some good product and someone else launches it before you can even talk about it with your friends.

The lessons here are twofold:

1) Know your business. Even if you are not from the business, or do not have formal training in the business, do your homework. If you want to create a pastry shop, don't focus on pastry recipes a lot; more than likely you like pastries and know how to make them; instead, focus on the business of a pastry shop. What does it mean to be a pastry shop owner? How many hours do they work? What clientele do they serve? What is the cost of good percentage they need to reach in order to make

a profit? What does it cost to lease a place of business? Should it be a manufacturing only place or should it also be a retail store open to the public?

The best way to do that research on the business is to go to a pastry shop, talk to the owner, see if they would let you stay a couple of days to follow them. If you are not going to be a competitor, they might let you in.

2) Be fast in determining what product the market is going to buy by prototyping and getting feedback from friends and family and folks at your church or in your community. The sooner you know what price they are willing to pay, what differentiates you from the competition, and whether or not they will repeat their purchase, the better it is for you.

Going to Market

Like the proverbial tech entrepreneurs of the 20th century (e.g., Jobs, Hewlett and Packard, Bezos) you will start in your garage with nothing. Or in your basement, or somewhere in the house. You will create a prototype and you will show it to your friends and family to get feedback. As we have eluded before (See Chapter 3) you need to create a product or service that is unique or different or both. Ask yourself the question, how unique or different is your product? The second question you need to ask yourself is what kind of margin you will make on that product. That implies knowing the price consumers will be able and willing to pay (the value they see in your product) and it also implies that you control the cost to manufacture the product. You are seeking a margin in the neighborhood of 50% to 70%.

Let's take the example of the pastry shop. Let's break it down, first assuming you want to focus on party cakes (See *Cake Wars*, *Next Great Baker*, or the *Great British Bake Off*). A wedding cake might cost $5 per slice with a minimum of 100 people or $500. A birthday cake might be more expensive per person because people tend to have more servings, but there are less people at the birthday so the slice might cost $7 and the cake might be serving 30 people, thus, $210. No matter what, you will have to make that cake for 30% of the price (your cost of goods. Remember Chapter 3, Profit & Loss statement?). For the wedding cake that will be $150 of raw ingredients. For the birthday cake it will be $63. Can you do that? Factor in a professional cost for sugar, flour etc. That means wholesaler's price on raw goods, not just your regular food store. Second question is your talent. When you sold the wedding cake to the bride and groom, did they see a $500 value? If they were not ready to spend that much, then maybe your talent isn't appreciated, or you don't have the right customer in front of you, or maybe your talents are not worth this much after all. Better to know now rather than later.

Let's say everything is good. The newlyweds are very pleased with your $500 wedding cake and everyone raved about it. And it cost you $150 or less to make it. Now, factor in your time and your salary. If you had to pay yourself full-time to make that type of cake year-round, how many cakes would you need to make per day in order to sustain your income? To figure this out, and after talking to the pastry shop owner, you might find out that usually keeping salaries around 30% including benefits and taxes is the target the shop owner has. That allows them to still be able to pay for equipment repairs, the lease, rent, utilities, insurance etc., and make a small profit.

If you want an income of $40,000 as a pastry shop owner, then first factor in your benefits and taxes. As an owner and operator, you will need to pay for the business payroll taxes, which are 7.65%, plus some other payroll taxes, so let's round it up to 10% of payroll (check with your state), in our example $4,000. Your payroll is going to be

$44,000 and if that represents 30% of sales, then your sales must be $146,667 ($44,000/0.30) per year. If your sales must be $146,667, it means you need to sell 293 wedding cakes in a year, or a little less than 6 per weekend. That brings us to our next question: can you do that? Is there a market around you with these many weddings? Can you access and reach that market and win their business against the competition?

If all is good, then you would manage to have $58,667 to spend on equipment, lease, repairs, insurance, and administrative things including website hosting and marketing expenses, and if you spent only $50,000 per year on that, then you can manage a profit of $8,667 or 5.9% of sales. I did not account for sales taxes here, but don't forget that licenses and taxes are inevitable. At some point you will need to get out of the garage or the kitchen and establish your business properly, organize your company legally, be food certified by the local state inspections, and pay taxes.

Distribution

If you are already selling 5 or 6 wedding cakes per weekend, you are already on a good path. As a pastry shop owner, what you have to do now is diversify into other types of cakes. That will give you some form of protection against wedding cake wars your competitors might launch. Maybe corporate cakes. Think about spreading your business production load throughout the week, as well as across several promising segments. And maybe if you have a particularly good idea in terms of cake, but also in terms of transportation, maybe you can also think about distribution. Can you sell and deliver the same cake that made you famous two states over? What does it mean in terms of equipment needed? And what does it mean in terms of a production schedule for you. Can you handle it, or do you need to hire help? If you hire help, what is your new number of cakes you need to achieve to keep payroll at 30% of sales? One major drawback of the food business is that you cannot protect yourself from someone else to reverse engineer your cakes and make copies. So, the only way out of that is to get new ideas fast, and to change recipes or decorations before the competition copies you. You can keep recipes secret for a while, but the help that just quit has gotten a 50% pay increase with your competition just so that they can extract your unique recipes out of them. Yeah, that hurts. But business is brutal, or as Michael Scott would say, "Business is personal. It's the most personal thing out there."

One thing you can use to protect your business is branding. You can copyright logos and trademarks, and if that is how you are known, then the brand means something to the consumer, and that is protected (count $3,000 minimum to get some trademark or copyright done). The copycat will always (actual not always) be the second to market, the knock off, the copycats. Who copied whom: McDonald's, Wendy's, or Burger King? KFC, Popeyes, or Chick-fil-A? You can see the limit of that strategy.

Exit Strategy

When a business owner tries to retire, it is often difficult. Who wants to buy the business? If the owner was very visible, as a pastry chef might be, then how could someone else really be better? These issues are at the core of what is called the exit strategy. Angels (people that help startup businesses at the very beginning, think garage or just after), venture capitalists (think *Shark Tank*, and people that will invest larger sums in your venture than angels), and other investment banks (banks specialized in startup investments and venture capital) will want to get out as well at some point, sooner than later, with a multiple of 10 (10 times their investment) at least. How can one investor leave? Usually, it is because the business is sold to another private investor or a group of investors, or if the business makes an IPO and the public is buying early investors' shares. For the business creator it is not easy to either leave the business to someone else because of the psychological attachment to the business and because of some personality issue like being the face of the business. Sometimes businesses have the creator's name on them. You have seen the "Joe's Pizza" parlor, and you ask if Joe is there and get a blank stare from the staff (like when Michael Scott asks for Alfredo at the pizza place, then asks for the manager. Or the time he called Wendy's and asked for Wendy... because that's who Kevin tried to set him up with). Joe has not been the owner for years.

When the exit strategy for the original investors is an IPO, then the original owner is stuck even more. The public and the financial analysts want the owner, the creator to stay. That is part of what they are buying. Think about Apple going public in 1980 and Steve Jobs saying "Ok, I am selling all my shares and I am retiring." That would not have made a good impression on the market (He later was fired, then came back, but that's another story).

I was managing a hotel for a private owner once. As I was the turnaround specialist, when I arrived at the hotel it was bleeding cash pretty bad and the ownership was forced to keep the hotel afloat by reinjecting cash because it was losing money every year (we were in the red). After assessing that the issues were not getting enough revenue and having too many expenses, I trimmed expenses and created a sales organization that performed extremely well. So well, that three years later the hotel was profitable, was the leader in its market, and enjoyed great customer feedback and good employee satisfaction. Several of the employees had been promoted within the hotel and within the organization (that hotel was also part of a chain). We (the

hotel and by association the staff) had gone from pariah in the organization, to stars. For the owner, the opportunity was not missed. He
knew that my time at his property was counted and that I might be
sent somewhere else, and he might see a reversal. So, he decided it was
time to sell. Only because of the market share results and the profitability was he able to sell the hotel at a premium. Who would buy a
business losing money?

Selling small businesses is not really like selling big corporations.
Public corporations are purchased via the stock market, and a rough
idea of their price is their market capitalization (a.k.a. market cap),
which is the share price multiplied by the number of shares. If you
can buy all the shares, then you own the company. Medium size companies, like the hotel I was managing are private, and do not really
present the same opportunity for buyers. The price is usually a multiple of sales and/or profit before taxes. A usual ratio is three times annual sales or revenue, or ten times profit before taxes. For the pastry
shop and any other small business, the price calculation is different.
First of all, most of the small businesses do not own the property in
which they are located. They usually lease it from a landlord. If you
think landlords of apartments are ruthless, wait until you deal with
a commercial landlord! A commercial lease will typically be a 3/6/9
type or some other numbers. The idea is that you lease for the first 3
years, then if the landlord likes you, you can lease for another 6, then
another 9. You get the idea. But the lease is obviously tied to the location, and location might be very important. Think about a pastry
shop that has a retail shop with very good foot traffic (foot traffic =
lots of people passing by the shop = potential customers). You want to
sell your business with the idea that the retail store will stay at the
same location. So, you are also selling to the landlord that the new les-
see (the renter) will be a good person, a successful person, and you're

asking for the landlord to transfer the lease to them, which they can decline to do. If the landlord says no, and it was not really formally agreed upon in the lease, then you might be stuck paying the lease for the next 6 or 9 years, and/or will not be able to sell that business of yours. Small businesses that do not have real property have value because of the transferability of the lease, and because of the good-will they have. The goodwill is the customer base, the regulars, the loyal customers, that will continue coming to the pastry shop even if there's a new chef. The rest of the business might have some value, such as the name recognition, the logo, the website and its traffic, the recipes, the staff, and all the inventory, but at the end of the day once the new buyer looks at the P&L and balance sheet, they will buy the business on the basis of one time the cash flow. The cash flow the business generates is defined as all the profit before taxes and before it pays the owner's salary. So, in the case of our pastry shop the cash flow is going to be $44,000 (owner's salary) + $8,667 (profit before tax) = $52,667. Disappointed? Yes, you are right; you should be. But think about it, you put your blood and sweat in that business and you get $53k out of it, which isn't really that bad. But that is not how you become a millionaire.

Your path to becoming a millionaire while being a small business owner will be in your capacity to leverage your idea. Leveraging is the idea that we saw in Chapter 3. You have to find a way to make that business gain market share without really requiring you to work 48-hour-days, which by the way is not possible. You need to hire staff that will be able to replicate your recipes without much supervision, so that you can develop and market the business and maximize your manufacturing capacity until you need a new and larger facility, and so on.

Or you'll need to sell your way of being successful via franchise.

In our pastry shop example, if you want to sell for $1 million instead of $53k then you need 20 times the cash flow you have. That could mean 20 shops, that could mean 3 shops but 20 times the revenue. Whatever it means, you have to figure it out.

If your idea is replicable and you feel you can train owners that have little expertise in being pastry shop owners, and owners that would like your recipes and your business methods, then maybe franchise is for you.

Should You be Thinking About Franchise?

Franchise is a way for you to copy and paste your success story throughout the U.S. and possibly the world. It is how McDonald's made it thanks to Ray Kroc. Before you start writing a franchise agreement you will need to have two or three successful shops running for at least a year. Future franchisees are going to want to see that in different markets your concept is a success, and that it makes enough money to give them a return, or a salary. Once you have that, then time for the lawyers.

A franchise agreement is a legal document prepared and filed in each state. It costs quite a bit of money to get that done by specialized lawyers. Count about $20,000 minimum (by state!).

You will probably start with one state, possibly the one next door. Once you have the agreement written up, it is time to sell the concepts to potential franchisees. Entrepreneurs that do not have unique ideas still have the motivation to be entrepreneurs. And if they have the money, then they will go shopping, usually online or at franchise shows for an idea. Once they apply to your franchise, you'll do an evaluation of the potential franchisee's ability, both financially and psychologically to become a good franchisee. A good franchisee is one that is not going to destroy your brand by changing all the recipes or stealing your concept and renaming it another way. Usually, the franchisee will pay an entry fee of something like $20,000 (sometimes more, sometimes less). That is how you get the franchisee legal fees to be paid back. Then, each month the franchisee will pay a percentage of sales for marketing (something like 6%), and management (something like 6%). There are other more complex schemes, but that one is the basic idea. So, as a franchisor you will get 12% of sales from that franchisee. If they are as successful as you, thanks to your method, then their yearly revenue will be $146,667 minimum, and you will get a check for $17,600, plus the initial $20,000. How many franchisees do you need to get $1,000,000? The answer is 30 more or less, and that depends on the revenue they can achieve of course. That million is not all profit for your franchise because you have agreed to help with marketing and management, so you need to spend money on marketing (TV commercials and online marketing), and you need to go visit and help management improve the operation. But you get the idea, and should you be able to sustain growth in several states, then you could really hit some serious money and possibly headaches as well.

Calculate Your Net Worth

Remember the balance sheet from Chapter 3? Well, you have a balance sheet as well. It is called a Net Worth calculation (See Figure 11). Your net worth is important to calculate and to know because bankers will ask for it. For instance, if you are buying a business or if you are applying for a small business administration (SBA) loan, your net worth is the basis for lending you money. A net worth is the result of a subtraction: your assets minus your liabilities. What are your assets? The value of your house, your cars, objects of art (statues and paintings), furniture, jewelry, boat, RV, summer house, whole life insurance cash value, cash, and retirement accounts. Liabilities are what you owe: mortgage, HELOC, credit cards, student loans, and car loans. When you hear people say this celebrity's net worth is $10 million, then what it means is that their assets minus their liabilities equals $10 million. If they would liquidate their assets today, meaning they would sell everything they have (and get the highest price), then after paying all their debts, they would be left with $10 million in cash. Kanye West's net worth is reported to be $3.2 billion and Beyoncé's is "only" $400 million. Johnny Depp's net worth was once $500 million, but today he's reported to be near bankruptcy. Calculate yours.

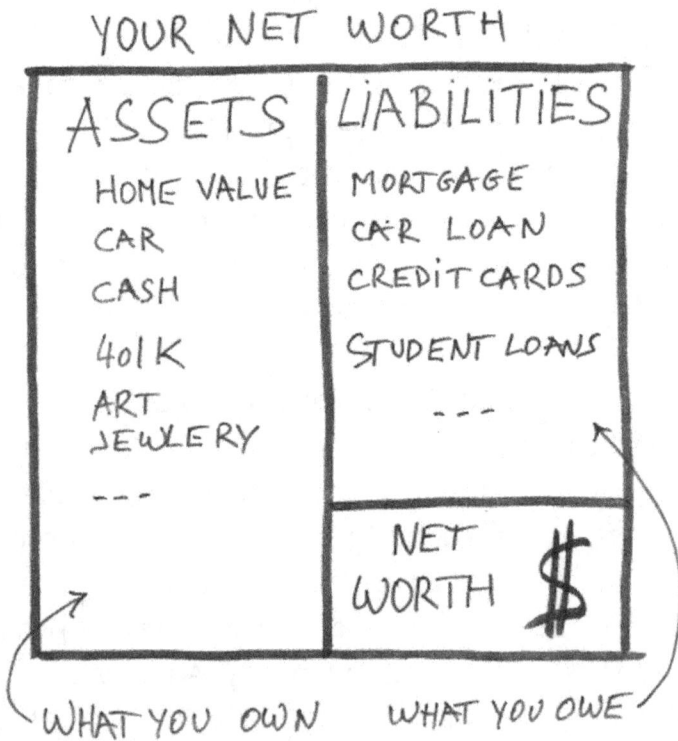

YOUR NET WORTH

ASSETS / LIABILITIES

HOME VALUE / MORTGAGE
CAR / CAR LOAN
CASH / CREDIT CARDS
401 K / STUDENT LOANS
ART
JEWLERY
- - -   - - -

NET WORTH $

WHAT YOU OWN   WHAT YOU OWE

Figure 11   Net Worth

Note: Million versus Billion

Becoming a millionaire is a reachable goal. But I need to put that in perspective. Think about a million seconds. If you think about that million of seconds in terms of days, how many days are there? 1,000,000 of seconds divided by 60 seconds for a minute, then divided by 60 minutes in one hour, then divided by 24 hours in a day equals 11 days and a half. Compare that to a billion. A billion of seconds is equal to (drum roll) almost 32 years!!! 11 days to 32 years is the equivalent of comparing a millionaire with a billionaire. In other words, a million is a lot to achieve, but in the end, it is not a lot. So, chill. A.K.A. be philosophical about it (See Chapter 9).

Chapter 7 Appendices: Calculate your Net Worth

Example:

Assets		Liabilities	
Home Value	130000	Mortgage	100000
Car	7500	Car Loan	7000
Cash	2000	Credit Cards	1500
401 K	3000	Students Loans	30000
Art	0		
Jewelry	500		
	143000		138500
		Net Worth	4500

Your turn:

Assets		Liabilities	
Home Value		Mortgage	
Car		Car Loan	
Cash		Credit Cards	
401 K		Students Loans	
Art			
Jewelry			
		Net Worth	

THE LAST TWO CHAPTERS

So far, we have concentrated on how to acquire material things. Getting a job to get money and buying stuff with that money. But, of course, there is more to life than material things. It took me several decades to understand that life was about something other than a car, a house, a bank account. Of course, without a house or a bank account (with money in it; I guess you can try to avoid the car), life would suck or be very harsh so don't overdo it.

Getting a house you can barely afford is not prudent in case of a reversal of luck at work. Buying a mega mansion will not necessarily bring you joy and happiness. Aren't we all pursuing happiness after all?

In fact, many other researchers have studied what makes people happy or what motivates people to wake up in the morning. One theory you might know is that of psychologist Abraham Maslow known as the "Hierarchy of Needs" (See Figure 12). The bottom two levels of that pyramid deal with basic needs. The need for food, water, and shelter which are linked to the need for employment in order to get the money to get the food, water, and shelter. We have seen these topics in the first chapters.

SELF, ACTUALIZATION

RESPECT
SELF-ESTEEM

LOVE : FRIENDS, FAMILY

SAFETY : SHELTER, INCOME...

BASIC NEEDS : FOOD, SLEEP...

MASLOW'S HIERARCHY
OF NEEDS

Figure 12 Maslow's Hierarchy of Needs

In these last two chapters I will talk about my journey so far through life with respect to activities that have helped me be a better person (at least I hope) and be a happier person (that I know). These activities have also contributed to my self-esteem, confidence, achievements, and respect for others, which in turn have rewarded me with the respect from others (ok, not all others), Maslow's higher needs. Finally, we will touch on my favorite topic, and what usually separates my friends from the rest (my non-friends). I call it philosophy. Others would call it rhetoric, dialectic, argumentation, or discussions. I want to try to walk you through my thought process when engaging in a discussion with someone else. My process is far from perfect and cost me several relationships. But each time I learned a little more about myself and that made me stronger. Paraphrasing Kelly Clarkson and Friedrich Nietzsche: "What does not kill me makes me stronger."

CHAPTER 8

Etiquette and Other Miscellaneous Life Skills

"He who laughs, lasts"

It is sometimes difficult to "keep the fire going." I have been in situations where I was not motivated to wake up and go to work. I don't know about you, but I would guess you also have been in situations where it was a drag to go to work, or to class, or maybe even to go to a family event. Today I cherish my memories of family vacations or Christmas dinners, but at the time I also remember that some, if not all, were a drag. Particularly when I was a teenager. You know the feeling, when you are a teenager you want to be cool, you do not want to be associated with your parents, you want your independence, you want to belong to a group of friends or any group as long as your parents or sometimes siblings are not there. That allows you to experiment freely, and to "find" yourself without having to suffer the judgment of your relatives. Let me share a few stories here and what I drew as life lessons.

Adventure and Seeing the World, Hobbies, and Bucket Lists

One very difficult decision I had to make when I was a teenager was choosing between two expensive gifts that my parents could likely not afford but had planned to offer me if I was to get my middle school certificate (in France you have an all-day exam at the end of the year between middle school and high school that you need to pass, otherwise you stay in middle school another year). If I passed that exam, I could pick either a moped or a scuba diving gear. This was a dilemma. A moped for a 13-year-old is synonymous with freedom and autonomy. I could go anywhere my friends were and hang out with them all day instead of relying on taking a bus, riding a bike, or sketchy hitchhiking. Plus, a moped is cool, so I was going to be cool. Why the scuba gear you ask? My dad was one of the pioneers of scuba diving in 1950's France and every week of his youth he would go spear fishing or scuba diving. He passed it on to me of course, and I would also spend my summers and most weekends each spring spear fishing with him. I was using made up gear and old suits that had been glued together. So, to get a brand-new wet suit, fins, mask, spear gun, and depth meter was big. My choice was to either accept the diving gear and please my father and spend most summers with him or accept the moped and go with my friends. I chose the scuba gear.

Over the years I gained knowledge in the discipline and got my diving instructor diploma when I was 20. That allowed me to start teaching others and develop a sense of pedagogy I used later on in my professional life (well, according to some of my students I am the worst teach. But most students are happy, so let's focus on them). In addition, being a scuba instructor is cool, and now we come full circle, leaving these knuckleheads on their mopeds at the dock while taking off on the dive boat along with good company.

You do not become a diving instructor without getting a first aid and CPR certification or without getting your boat driving license. In getting these credentials I also picked up a lifeguard certification allowing me to work on the beach as a lifeguard. Imagine yourself at 17, walking up and down the beach with your official t-shirt, official speedo (it is France after all), Ray-bans and whistle, using the Zodiac inflatable boat once in a while to "test" it when the proper gallery was on the beach. You know what I am saying?

Another passion of my dad's when he was young was judo. My dad was a very young black belt that trained with the early Japanese masters, like Michigami Sensei, who came to France post WWII. So, when it was time for me to pick a sport, guess what I did? I honestly don't really remember actually picking judo. I was hanging at the dojo from when I was 2 years old until it was ok for me to actually be part of a class. And then I was there, competing. I can't remember when that happened. Anyway, I competed in judo until I was 16, but one day I found Bruce Lee. That took me on a completely different trajectory. I was still involved in Japanese martial arts, so my dad would approve, but I was now adding kung fu, karate, nunchakus, and more. That led me to start practicing aikido (See Steven Segal's movies). I still practice aikido and hold a black belt now. I love the esthetic and the non-competitive aspect of aikido. It is also heavy in weapon techniques and self-defense. Given my background I would get creative with a little bit of karate or judo here and there and created my own style. I could express myself; I could gain confidence and it showed in my demeanor and approach to situations.

All these activities gave me assurance, self-esteem, self-discipline, and acceptance. I do not regret one moment for having let the moped go, although I had to rely on my bike, and did a lot of bike rides to go places when my friends had graduated from the moped to the dirt bike to the full-on bike. That was ok, though. In Europe it is ok to ride behind your buddy on his bike, right?

What is the activity or the hobby you have right now? Can you see yourself doing that hobby or activity for several decades? Can you grow within the organization or association that you are in right now? For instance, if you are an online gamer, or you enjoy fishing, or the outdoors. Do you see yourself progressing in that field, and could you potentially see yourself gaining responsibilities in a related organization or in tournaments?

Professional Organizations

At some point in my life, I was part of the Junior Chamber of Commerce known as the Jaycees. The Jaycees are young leaders under 40 that meet, take actions, and create events that benefit their community. It is part Rotary or Lyons, part Toastmaster or Political party. You learn to speak in public, argue your point of view, organize campaigns, network in the community, fundraise, and lead at the local or national level in typical association positions such as treasurer, secretary, or vice-president, and president.

This served as a tremendous benefit for me. Public speaking is frightening for most people. Even professional actors have stage fright every time they perform. Convincing people with your words is also a very important skill to have. Knowing how to set up an association and to run one is crucial to contribute outside of work to your community. I have served as treasurer, secretary, vice-president, and president of multiple associations along the way.

Every profession has its local or national organization. The National Association for Business Economics, the American Hotels and Motels Association, the Professional Association of Diving Instructors, the U.S. Chamber of Commerce, and so on. Find yours and join. Then, make your way through the organization. First at the local level, then at the national level. Be involved.

Get Out of Your Comfort Zone; See the World, Open Your Mind, Learn Stuff

Seeing the world is very important in life. I have not been to many countries; however, I have not shied away from traveling. I went to Spain and the UK many times, a few times to Switzerland and Italy. A few times to the Middle East and North Africa. A couple times to the Caribbean and once to China. I lived in Canada and the U.S., of course. These trips pale in comparison to some of my friends and colleagues in the tourism field that have "done" more than 100 countries (that is still only half the number of countries on earth by the way). Why is it important to go see the world? I think the statistics is that less than 25% of Americans speak another language (and most who do are probably recent immigrants), and less than 45% own a passport. I actually have always been flabbergasted by how many people have never left their city or state! On the other hand, and most likely because English (thanks mainly to the UK, not the U.S.) has been the "world language of business" (read here the language of the conqueror since most colonial nations impose their values, cultures, and languages on the country they control. The reason why Brazil speaks Portuguese, the rest of South America Spanish, West Africa French and so on), most of all other countries speak English along with their native language. So, most of the world is at least bilingual, even the Brits and the Canadians are bilingual, the former because at some point they have learned French (note: French was the official Crown language up until very recently), or for the latter they have lived alongside French people within their own country. Australia is in the same "bag" as the U.S., but I digress.

You need to speak at least one other language. In the U.S. that language is not French (too bad, we lost the opportunity when Napoleon sold Louisiana to the colonies to finance his wars) or German or even Portuguese, it is Spanish. According to the Census at least 13% of the U.S. population are native Spanish speakers. Spanish is the spoken language for 29% of Californians!

Gen Z POV: "After a study abroad trip that we did in France I just loved it so much that I studied abroad last year through the University, but then I just loved it so much that I decided to transfer over. I enjoy living by myself in Paris; all my friends are here now."

Back in France when I was in high school as I said before I was not really a good student and that included the languages we had to learn. Mandatory English, Latin (a dead language, what a drag!), and one more language, in my case Spanish because I had briefly been to Spain crossing the border with my grandparents once; it was sunny and different, with great Fanta orange drinks (no coke there). I was a very "rational" decision maker (sarcasm alert). Major life decisions are sometimes based on a memory or feeling that could be perceived as mundane by others. It was a trip done during the dictator Franco era pre-1975, and I remember the Guardia Civil uniforms and their little funny hats known as "medio queso" (half cheese). It was funny, but the Guardia Civil was not fun at all and the feeling of being observed as a foreigner, even on vacation, was real.

It took me another three years once in the vocational school, to start appreciating English and Spanish. I first started to appreciate English mainly because of music and coding. I remember being at my first waiter's job and the bartender for the summer was an English teacher during the regular year. I was deep into rock 'n roll at that point in my life. I was able to play smoke on the water on the guitar using two strings (that means I knew nothing)! That must tell you that I was committed to the craft. Listening to the Beatles, Pink Floyd, Led Zeppelin, Deep Purple, the basics. But not really understanding what they were saying. I was able to pick up a word or two, but that was all. The English teacher said it's easy to speak English, imagine you have a hot potato in your mouth. That's it! Not sure she was a real teacher. My real incentive came from coding or programing as it was called back then. All computers were and still are programmed using some form of English. The programming languages of the times were Fortran, Cobol, or Basic. They all had similar commands like IF/ THEN/ELSE or START/GO TO/END, etc. (See the example at the end of this chapter). Today everyone should learn a little bit of coding like HTML or Python. In the end you will find that they are all similar and not this obscure. Think about English from the UK, Australia, and Canada versus the U.S. Computers of the time were a little easier to program, and very limited in memory, but for us teenagers it was a completely new world out there. So, English became interesting in order to achieve something. Complete that with a couple trips to the UK and now you could say you were "fluent" on your résumé, even though you were not really fluent.

Spanish was more of an opportunity to me than anything else. I became more interested by Spanish than German or Arabic (the alternatives) because I guess of that trip with my grandparents, and the fact that we lived closer to Spain than Germany, so we had that "south west" feeling (Germany is to the northeast of France). One summer I had the opportunity to go work for four months in a five-star hotel in Pamplona. You know Pamplona because you have seen the running of the bulls (See *City Sleeker*, the movie). Well, I ran with the bulls!

Beret, scarf, and white shirt and pants, the works! San Fermin, the official name, starts from July 6th and lasts until July 14th and is only the third most attended "fiesta" in the world after the Carnival of Rio and the Munich Beer Festival (See *Beerfest*, the movie). People sleep on the street after partying all night (not me of course), and they are awakened by others giving them more Sangria (as if they needed more) for breakfast (don't ask me how I know that).

I was a cook apprentice there for these four months, and I loved the easygoing pace of Spanish life. No more dictator Franco at that time, everyone was smoking something that smelled funnier than tobacco, life was a party. One day the Chef received an invitation to participate in the Pamplona paella contest along with all the other chefs in town. I believed that the Chef was quite cynical as he said to me: "You are going to represent the hotel in the contest." I was immediately flattered, but then realized that I knew nothing about paella. He taught me, and I went there and won the contest. A French guy, barely speaking Spanish, definitely not completely enculturated, wins the best paella of Pamplona contest in 1979. After that I was on cloud nine. By the end of the summer, I was fluent in Spanish. Not fluent like I said before, but really fluent. To this day I can watch Spanish movies in their original language and understand. I have some issues with accents, like Mexican or Central American Spanish, which is not as easy as Argentinian or "Castellano" Spanish, but I get by quite well.

In my life in the U.S., speaking Spanish served me a lot. In the restaurant industry and the service industry in general many workers speak Spanish, and sometimes only Spanish. So being able to converse is a strategic advantage in terms of employment and management. Learn Spanish now! Go to Mexico or Costa Rica, not with your friends, but by yourself, and survive while having fun.

Besides the strategic advantage of knowing another useful language for the career you want, going to see places, even if you start with just getting out of town, or out of the state, has tremendous advantages.

It is sometimes difficult to understand someone else's point of view. Very difficult to put yourself in that other person's "shoes" as we say. Going to another city, state, country, and making the effort to live the culture and communicate with the "locals" is paramount to understanding the culture and getting an appreciation for what makes that culture as good as yours. Most, if not all, cultures are as good as yours. There is always something to learn that you can use back at home. Now, culture is sometimes different at your doorstep. I lived in New Jersey and going to Manhattan was a culture shock. Mind you, I arrived in New Jersey from Canada, and that was a culture shock as well that several years later I appreciated while watching *Sopranos* (the TV series). Crossing the Mason-Dixon line is a culture shock. Going to Canada or Mexico is a culture shock. Going to China is a BIG culture shock. Going to Europe is a culture shock. I took many students on study abroad trips to France, and they are always surprised that France is not like the U.S. It looks like the U.S., you have your McDonald's, your Starbucks, your Zara and H&M, and so on. But start interreacting with people and you are lost. Etiquette is different, what you do and how it is interpreted is different. The way people greet each other by kissing on the cheek is different. What people eat is different.

The more you live with people who are different from you in some or most ways, the more you will develop an understanding for where they are coming from, and the more they will do the same about you. It does not mean that you will accept or agree with the way they do things. It does not mean you will eat frog legs with them

(Note: French people do not eat frog legs anymore; it is only on the menu of some tourist trap restaurants in Paris). My point is that you need to open your mind to possibilities while you are young, because believe me here, that window is going to close fast once you get older. Case in point, your parents (mine too). Do you see them passing judgment on "others" (i.e., the people with different views or different cultures)? Did you look at your parents' photo albums from when they were young? Notice anything? Your parents were rebels. They went to rock concerts, or marched in protests, or did plenty of "stuff" that they don't want you to do. Hypocritical parents they are, and I am as well. Experimentation is good and must be done early on, not later in life.

So, while at school take a study abroad trip, or take a summer trip abroad. You will remember that for the rest of your life and have great stories to tell at parties (that's a song, right?).

Let's talk about etiquette and about what you need to know to fake it until you make it in life.

Making a Great First Impression

I forgot who said, "you only have one chance at making a good first impression," but it is so true. Amongst the many things we don't teach at colleges is etiquette, or the art of following cultural expectations of polite behaviors in groups. Etiquette comes in many forms, from the proper way to dress given the occasion, to the proper way to say hello, to eat (See *Pretty Woman*, the movie), to interacting in meetings, to sending correspondence (e.g., emails and stuff), to speaking in public with (some) eloquence.

In many life situations you probably want to make a good impression. Think about yourself in a bar on a Thursday night (Yes, most students are partying on Thursday I learned. And all other nights as evidenced by dollar pitcher Mondays, taco Tuesdays, bring your own cup Wednesdays, thirsty Thursdays, TGIF, it's Saturday, Sunday scaries) and you're approached by someone else (See *A Beautiful Mind*, the movie with Russell Crowe). What are the clues that will make you stay with an open mind (Read "Blink," by Malcolm Gladwell), versus the ones that will be a major turn off? Are these clues nonverbal first (i.e., the dress code, the body language, the esthetics), then verbal (i.e., the first word, the first sentence)? Do you compare these clues to the ideal in your mind or to the current state of choices at the bar that very minute? Are you looking at the clues based on a long-term or short-term goal? And in the end, do you have a strategy like Russell Crowe when he played John Nash? Is that a win-win strategy or a zero-sum game?

Dress Code

Up until I was 20, I couldn't care less about knowing how to tie a tie. My dad tied my only tie, and I was careful to remove it and put it on without undoing the knot. You need to know how to tie a tie. You don't have to learn several knots, just learn one very simple knot and go with that. That's what I did. I fell in love with the simple knot. And that's what I have been using since. Although nowadays not wearing a tie seems to be more common. You will need a tie for your job interview (See Chapter 1), or for going to a wedding (See Figure 13). Make sure the front part of the tie is just lined up with your belt, no longer, no shorter. Make sure the thin part of the tie (the one that is hidden by the larger part) is long enough to tuck in the little retainer loop sewn on the back of the larger part.

Also, if you want to keep your look "classic" stay away from jewelry, no earrings for you gents, hide your tattoos, make sure your nails are done properly, get a simple haircut.

What suit do you need to wear? Fashion moves the needle once in a while (See *The Devil Wears Prada*, the movie), but in general when you are in your twenties you might want to experiment out of the "traditional" suit. I recommend that unless you are going to some family function, or New Year's Eve party, you don't deviate from tradition.

Stick to a two-piece suit, dark colors–charcoal, black, grey, dark blue. Make sure you can button your pants without them being too tight, make sure the pants are not "Rock 'n Roll Star" tight (See early Led Zeppelin's Robert Plant), make sure the pants are altered (hemmed) or sized for you [Note: that means you should have one (not two) small (not big) breaks over the shoe that don't show your socks while you're standing- See Figure 14]. Pants off the rack that are too long will make you look like you don't care. Pants that are too short and show your red socks make you look like you want to be noticed as a trend setter, but you won't. Stay classy San Diego (See *Anchorman*, the movie).

Your jacket should be able to button without being too tight. If the jacket has two buttons, button the top one. If it has three buttons, then just button the middle one. The color of your tie should complement your shirt and suit and the pattern should not be the same as your shirt or suit. For instance, if your suit is a pronounced striped suit (which I do not recommend for an interview), then your shirt should not be striped. Pick a white shirt. If your shirt is striped, then your tie should not be stripped, pick a plain tie or one with a small pattern. And for the love of God, guys, tuck your shirt in and wear a discreet and classic belt.

For the ladies, accessorizing tastefully without being excessive is the challenge. Think about what you could do with a simple pearl necklace or a scarf.

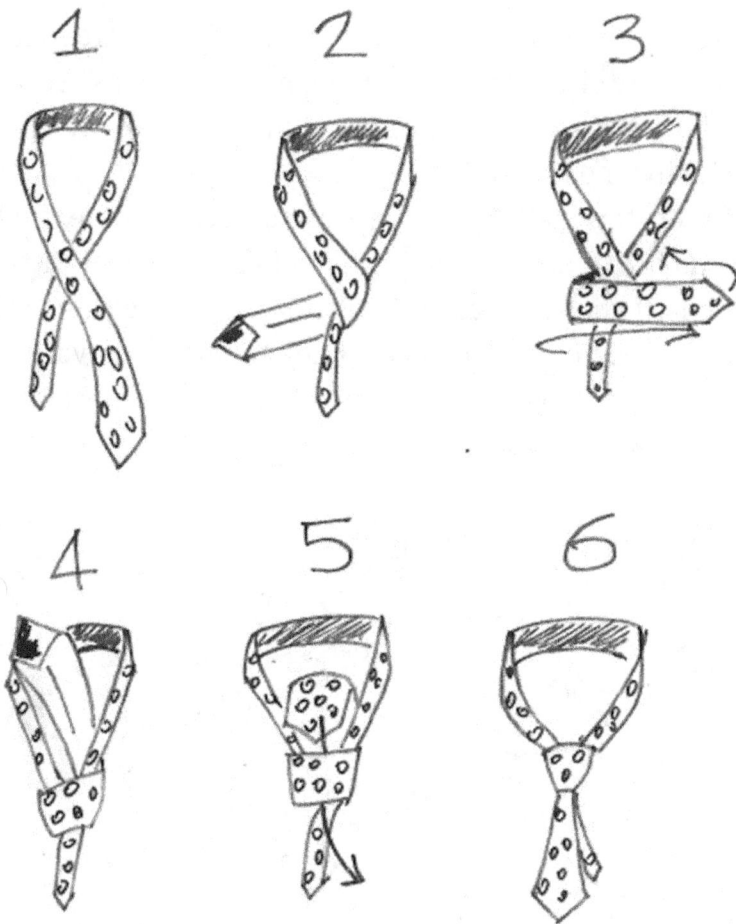

Figure 13   How to Tie a Simple Knot

Interviewing in a two-piece suit is not a bad idea. Think about the FBI look (See *Miss Congeniality*, the movie). Either a skirt or pants is fine. Heels are ok as long as they're subtle; no stilettos, no more than 4 inches high, with a little larger heel rather than a skinny one. You want to be middle of the road. This is not a seduction game. Do not show too much cleavage. It does not mean that you should have a buttoned-up blouse but be cognizant of where the proper limit is. Safe to say that no one should be able to see anything more than 2 inches down the base of your neck. Should you wear nylons? Yes, probably. I would even suggest nylons in the summer. It will give you a uniformed skin tone.

Easy on the makeup, no flashy red lipstick, no extra-long eye lashes, no bright or unnatural colored hair, hide your tattoos if you have some, if you have painted nails, make sure they are freshly done and not a week old and chipped. Keep them "conservative," i.e., no bright colors, no longer than a tenth of an inch, hide them if you bite them.

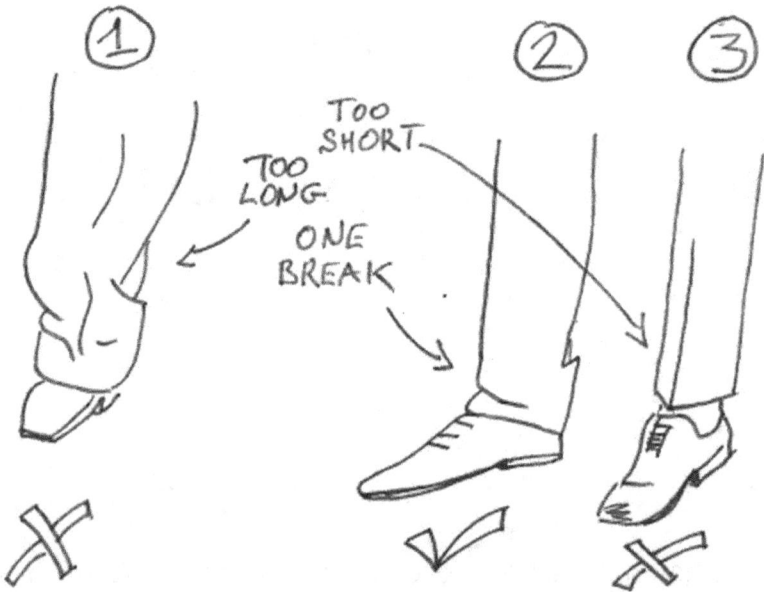

Figure 14   Hemmed Pants Examples

Business Etiquette

You should look at the person who's greeting you in the eyes. If that makes you uneasy, then try to look at them between the eyes, in the middle of their forehead, or at the base of their neck if you are far enough (about four feet away; if you are too close, one might feel like you are staring at their chests...). I do not mean that you should be staring intensely, but once in a while look in their eyes to project confidence and foster trust. Other cultures will want something different, but that is for another time (Check out the book "Kiss, Bow, or Shake Hands").

Shake hands with a little bit of strength; not too much, not too little. The person you are meeting should be able to "feel" your determination. The test here is to try to mirror your interlocutor's strength or just a little less. Rehearse with a friend.

If you are the type of person who doesn't smile or looks too serious, a.k.a. the "resting bitch face" (like I am), force yourself to smile when you first make eye contact with the person you are meeting. That sends a positive friendly message. Then, once in a while remember to smile again. If you are the kind to smile easily, then maybe check yourself once in a while, and stay a little more serious than you would naturally to project strength and determination.

When walking with a businessperson that is or could be your boss or client do not pass ahead of them, stay in line with them or just slightly (a couple inches) behind them. Make sure to say hello to anyone you encounter along the way.

I had a manager tell stories of potential employee trips from the hotel lobby to the office where the interview would take place, and all along the way they'd be observed and judged on their ability to be polite, friendly, straight forward, and also observant. One manager would also plant papers on the floor to see if the interviewee would notice and do something. Attention to detail and willingness to step up and do something that would not necessarily be your job was the test here.

Office Space

If you are given an office, or just a desk, make sure that it does not get out of hand. It is ok to have a desk look like you are working on different projects at the same time, but if it starts looking like a mad scientist's desk overflowing to the floor, and it takes you several minutes to find something on your desk, then it is going to reflect on your boss' perception of your ability to get and stay organized.

The test is that if you are sick, or on vacation, your boss should be able to go through your desk and find what they need fast (unless your boss wants to hear your voice and needs to be handheld all the time, but that's for another discussion).

Public Speaking and Presentations

Public speaking is difficult for most people. Do not think it is easy. Take a course on public speaking like Toastmaster; you won't regret it, and it is a lot safer to screw up in front of fellow classmates than to fail in front of your boss or clients.

In general, a speech or a presentation has to be timed, it has to be rehearsed, and you need to memorize all of it. I see many students put presentations together from individual group members' work at the last minute, not rehearsing, and reading the slides in front of the professor or client, or worse, reading cue cards. I know you say that even the best politicians or celebrities have cue cards or teleprompters. Many famous singers have to have their own lyrics on a prompter in concerts. But you are not there yet. Take a look at young comics at stand-up clubs. They do not have cue cards; they even have to read the room and pivot their jokes and effects accordingly. That is more where you are now.

The time will come when you will be able to hide behind a prompter, but even then, something might go wrong, the prompter might not work, the speed might not match your delivery, etc. Always be prepared.

Another tip I give my students is that you should assume that because you do not know the room in which you will present, and even if you do, you can be surprised at the last minute with some big issue, often technology related, sometimes layout related. For instance, the Wi-Fi in the room might not work. You might have your presentation in a "Mac" format and have to use a "PC." The room might be very large or very small and your routine might be destroyed. Be prepared for all possibilities. For instance, email yourself your presentation in a PDF format. Have your presentation in several formats on a thumb drive with you. Bring your own laptop. Bring your own clicker to advance slides while talking and strolling "on stage." Have a bottle or glass of water ready in case you need to pause or need water.

Business Meetings

I hate meetings. They are a waste of time. Yet, most organizations do a lot of meetings. "They are in a meeting," you often hear from the staff. There is a way to make meetings more efficient, but of course you will lose a lot of the "small talk" feel and people would rather feel important by the length and numbers of meetings they attend rather than by the synergy they achieve through them. I have worked in organizations where meetings during lunch or on Fridays at 5pm were ways bosses would make you feel you were less important and under their control. A few rules are needed to make a meeting efficient.

First, you need an agenda distributed in advance, well-timed so that it is not too optimistic. Outlining information that needs to be read prior to the meeting and asking participants for a clear objective to be achieved during the meeting. If you do that, 80% of the time you will realize you do not need a meeting. By the time you have researched prior information for your meeting, the objective might have change even slightly. Your objective might no longer be achievable during the meeting, and you might need to ask particular people to do a very directed task rather than hold them and the entire group up around a table. At that time the opinions that will be expressed might be irrelevant or redundant. So, if you can have a few people solve an issue outside a meeting, then do not hold a meet to solve that issue.

Some time you have solved the issue yourself before the meeting. Do not hold a meeting and ask folks to work on something you have already solved. They'll know you're wasting their time when you say: "Actually, I thought about that and think we should do this." Once you have done that preparation work, then you will realize that a meeting is needed maybe with half the folks you usually invite. Take care of explaining to the folks that do not need to participate why they do not have to participate or invite them on a voluntary basis if you care about their FOMO.

With the right folks around the table, now is the time to foster synergy. Synergy is what you will achieve with a group of people that you could not have achieved with each participant working individually (remember the high performing team discussion in Chapter 3). In other words, it is the added value of the meeting. Here again you will quickly find that meetings do not add value for the most part. Why? People in groups have a tendency to fall for what's called the groupthink syndrome. They tend to decide middle of the road things, and use "average creativity", often ideas that are not middle of the road, are stifled by the group. The leader needs to set the stage, the rules, and show the example on how to foster synergetic achievements during meetings.

Some meetings use the Robert's Rules of Order during meetings to frame the talks. You have listened to meetings where someone says, "move to approve," or "I second the motion." That's part of the Robert's Rules of Order. The main advantage is that if done lightly (i.e., not like Congress. Watch CSPAN), each person will speak in turn and all voices will be recognized and heard. Decisions will be formalized with voting rules known in advance. That system is good, but it probably does not foster much creativity.

What do you write on the minutes of the meeting? That is also a job in itself for some organizations. I have always dreaded the position of being the secretary in associations because you are expected to write everything just like a court reporter. You know: "Mr. Smith said: "I do not agree," then Mrs. Robert said: "What do you not agree with?" etc. The most efficient minutes are simply writing down decisions. Take the role of the people present, and then for each topic write down the decision made using the SMART goal format we saw in Chapter 2. Who will do what and by when?

This becomes what you can review first at the next meeting, and it also holds people accountable.

What About "Zoom" Meetings?

Remember the Progressive Insurance Ad mimicking a Zoom meeting? I laugh each time I attend an online meeting on Zoom, Webex, Skype, Teams, or the likes. It reminds me of the Ad, and it is so on point. People doing something other than participating, like using their phone, answering a call, going to attend to something on the stove, leaving the meeting and coming back, too close to the screen, too far, shooting too low or too high, not enough light or too much, bad sound, speaking while on mute, feedback sound from being connected to the phone and the laptop at the same time, not being dressed or groomed professionally.

An online meeting is just like a regular meeting. If you would not show up at a meeting in shorts, do not do it for a Zoom meeting. Rules of an online meetings are very similar to social media rules regarding posts. If you would not want your grandmother to see that post, then do not post it. If you would not want your boss to see you like that, then do not do it. Learn the platform. Don't be that guy that leaves the mic on and talks bad about that "boring meeting" live.

Etiquette in Correspondence

I find that most young people do not know what to say or what to write when communicating with me. When I was in management school, and mostly because it was a vocational curriculum, we had to take a class in typewriting (on a typewriter, not a computer. The difference? You cannot, or it is very difficult to, correct typos on a typewriter) and a correspondence writing class. The typewriting class goal was to get us to type using all of our fingers on the keyboard, while reading the text being typed and not the keyboard, and to type at the speed of a metronome (the tic-toc instrument used in music). Your grade was a function of words per minute minus the typos. Our hands were covered with a sheet of paper so that even if we would want to peek at the keyboard we could not. Torture.

The correspondence class was to prepare us with a set of rules based on different situations (answering a client's complaints, acknowledging the receipt of an invoice) and proper formatting of a letter or report. The basic rule is to mirror the person you are communicating with or do better. For instance, if the person starts a letter with: "Dear Sir," then you cannot start with: "John," unless you are higher than John in some hierarchical way. If the person has a title, like a Doctor, start with: "Dear Doctor Smith." Start the conversation with a little "small talk" like, "I hope you are doing well." Then the body of your communication needs to be succinct but state the basis for your correspondence. For instance, if you are responding to a client's complaints, then start by saying: "I acknowledge receipt of your letter dated July 6th regarding your stay at our hotel." After which, in this particular case, you need to acknowledge the problem, thank the client for having taken the time to voice their concerns, apologize for the situation, and suggest a concrete solution to resolve the issue. The end of a correspondence needs to be polite and forward looking. You could say something like: "We are looking forward to your...and wish that you would... Sincerely." I usually mirror my conclusion to that of my counterpart. If the person says, "Cordially," then I say "Cordially;" if they say, "Very Respectfully," then I use the same.

Using email rather than paper has created several issues. First, it is very easy to fire back an email without much thought. Do not do that. Take the time to write your answer; if it is charged with emotion, then save the response and look at it the next day. For the most part, people do not expect an answer within the hour, although it happened that an advisee of mine complained to my boss that I was not responsive enough, when I had responded within the hour of his initial email. Ok, boomer! I mean ok, Gen Z! But do not wait too long either because people rightfully should get an answer within 24 to 48 (business) hours. And if you are like me, the emails received last week are buried below my screen fold, thus I do not see them, and I have to force myself to scroll down in order to see which email I need to answer. Not a good practice.

Do not write long emails. I have colleagues that want to put everything into one email so that they do not forget anything they want to say, and because they think it will be more efficient. Whatever the reason, you know as I know that no one reads a long email completely. Keep it above the fold. I'd rather receive three emails that talk about one issue each, than one email with three issues within it. Because I know I will forget something. Plus, in terms of saving emails and organizing your folders, each issue can go to a different folder, when a long email will have to be classified in some broader subject folder. Very often I find that people who write long emails keep the most important for the last bullet point/paragraph of the email. It is a mistake since not many people read the last bullet point. Bring the main issue first.

Being Organized

One of my bosses once said, as we were sitting for my annual review, which would trigger potential training, promotion, and a pay increase: "I don't understand your system, but you seem to be well organized since you are meeting the deadlines."

Organization is important in order for you to meet deadlines. Your boss will set deadlines, and if they do not, you should ask for one. Then, unlike what you might have done in college, you need to think about the steps needed to do the project on time, and back track in time from the deadline, by setting milestones or mini goals for yourself all the way to the start of the project. What do you need to do first, second, etc. Leave yourself one week before the deadline to think about the end result and prepare the presentation and the way you will answer questions. That is also a way to trick yourself into meeting deadlines if you tend to be a procrastinator.

Personally, I like to start on paper. It is more visual for me, and I can draw the entire plan, or process on one sheet of legal paper. Then from that point on, I will set goals with dates, and will put these goals into my agenda (paper agenda, or phone, or desktop, whatever you use is fine, but use it). At the start of the week, look for what you have to do that week. And then work every day on the project or set of projects. I personally like to have some physical binder with the project in it so I can see it on my desk, my boss can see it, I can move from folder to folder as I progress, I can have three or four project folders on my desk at the same time and move from one to the next easily. Whatever you are doing, the goal is to not miss deadlines. Think about the projects in terms of what and who in your organization will slow you down. If one department needs to give you some report before you can do one task, then make sure you understand the issue before it happens, and if what takes one week will take three with this particular department, then plan for that. Your deadlines should not be missed because you did not anticipate the lack of organization of others (within certain limits, that you will raise with your boss if needed). Inform your boss regularly of your progress. Reassure them that you will meet deadlines. Every day, break down what needs to be done in order to meet the weekly goal on each of your projects. Put these micro tasks on a post-it note and stick it to your desk. Take 10 or 20 minutes in the morning with a cup of coffee or tea to update that list. Each time you have done one micro task scratch it off your list. The feeling of accomplishment attached to seeing a micro task scratched off is real and empowering. Your goal is to see a complete list scratched off by the end of the day. You know you are moving towards your goal, and it feels good. It lowers anxiety. You feel you are doing what needs to be done, and you do not feel overwhelmed, drowning in tasks that do not seem to disappear from your list. Caution: do not make weekly lists if it is too long. Here, you are tricking your mind to make a daily list and avoid thinking about the weekly one to lower anxiety. The daily list might not get done, but 80% or 90% will be done. That's the goal. "80% is perfection."

> *Gen Z POV: "No matter how organized I stay and no matter how many emails I send with specific instructions for each client, it never ceases to amaze me how many texts I get asking where something is. Job security, I guess."*

Basic Verbal or Non-Verbal Communication Skills

More often than not I see students presenting a project using words or sentences similar to: "like I said," "basically," "you know what I mean." At the same time, they cannot stay put while others are talking or sometimes even when they are talking and seem to act as if they were five years old, fidgeting back and forth, hands in their pockets, making noise with their keys or loose change. When you are on stage, act as if everyone was watching you, because everyone is watching you. Do not project a five-year-old image. That is only cute when you are five years old. So, start taping yourself rehearsing your presentation. Then watch the recording with someone that can coach you or at least give you honest feedback, i.e., not your mom. Then start re-wiring yourself by changing one thing. For instance, if you tend to put your hand in your pocket, then don't. Think about not putting your hand in your pocket. If you still do it subconsciously, then sew your pocket closed (I did that when I was in the Army, 'cause hands in the pocket are a no-no and lead to many punishing tasks).

If you cannot for the love of God remember a text you need to say during your presentation, then cut it into small pieces and memorize only the topic, or the first words. For instance, maybe your part is: 1) We had a problem; 2) We looked into its causes; 3) and found that; 4) We have thought about solutions; 5) but we stay open for input from the team. It is easier to remember steps rather than trying to remember a full text you will stumble through. Train yourself to not use those filler words–like, you know what I am talking about, right? Record yourself and try to catch yourself. It is best to pause a presentation and use words such as, "Is this part clear to you?" or, "At this point I'd like to stop to see if there are any questions," rather than saying: "You know what I mean." You know what I mean?

Active Listening

Some people use the sentence "I hear you" to signify that they understood you. But sometimes they have not (listened or understood). It is best to use what is called "active listening." Active listening is a technique that consists of re-phrasing what someone just said in order to get their approval that you actually understood them correctly. For instance, someone says to you: "I think that the department should really get rid of meetings because they are not efficient and too long." You might say, "I hear you," which might imply that you understood and that you agree. But you might alternatively say: "So, if I heard you correctly you want less meetings, or shorter meetings because you feel they are not efficient or too long, is that correct?" Once the other person replies with, "Yes, that is correct!" then maybe you can start voicing an opinion on the matter such as: "I agree on the number of meetings, but the length is dependent on the agenda, don't you think?"

Eating in Public

Your boss is coming to lunch with you. You are a new employee. You want to impress. What should you do?

I have used several strategies in these cases. They all work for different situations. For instance, your boss invites you to a formal dinner (i.e., your boss bought a table at a charity dinner and needs you to fill in for a client that said no at the last minute), to a lunch at a fast food versus a lunch at a steakhouse, to a cocktail reception for the grand opening of a new store, and so on. The main idea is that you want to show that you fit, that you have some education, that you are smart, that you can become that supervisor one day (See *Starbucks Glen*, the supervisor Ad). In general, do not order something that is too spicy (you don't want to cry or choke on a piece of curry chicken), too hot (you will burn your tongue trying to speed up in order to finish by the time your boss is done), too messy to eat (no spaghetti and to-mato sauce, no triple decker pastrami sandwich too big to put in your mouth), too expensive (pick the middle priced item, always a safe bet). Of course, no alcohol unless your host is ordering some. So, I will wait for the lead and if the boss says, what will you drink? I'd say: "Do you have any suggestions?" or I would say: "I have not quite decided yet, please go ahead." When in doubt, go for mineral water (no ice) and see what the boss is going for. At any rate, it is better to stay sober, and if the boss orders a bottle of wine, then that would be the opportunity to try it.

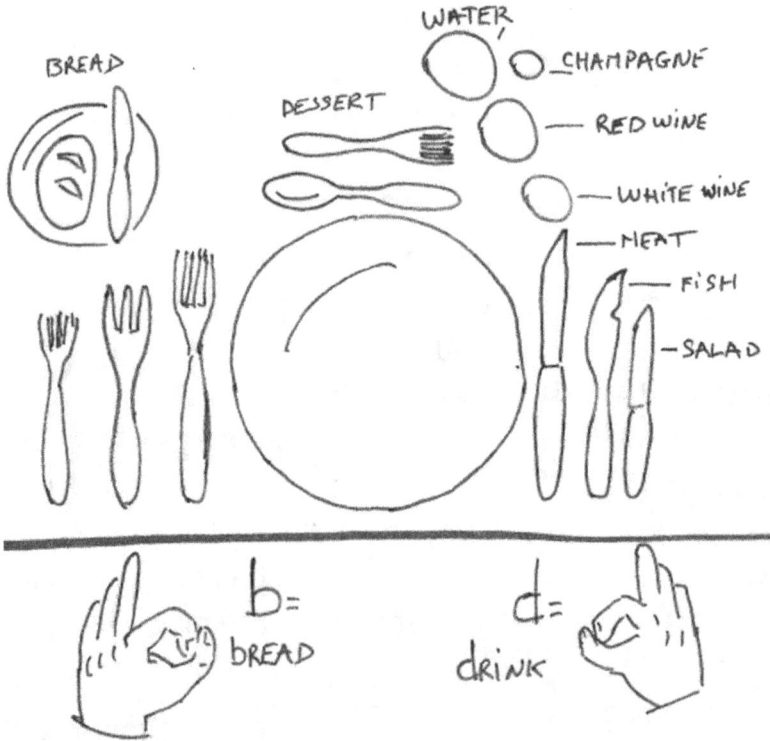

Figure 15   Example of a Banquet Table Setting

Take a look at Figure 15. Do you know what to do with all this cutlery?

The basic idea is that you work your way from the outside in. And when you have no more utensils on the side of the plate, you move to the ones on top, which will be for cheese and/or dessert.

As far as glasses, the small wine glass at the top of the knife is for white wine, the next wine glass in line towards the center of the table is for red wine, the largest wine glass is for water, the flute would be for champagne, the smallest glass for port or liquor, the shifter for Cognac or Armagnac.

How about the annoying bread and butter plate? Which one is yours? Think of it as the symmetrical answer to the fluids, the wine glasses. So, your glasses are at the top of your knives, then your bread and butter plate is to your left at the top of your forks. A trick you learn if you watch the movie *Hillbilly Elegy* or read the book is to use your hands to make a "b" for bread, or a "d" for drink (See Figure 15).

Your napkin will rest on your lap for the entire meal unless you have to go to the bathroom, at which point you will place your napkin on the chair. If you are not done with the dish leave your fork and knife at the eight and four o'clock mark. If you are done with a dish signal it by placing both fork and knife parallel to each other and at three o'clock on the plate.

When the meal is over and you are ready to leave, place your napkin folded on the table left of your setting, or centered if no dishes are present.

To set up a table there are some simple and useful rules. The plate needs to be lined up with the table edge, distant inward by the length of a thumb (one inch) from the edge. You must be able to run your finger all around the plate without touching or displacing the utensils.

Knives' cutting edge must be facing in towards the plate so that you don't cut yourself.

Wine Knowledge

Most people assume that because I am French, I know about wine. They should not. But I do know about wine. Not as much as perceived, but enough to be able to make distinctions. That is really all there is to wine tasting. You need to become an educated consumer about wine, and about everything. Don't you want to know the difference between a mutual fund and life insurance? Between a $99 hotel room and a $300 one? Between a $15,000 car and a $30,000 one? Of course, pick your battles, you can't know everything on everything. But if you are buying, then you should know enough. For instance, do you know why you should not put ice in mineral water (then read on)?

One way you can start shining is with your knowledge. Do you know what makes mineral water "mineral"? What is the difference between Evian, Fiji, Deer Park, Aquafina? Did you know that similar to wine, some people are tasting waters and are able to recognize them blind? To make it short, water comes from rain and is stored in one big container to make tap water. A city will purify the rainwater to make it drinkable using chloride (like the pool) and filters to eliminate that taste. Water will be seeping through the ground into wells, and sources, and will be extracted to make spring water. Water can be filtered through the rocks of a mountain, a process that could take hundreds or even thousands of years, picking up minerals from the rocks in the process, and end up in a source. That would make mineral water. Some are carbonated, some are not. Any non-carbonated water can be carbonated using an injection of CO_2. Think about the way you make soda or some sparkling wines. So, in the hierarchy of waters, mineral water is at the top. It has a natural addition of mineral that could be good for your health. Due to the process, it can only come from one source. Thus, Evian comes from the city of Evian, Fiji comes from the island of Fiji, and should not be tainted with other less pure additives, especially ice cubes, which are often made from tap water, and often taste too much chlorine. Should you ask for a mineral water with a slice of lime or lemon? Sure, that's ok. But always say no ice, just cold. So, do your homework, and understand product categories. That is the beginning of acquiring knowledge that would make you be perceived as a little more sophisticated than maybe you are. From water move to wine, then food, then to other subjects.

Wine is the same as water. There are three big categories of wine: red, white, and rosé. Wine is made from grapes. Not the same grapes you buy at the grocery stores. The ones used for wine are less sweet. The basic recipe for wine is simple. You pick the grapes on the vines when they are ripe. You crush them (See *I Love Lucy*, the show), maybe not with your feet anymore but with a big press. You put the juice in a vast, and you wait. The juice will ferment. You clarify (take the impurity out) the wine and put it in bottles. Bingo, you made wine. If you use red grapes, the skin will contain red pigments that will taint the juice red, thus, you have red wine. If you use white grapes, you get white juice, and white wine. But if you use red grapes and you leave the skin a little bit in contact with the juice but not too much, you get rosé. You can make a much cheaper version of rosé by mixing red and white juices, but that is not the best way. You can make white wine with red grapes too. Just make sure that the skins do not touch the juice, and bingo, you've got white wine. Why would you want that? Maybe you only have red grapes in your vineyard, or maybe it is cheaper to do that. White wine made from white grapes says that prominently. As a sign of quality, you will read "blanc de blancs," which means in French, "white made from white."

How about champagne? Champagne is white wine made from red or white grapes, but instead of leaving the juice ferment in a big vast until all the gas has left the juice, it is bottled early and continues to ferment in the bottle that is sealed, therefore, trapping the gas inside the bottle. Some sparkling wines use an injection of CO_2 (CHEM 101) in the white wine to mirror the natural process of champagne. See a bottle mentioning "méthode champenoise" or "méthode tradition-nelle" which translate "Champagne region method" or "traditional method" both without the CO_2 injection but with the better more natural process of trapping the gazes in the bottle.

So why are wines so expensive?

If you browse the wine store you will find relatively cheap wines, around $3 a bottle, then a $15-$20 range of wines, then $30+ wines, all the way to $100 or several "Benjamin" ones. What is the difference? In short, it is the same difference between Evian mineral water and Aquafina, or between a BMW series 700 and a BMW series 300, or be-tween a Louis Vuitton handbag and a Nine West one.

Take a wine tasting class. Start appreciating wine as a crafted bev-erage made by professionals as opposed to a cheap way to get a buzz.

If you are invited to someone's home, bring a bottle of wine and bou-quet of flowers. If you do not know what to pick for wine, pick a well-known producing region, and one in the $15 to $20 range. Pick a vintage (very important) that is at least 3 years old. So, if this year is 2020, pick a $15 wine that has a 2017 vintage or older. The older the vintage, usually the better. The wine has more time to mature inside the bottle. Some vintages are better than others (more sun that year or less rain) but not always.

What region should you pick the wine from? With France you cannot go wrong with Bordeaux or Burgundy wines (I am bias). With the U.S., Sonoma Valley and Napa Valley are good picks. Argentina, Chile, and Australia all have good imports, as well.

Should you buy a Cabernet Sauvignon, or a Pinot Noir (See *Sideways*, the movie)? Grapes have varieties. Most used red grapes to make red wine are Cabernet Sauvignon ("cabs"), Pinot Noir, Merlot, Shiraz, or a mix of different varieties. White grape varieties mostly used are Chardonnay, Sauvignon Blanc, Semillon, Pinot Gris (or pinot grigio as Italians say). Heavier reds will be made with Merlot and Cabs. Lighter reds with Pinot Noir. Woody tasting whites will be made from Chardonnay; dryer, lighter, fruity whites from Sauvignon and Pinot Gris.

You have seen many movies or people tasting wine like pros. They first swirl their wine in the glass. That will release the essence trapped inside the wine and will leave some indication of alcohol and complexity on the glass sides (the "legs"). Then they smell the wine (the "bouquet") and try to identify the smell or scent associated with fruits, forest, mushrooms, flowers to describe the wine. Then they finally sip the wine and make some weird sound with their mouth (they let air in contact with the wine so that the wine gets more oxygen and releases all its flavors on all the areas of the tongue and palate). That last taste allows the expert to express the feeling of dryness created by the tannins (the particles released from the red grapes skin and a sign of conservation), or the fruity taste of a white wine.

The wine is short if the taste does not last long after swallowing (or spitting out in a bucket). The wine is long if the taste lasts longer, and that is a good sign. The wine is round if you get a feeling of drinking something thicker than it appears; it is flat if it feels like water.

Cooking Skills

I love watching my Tasty feed on Instagram, or TV series like *Iron Chef*, *Hell's Kitchen*, or *Chef's Table*. Always a lot to learn and good entertainment. But I feel that it is sad, to a certain extent, that a lot of folks watch these shows and never try to cook because it is easier to order delivery from some local place. Cooking is full of emotions. Cooking for someone or for a family is a very fulfilling process. Ok, not all the time. When you do that every day, and the people you do it for do not appreciate the effort, then it is frustrating. But like anything else, I guess.

Try cooking for one person, your girlfriend or boyfriend. Try something simple. Then learn new recipes and start making a recipe book. A recipe book will be the greatest gift you will give your kids in 20 years. I have the recipe book of my grandfather's uncle (he was a pastry chef in 1885).

Let me give you a couple of very easy recipes that you can make to impress. The first one is a fish filet in papillottes (papillottes is a French word for a little paper bag you use to cook the fish in. It just sounds fanciest in French, doesn't it?). Take a fish filet (you can buy tilapia, sea bass, or a salmon filet. Remove the skin, or make sure the skin is scaled). In a foil sheet of paper, about 10x10 inches large, place carrots, zucchini, and leeks cut in "julienne," which means in three-inch-long thin strips, in the center. Place your raw fish filet on top, skin down. Fold the sides of your foil to create a little container. Add a shot glass of white wine on top of the fish. The wine will stay in because you have made that container tight with the foil. Add a teaspoon of butter on top. Salt and pepper. A slice of lemon and a branch of thyme. Close the foil all around the fish and veggies as you would do a doggy bag in a restaurant. Place the bag on a cooking sheet and place in the oven (when ready for dinner, sometime after aperitif and the appetizers) on 450F for 15 minutes or until you see the bag all puffed up. Remove the bag (papillottes) and place it on a plate and serve with rice, or just as is. Your guests are supposed to rip open the foil and enjoy the meal right from the papillottes.

How about bananas flambées? I race a schooner (a schooner is a type of boat with two masts) down the Chesapeake Bay for a charity every year and it is a lot of fun. But we have established a tradition that when in port after the race we cook the left-over bananas (note: bananas on a boat is a big no-no for the superstitious sailor due to many commercial boats carrying bananas sinking. Obviously not due to the cargo, thus. Don't be superstitious 'cause it is bad luck!) with the rum on board and relax for a moment with stories and sea shanties (sailors' songs).

Take one or two bananas per person. Peel and cut in half sideways. Take a frying pan and place it on the stove with a tablespoon of butter for 4 bananas. Let the butter melt and add one spoon of granulated sugar (brown or white) per spoon of butter. Let it cook and caramelize. The sugar will get dark and thick. When the caramelized sugar is a nice brown color, add orange juice (measure before in a large cup about half a glass per person) and mix the caramel and the orange juice to liquify the caramel. When it's done, add the bananas, round side down. Let them cook two minutes. Flip them over. Let them cook another minute. If the orange juice has evaporated, you can add a little more. If not, then at that point, add one glass of rum (any rum, but dark rum is better, spiced rum is less favored as it will overpower the orange/caramel taste). Use a fire source (match, gas burner, lighter) to get the rum to light (flambée in French means burned or flamed). Serve and enjoy!

Carving a Turkey

A skill that allowed me to "shine" in company, believe it or not, is knowing how to carve a turkey. Most people do not know how to carve a turkey. Most You Tube videos show a kitchen way of carving a turkey using your hands that is not practical in front of people at the Thanksgiving table.

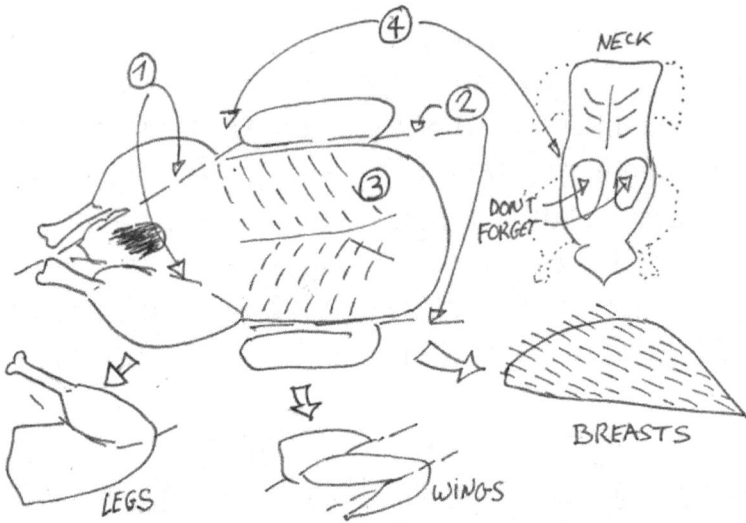

Figure 16   How to Carve a Turkey

You carve a turkey like you would carve any bird. You cut the legs first, then the breast. Remember the mnemotechnic (some words that make you remember something not easy to memorize) "knife-neck." You have the knife in your right hand and the fork in your left hand (reverse that if you are lefty). For a turkey use a longer knife and a longer fork, sometimes called a carving fork and knife. That will allow you to carve without having your hands too close to the turkey. For a chicken you might use a regular table fork and knife, but most chickens today are so badly grown that as soon as you take the elastic holding it together off, the bird is basically falling off the bones. It is terrible, but back to the turkey. With the knife in your right hand stick it inside the turkey through the neck, or where the neck was, through the skin. Hold your fork in the opening opposite of the neck where the belly was and turn the turkey sideways so that one side faces the people sitting and the other faces you. Best to use a cutting board and to have a long dish in front of you to place the cut pieces on it as soon as they are carved. Start cutting the leg closest to you by holding the leg with the fork stuck in it and cutting down following the side of the turkey breast all the way to the leg joint. Find the hip joint and cut through. Place the leg on the cutting board and cut the drum from the leg by finding the joint (See Figure 16). That is the most difficult part of the operation here because the joint is not where you think it is, so the best thing to do is to follow the roundness of the drum meat and use a circular movement of the knife to find the joint slightly off the imaginary triangle made by visualizing the two bones. Place the two pieces on the serving dish close together as if they were still attached. Do the same thing with the other leg. Cut the wings off and place them on the serving dish. The next move is to slice the breast one after the other from the neck to the end to make long thin slices. Hold your bird with the fork in the rib cage and start cutting horizontally with ample movements (your knife needs to be sharp enough) from left (the neck) to right. Once you have one slice cut, take it with your knife and fork and place it in the dish. Repeat the same movement to cut the entire breast. Repeat that on the other breast. Turn your turkey carcass over and cut out the "oysters". They are small, dark meat pieces lodged into the bones, where you would picture kidneys to be, but it has nothing to do with kidneys, it has more to do with back muscles. You are done!

Chapter 8 Appendices

Your Bucket List.

Write down things you want to get, experiences you want to have, places you want to visit.

1 _____

2 _____

3 _____

4 _____

5 _____

6 _____

7 _____

8 _____

9 _____

Coding Example

The logic of if-else code.

If some test is true, then have the computer do something. But if the test is false, then have the computer do something else. In the following example we want the computer to print the phase "Positive or Zero" if the number we observe is greater or equal to zero. If the number we observe is not greater or equal to zero, in other words, if the number is lower than zero, then we want the computer to print the phrase "Negative number." Notice how both language Python and Java are basically the same, with some minor, yet very important, different details. It is an example of two coding languages.

Python if-else code

```python
if num >= 0:
    print("Positive or Zero")
else:
    print("Negative number")
```

Java if-else code

```java
if (num >= 0) {
    System.out.println("Positive or Zero");
} else {
    System.out.println("Negative number");
}
```

CHAPTER 9

Be Philosophical

"People would rather be right than be happy"

In this final chapter I want to get a little more philosophical and maybe mystical or even metaphysical.

I am keeping the least numbers-oriented chapter for last as a way to finish with a more relaxing read. Or is it going to be the most difficult? I guess it depends on whether you like numbers or words. But let's start asking ourselves if that is a fair categorization of people. True, some people are better at numbers than others, and others enjoy reading more than the average person (not a problem since the average person does not statistically exist).

In fact, we should all be at least minimally motivated by wanting to understand others and the world around us, which means that we all need to read, listen, argue properly and respectfully, and know our way around some key quantifiable questions we need to decide on throughout our lives. We need to be decent with both words and numbers. There is no way around that. It does not mean being a wiz at math, or at philosophy. It just means being in control of what is needed to make it through life with a better chance at happiness than if we would not.

The premise of this book was to introduce and discuss topics that are rarely touched on in college, yet essentials, in my view, to succeed in life (although you will not get a gold star for that). These have to do with what it takes to actually live, in the sense of making a living, and maximizing your buying power in search for a better life or a happy life. In essence this book is about "life, liberty, and the pursuit of happiness." A phrase you know from the declaration of independence.

The previous chapters might have taught you a few skills at life: getting a job, making the best investments, navigating life given society's expectations. But the question remains as to whether it will lead you to happiness or not.

In fact, the use of the phrase "pursuit of happiness" in the declaration of independence was not the first drafted set of words, and it took Jefferson (age 33 at the time) and the other creators a few trials to come to that particular set of words. Some of the original ideas were more materialistic and talked about the protection of estates or property instead of happiness. Funny enough, we today still equate happiness with materialistic possessions. The more cars, the more money, the bigger house I have, the happier I will (should) be.

We know, I know (you might not know yet) that this is not true. The proof is fairly easy to demonstrate. Find an indigenous society living in the deep Amazonian rainforest and you will see, feel, and understand that they are happy, yet they do not have many possessions or material things. No TV, no internet, no cars, etc. Therefore, happiness is not about things (Listen to John Lennon's "*Imagine*").

Of course, it is not as easy to get rid of all your possessions as John Lennon would suggest, to find happiness. His argument is less about a society with no possessions or no borders, otherwise, he would be the biggest hypocrite there is since he fought so hard for his green card. He might have been a bit of a hypocrite after all, but I think that the idea of a limit is a message that we need to incorporate in our society. How much is enough? How much is too much?

So, how are we supposed to pursue, and supposedly achieve, happiness? Jefferson et al. did not tell us. It is up to us to figure it out. Marketers, Economists, and Politicians have been quick at creating an illusion that material things equal happiness. One U.S. president told us to "go shop" as a way to deal with sadness and loss, therefore, implied that shopping would make us happy. Was he wrong? Yes. He did not believe in what he said, rather he wanted the economy to restart via consumerism. And if the economy goes well, then he could claim reelection victory. You know that some people use "shopping therapy" when they feel down. You and I have had some impulse to purchase something we "always wanted" and have felt great right after. I would argue it is equivalent to a sugar rush, which doesn't last. We felt happy after buying something we wanted, but not for long. We feel happy after buying anything most of the time. Do we feel "more happy" after buying a $35,000 car rather than after buying a $10,000 car? Maybe not. Is that happiness adding to the happiness level we had prior to the purchase? Not really. It does not feel that the more we collect things the happier we get.

How do we explain that? And more importantly, how do we achieve happiness if not via possessions?

Over the years I have come to appreciate philosophy as a way to help me make sense of the world around me, and as a way of guiding my existence and my behavior. Philosophy, from the Greek "love of wisdom," is the study of human beings in what makes them different. Philosophers study the nature of our existence, our origins, our knowledge, our minds, reasons, values, ethics, and more.

Know Thy Self

In my life, I have participated in many team building exercises (See Chapter 3). Team building exercises are these group meetings led by a "facilitator" (half shrink, half consultant) that helps your boss make sense of the team's synergy or cohesion and eventually explains what does not work along with what does for the benefit of the company. During these very intense weeklong meetings that feel like group therapy to some, I have seen some pretty disturbing things happen. I have seen team members quit on the spot after being singled out by the team or the facilitator for a behavior that was exposed as a child-hood unresolved wound. I have seen grown-up colleagues cry in front of their peers and boss about issues they were having in their family with their spouse or children. I have seen employees truly believe that the space of the meeting was safe and that they could really tell their boss how they felt about the company's culture and about the working conditions, only to see themselves ostracized and warned that the next time they do that they'd be fired. In a word, I have seen more bad than good come out of these "team building exercises."

But one thing that I have always appreciated, in a weird sadomas-ochistic way, is what I learned about myself. I grew personally from each of these meetings, and then I continued the introspection deep down into my soul by taking on a life coach and attending actual group therapies and other cult-like retreats (See the last episode of *Mad Men*, the TV series).

I want to share a few of the things I have learned here because I believe that it will make philosophy a little more practical, and it might even be interesting to the point that you might pick up a phi-losophy book next, or you might start talking philosophically with your friends next time you are at a BBQ instead of talking about the usual sports stats or home decor tips. Philosophy gives you access to deep discussions with friends. But in order to not alienate your friends next time you see them, you first need a little knowledge about the philosophers' theories, and then you need a little technique on how to hold an argument. You need to know a little rhetoric, the art of persuading someone with your words. That is not only if you want to persuade, of course, but it is also if you want to have a discussion that will not end up with your friends avoiding you for a while (I know what I am talking about).

> *Gen Z POV: "You're never complete in your learning. I definitely graduated and felt I was at the highest level of education; my interview and job search process went very smoothly, but for the last five years I learned a ton more, and I am still learning, as I am thinking about the next chapter of my life. Don't get too arrogant about thinking that you know what could come next, 'cause even when you feel like you know a lot, there is still a lot more."*

Deal with the Past; Understand Why You Are Who You Are Now

At a three-day long retreat that felt like an introduction to a cult and a multilevel marketing scheme [Note: a multilevel marketing scheme is very similar to a pyramid scheme, although it is tolerated by the authorities where the pyramid scheme is illegal in the U.S. Think about your network of friends and family members as your first customers in a new venture that asks you to bring customers to them, as opposed to getting new customers from advertising or word of mouth. When the only way a business gets new customers is by asking its current employees to bring their family and friends to become customers, then it is a multi-level marketing scheme], I took note of several good points I had never really reflected on.

My coach, thanks to her, had suggested while warning me, that the retreat would be intense but that I would, more likely, get a thing or two out of it. I trusted my coach, because I am a coachable person, so I went there without too much research or preparation. Curious, and ready to learn. Not really ready to share my life on stage with 200 of my new friends, but nevertheless ready to let the door open. It was harsh to say the least. The leaders basically secluded 200 people in a large ballroom without windows. No one was allowed to leave or enter. Breaks were sparse and short. Volunteers blocked the doors (Seriously?). We were yelled at and insulted, telling us we were losers, idiots, and that we were stupid. But that is beside the point. There is always something to get out of any situation. My coach trusted it would teach me something. My job was to find it.

The very first thing I found was my story. As a child I was fascinated by Disney, as I assume a lot of children are. I loved particularly *Sleeping Beauty*. The story of the prince, named Phillip (coincidence?), fighting evil to save the princess and saving the day was my story. I found energy in saving people later in life. Sometimes saving them despite their will. I'll give you a few examples. Becoming a lifeguard was for me all about finding meaning in being on the beach. I was not a simple dude sunbathing. I was the authority, but more importantly, I was the reason others would not die, and if they would hurt themselves, I would be here to save them. And I did. A few people owe me their lives. One drowned and was revived on the beach by CPR and oxygen. Another one was this large size man who got stuck in a rip current where I slowly dragged him sideways to where he was able to get his footing and left me so tired on the shore panting. Another had his forehead cut open from left to right. We could see his skull, but not his face because of all the blood and because the scalp was loosely hanging down. Later, as I was scuba diving with someone older and supposedly much more experienced than me (he was a professional diver farming (illegally) red coral from the Mediterranean Sea for jewelers), he went into a panic about 100 feet down and had no more air. The two of us had to resurface on my tank, while making the safety stops needed to evacuate the dissolved nitrogen in our body. I gained pride and a sense of worth through these episodes of my life. Later I focused my "saving" skills (or my need to be a savior I should say) on saving people from themselves. That is where I don't think it served me well. I tend to help by giving my point of view or giving my opinion on what people should or should not do even when they do not ask. It is ok to jump to help someone drowning, but it is not ok to intervene in someone's life if all they want to do is vent and have you as a sounding board. The problem is that very rarely do folks tell you "all I want you to do is listen, not give advice." We all have a story. That story is made when we are very young. We identify with the heroes and we live our story. It becomes our identity. All that starts maybe around 6 years old. The rest of our lives we are living that story over and over again like a script (if you want to know more read "Scripts People Live: Transactional Analysis of Life Scripts"by Claude Steiner).

Spend some time thinking about what your story is. What was (is) your favorite Disney movie or fable, or mythological story? Write it down. Then look at your life and try to find similarities. Sometimes it is best to do that exercise with someone else that does theirs next to you, and then you can share. Sometimes you just share with someone else and listen to what they say. Someone from your family, that you trust, could be a good person to share that story with. The goal here, once you have identified the script you live, is to try to recognize when you are living the script. And step back and reflect whether living that script is ok or not.

The Meaning of Life

Meaning is about what we think; it is a concept we hold in our mind. What a word or sentence conveys as an idea, a description, a feeling. The meaning of something, like life, is not about life but about something else that would represent or explain life. It is "extrinsic" or refers to what is outside of the word "life" itself. The meaning of a word is not the word itself. For instance, if we talk about a car, the meaning of the word "car" is not the word itself but the object that it refers to, which is a car. You might have seen that painting of a smoking pipe with the words written under the pipe "this is not a pipe." It is a 1929 painting by the surrealist painter, René Magritte, and illustrates our situation perfectly. The word is just a word, like a picture is just a picture, not the object itself. This is also what triggered Freud (the famous father of modern psychology) to interpret what we call "Freudian slips" or unintentional acts we do or words we say, not as they are but as what they represent.

By this logic if the meaning of life is not "life" but something other than life, then it is death (don't be scared, it is only a word. If you are scared, then you need to talk to your therapist, now!). This is where religion is brilliant as it gives a meaning to life by pointing to the possibility of an after-life.

Think about the following challenge. What matters to you? What do you love? Maybe you love your parents, your friends, your pet, life! Do any of these have meaning? Nope. Things, people, animals, concepts you love do not have a meaning. We do not need them to have a meaning in order to love them.

A meaning is a result. The issue at hand is not to search for the meaning of life since life does not mean anything, but to search for what gives you meaning in your life.

There is meaning in life, but life does not have meaning.

What you believe, the cause you fight for, the people you love all give meaning to your life. Life is absurd, Albert Camus often said (existentialist writer circa 1943). But what we do during our life is not because it gives our life meaning. We do not need a meaning to everything we do before we do it. We simply need to live our life with courage and love without meaning, but with wisdom and simplicity. This is the pursuit of happiness (for fun, watch Monty Python's 1983 movie *The Meaning of Life*).

The Right Moment is Now

"Live in the moment, in the present," you sometimes hear. That is fine, but what is time? It is a difficult question to answer. Time might be defined as the past, the present, and the future all combined. But for the philosopher, the past is gone, thus does not exist anymore, and the future has not happened yet, thus it also does not exist. We are left with the present. And the present does not last. What happens now has happened and is part of the past already.

Other philosophers, even if they agree with the fact that neither the past nor the future exist in terms of time, think that each one of us is experiencing time in the present continuously. In other words, we live in the present all our lives. When we die, we leave the present, but the present is still there for those who still live. Even the memories are part of the present since we remember them in the present. Even the hopes are in the present since we make them in the present. This is what makes memories more than nostalgic.

The present is the only reality. We live in the present all the time. It is always today and now. This does not mean that the past should be forgotten or that we should not hope for a better future. We need to remember the past in order to better live in our present. We need to form strategies in order to achieve our personal projects in the future. Our memories are happening in the present, and they last in the present as well. To live in the present is to not live in constant nostalgia or to solely live in the hope of better days. To live in the present is to live without regrets but with memories, without hopes of a better future but with a plan to make it better here and now. Memories are the secret of eternity. They are the reason the people you remember are still present.

The Love of Life

We live because of love. Any love. Love of life. Love of ourselves. Love of others. Love of work. Love of wine. Love of food. Love is the sentiment that points at the object of our love. The cause of our love is external to us, even when we love ourselves, we might actually love our image (as in narcissistic tendencies). We love our reflection rather than the person we are and cannot see. Aristotle said that love is joy. Plato, on the other hand, said that love is created by the need and the absence of the object of our love. We love something or someone because we do not possess it, and that comes with suffering and frustration because we do not possess it.

We love what we want because we do not have it, and we need it. Once we have it, we do not need it, and therefore we do not love it anymore. Aristotle's love is philia; Plato's is eros. Both are true and are on some kind of ladder. Eros is primal. A newborn loves his mother because of the milk she gives him when he needs milk. Or the smile and care she gives when he is crying. Eros is passion. We want someone because we love her. Once we "have" her and love is consumed (notice the word is very close to meaning of eating), then the person is no longer needed since she is here. When the object of our love is not in our bed, we suffer. When she is, we are bored (not me saying that, Plato does).

To escape the Plato predicament of suffering or boredom we need to transit from love-eros to love-philia as defined by Aristotle. Philia is love not as passion but as power. Not the power of force, but the power of joy in that case. The mother giving love to her baby is joy, it is philia. She has that power, and she is using it. But we can go higher on the ladder of love. We can give without taking. We can rejoice without possessing, consuming, or having. This is what the first Christians called agape (pronounce AW-GAP-EY). Love of others. Without ego. Without egocentric agendas. Without anything in return. Love with no limits, no borders. Love is all around us, and we need to live with love always because love is our path, our direction, our objective (another Beatles/Lennon song, "*All You Need is Love*"). We first have to love ourselves (self-esteem; See Figure 12)). We need to be careful to not love ourselves too much, or only ourselves, because that would be narcissistic, and indicative of dependency and childhood regression needs. But first-things-first (read *The Seven Habits of Highly Effective People*, by Stephen Covey), you need to learn to love yourself. How can you increase your self-esteem if you feel you need to?

To conclude on the pursuit of happiness, *live a life you love, love the life you live* (Bob Marley) with people you love, but more importantly, with people you find joy living with. Find a job you love. Do not focus too much on what you want, because as the Rolling Stones will say: "*you can't always get what you want, but if you try sometimes, you find, you get what you need.*" And get rid of your regrets while cherishing your memories, build a future for yourself and do not rely on the hope for a better day.

As my coach would say after each conversation: "...and if choose, have a great day." The power of having a great day is in your hands. Think about people in the world that live without running water, or safety, and watch them choose to have a great day.

Politics and Prose

Imagine yourself in Paris, lounging at a café terrace, watching pass-ersby, ordering an espresso and a croissant. Perfect time for spending time with a friend and as the French say: "re-draw the world," or more pragmatically, talk about life, politics, and beliefs (as in religion mostly) among other things.

In the U.S. talking about politics and, God forbid (pun intended), religion is a no-no, even with friends, and especially with family and neighbors (because it is difficult to avoid them, I guess). But the more you learn to talk about politics with your friends, the better you will understand your friends, and they'll understand you, and the greater (hopefully) the chance that you will love each other's company because it is not sterile, not boring, but rather stimulating, and makes you think, if not slightly change your mind one conversation at a time. For me one great example of a respectful political discussion among two sides is not the political debates we see on TV or the single invitee that agreed to be on the other camp's morning show among four angry adversaries. My model is the internet news show on The Hill (thehill. com/hilltv) called *Rising* with Krystal Ball (a democrat) and Saagar Enjeti (a conservative). Not only do the hosts make arguments that are grounded in facts, but they also have a good degree of listening skills and often even talk about the weaknesses of their "camp" politicians' actions or views. It is a refreshing sight in our polarized world.

Let's first review what both camps (yes, in the U.S. there are really only two camps: conservatives and liberals embodied in the main political parties, i.e., the republicans and the democrats) stand for in a few areas in order to make a distinction between them and to launch a potential conversation.

For instance, we could look at the way income is taxed and how these taxes are used by both camps. Remember that the economy is all connected, and that we should be looking at a system, not necessarily at just one issue. However, we can also look at one issue separately of the others, that should remind you of ECON classes, in order to study it and to understand it, then try to predict the impact of any change on the entire system.

A few questions to ponder:

Should income taxes be changed? Should their level be changed? Should their calculation and reporting process be changed? Should their schedule of payments and uses be changed? Should other taxes (corporate, capital gain, sales, property, payroll, estate, custom, etc.) be changed as a result?

What about the use of these collected taxes? Should we change the budgets for health, social security, military, veterans, education, the environment, energy, security, space programs, agriculture, international relations, and help to other countries? Should we change the way the money is used in each department or area?

Should certain laws be created, altered, or eliminated? Should states have their power changed? Should the federal government have its power changed? Should the constitution be changed? Should the constitution be interpreted differently than it is? Should the supreme court be changed? Should limits be imposed on "liberties"?

How about the political system itself we call a "democratic process"? Should it be changed in any way? Should the election process be altered? How? Should the process of passing a law be altered in any way? Should we change the use of money in the election process? Should we change the required qualifications of elected officials in any way? Should we change the process of removing elected officials from office? Should we change the rules governing political communications?

No need to have graduated from George Washington University (my Alma Matter) or taken Poli-Sci classes to understand the issues and debate them intelligently.

The information is at your fingertips, but maybe too much information is at your fingertips that it becomes a little overwhelming.

Let's pick at different views on a subject you must have an opinion about.

For instance, let's talk about wages and taxes. Let's listen to Jill, a liberal (a.k.a. Democrat) and her friend Jack a conservative (a.k.a. Republican) as they exchange points of views.

Jill: I want a minimum wage established throughout the country. It's currently set at $7.25 per hour, although, as you know, that level is lower for the tipped employees, like my friend Bill who is a waiter. He makes $2.13 an hour. Currently, states can also weigh in and change that minimum wage to impose on businesses a better minimum wage than the one the federal government set. But of course, that is a political issue, and some states don't do anything more, when others do, based on their leadership's political views.

I want the minimum wage to allow for a normal living condition. What I mean is that one person on minimum wage should not live in poverty due to the local cost of living (rent, transportation, food) or be forced to work two or more jobs at minimum wage in order to make ends meet.

Jack: Well, Jill, all that is fine, but my point of view is that no minimum wage at all is needed. At least no wage set by the government, whether federal or state. I trust the "free market" to set it on its own. You see, the idea of the free market is that supply and demand will find an equilibrium naturally, as with the stock market (See Chapter 6).

So, say, for instance that too many workers want the same job, then wages would go down. On the other hand, if not enough workers are available to be hired for the job opening, then the market would increase wages in order to get applicants.

That conservative principle is a little bit of what happens with celebrities of all kind. Teams fight with dollars to attract the best athletes ("Show me the money," see *Jerry McGuire*, the movie). So, the "free market" seems to be working here.

Jill: ...although some college football players are left hanging out to dry after the draft is over, and they have to scramble to find ways to wait a year and try again or change career all together.

Jack: Maybe, but it's rare, right?

Jill: On the other end of the spectrum, fast food workers or manufacturing assembly workers, that do not need many skills or education to get a minimum wage job have very little room to negotiate a higher wage. So, they need that minimum wage.

Jack: Maybe but listen to this. Often the situation is reversed and there are less jobs than applicants. Thus, if you imagine 100 available dayworkers for 5 contractors each needing 5 day workers, then 75 workers will stay without a job that day.

Jill: It means that the free market here will give power to the 5 contractors to hire the best or most motivated workers at the lowest possible wage.

Jack: The demonstration is a little biased since it looks like many more day workers will stay unemployed than college football players, but think about the fact that the college football players that are not picked during draft day might in fact find a job as a day worker.

Jill: As if that would happen.

Jack: I mean that it will all trickle down, and the football player might get a coach job, the coach applicants get another job... and so on.

Jill: Yet 75 or more dayworkers will never have a chance at the football draft, and will only be left without a job that day.

Jack: The system works because the college football player finds a job, and if the contractors are smart, they will set wages so low that they will be able to employ all of the day workers for the price they would have paid if minimum wages were imposed. In the end all of them have a job...

Jill: ... except the job is paid at a wage so low that no one would be able to live on it.

Jack: You are pushing it.

Jill: Let's do the math Jack: 1 dayworker that would make $7.25 per hour for 8 hours a day would cost $58 to the contractor. Each need 5 workers, so they're willing to pay $290 to get the job done. If that amount of money would be distributed among the 100 workers that need a job that day, then the per hour wage that would make each contractor spend no more than $290 per day for the job they have to do will allow them to hire 20 workers each at $1.81 per hour. Do you think that is a good solution?

Jack: America values a free market. The free market philosophy is what makes millionaires or billionaires possible (listen to *Billionaire* by Travis McCoy and Bruno Mars). This is one reason you and I could dream of becoming a millionaire and could actually become a millionaire. In some other democracy, like Europe, it might not be possible to become a millionaire, and that might be because Europe is "too socialistic" and has a very high minimum wage.

Take France, for instance. It has one of the highest minimum wages at $11.40 per hour; Germany is at $10.47; the UK (no longer in Europe) is at $10.

Furthermore, other countries that do not have a minimum wage seem to do well, such as Sweden, Norway, Finland, or Denmark.

Jill: In fact, looking at these countries in detail shows that minimum wage is set by trade between strong unions and the employers, and that wages are actually higher than the other European countries.

Jack: Why set a minimum wage? Why doesn't everyone want to become a millionaire?

Jill: These questions seem related when in fact they are not. One can become a millionaire in a free market America, and at the same time one can be assured that a minimum wage is set in case they do not make the draft and have to work a factory job.

Jack: Conservatives are trying to protect not just the idea of the free market and the possibility for all of us to become millionaires, but also the fact that a higher minimum wage means that entrepreneurs and businesses in general will make less profits if they have to pay their workers a higher wage, thus some would have to close shop, and others would see their profits plummet and negatively impact their stock price on Wall Street.

Jill: Listen, becoming a millionaire is a good idea and a good goal for people living in the U.S.A. I agree that it is aligned with our culture, and it is part of what we call the American dream. Hope is a very good motivator.

[even if we just saw above that we should live in the present, but I digress, simply have a plan instead of hope].

Jill: The minimum wage is here to protect the weakest of our society. Not unlike what is engraved on the Statue of Liberty: "Give me your tired, your poor, your huddled masses yearning to breathe free." In fact, the position in favor of a minimum wage could be defended by saying that if the U.S.A. has no limit in upward mobility, it has a set of "floor" protections that will create a safe environment for all to prosper from.

Jack: Historically, this is not true Jill. A cruel, harsh free market has always been present in the U.S.A.

Jill: ...until the crash of 1929, and the subsequent WWII that forced politicians to intervene in order to save people from starvation and restart the economical machine. What could be wrong with a minimum wage that allows Americans to be able to live without having to work a second job in order to put food on the table?

Jack: Many businesses will not be able to pay a minimum wage, or they will go bust, or will have to increase prices to still make the profit they need, thus forcing those consumers to pay more for goods, and in the end spend all their extra wages on the food they need.

Jill: Currently some profits or even business owners' incomes are unlimited. The Wall Street culture might actually produce

millionaires, which is a good thing, and at the same time justify a lower wage to protect that same profit. Thus, without
limiting profits or CEO salaries, or incomes, or dividends, business owners have to share the rewards of productions through
a minimum wage, if not further with profit-sharing schemes
and other benefits.

Jack: OK, but as mentioned earlier, Jill, in European countries
where the minimum wage is high, there are fewer millionaires, and businesses do not make as much profit.

Jill: You are partially right, Jack. Except that the reason might
not be due to minimum wage levels but rather to the culture.
Looking at soccer players contracts, for instance, shows that
becoming a millionaire is possible in Europe (and the UK). In
fact, the second richest person on earth is French (Bernard
Arnault of LVMH). So, what is the problem?

The discussion between Jill and Jack could possibly drift to the freedom of enterprise that, in general, is more rigid due to the regulation
constraints in Europe. Or maybe the discussion could drift to the cost
of living in general. A country with a higher cost of living requires
higher wages to survive than a country with a lower cost of living. The
U.S.A. has a higher cost of education and health than most European
countries, thus it takes more money to live in the U.S.A. than to live
in France, for example, because you need to spend more to go to school
or see your doctor.

Conservatives will then drift to the topic of taxes claiming that
in Europe higher income tax and higher sales tax help finance the
educational system and the health system, and that in the U.S.A.,
mainly because we want to give people freedom of choice in the
case of education or health, we do not tax as much so that the extra

money one is making from each paycheck can be used to pay for school. It becomes a discussion of individual choice versus collective choice. As most binary choice arguments, the solution is somewhere in the middle.

Why do we argue? I ask myself that question often because, as my friends will attest, I am an opinionated guy and I love an argument. But what many friends or observers miss is that I argue from my heart. I argue because I care (ok, sometimes it is selfish, or provocative, I'll give you that). I might actually suggest that I argue with a little selfishness, a little love, a little fun, a little fire all the time. Being agreeable and shying away from arguing could be misunderstood for being weak or being a "yes man" in my mind. I am often reminded to "pick my battles" when it feels that I argue on every topic all the time (just a perception; I don't do that).

If you are not an "opinionated" person, and you tend to shy away from arguing because you fear something, whether it's offending people, being seen as a contrarian, or being ostracized, then maybe you need a little technique to feel more comfortable arguing just a little more than you are today, and possibly to make your point when the "battle" is worth it.

Ammunition for a Good Discussion

Rhetoric, a technique in the art of persuasion, and logic are both ancient arts used by philosophers but also by the politicians of the days roughly 300 years before Christ. Aristotle (he is everywhere...a genius really) and company formalized a set of rules and techniques that people use today to their advantage.

A good argument starts with a premise and a conclusion. For instance: "You must exercise (premise) because it is good for your health (conclusion)."

Be warned that people you are arguing with will use what is called "sophism" to try to convince you. A sophism is a false statement. Let's look at a few examples.

1) You must exercise, everyone knows that.

    The goal in using "everyone knows that" is to make you feel stupid using a conclusion that implies that everyone knows the premise of the argument is true except you, so you better agree (and feel stupid for not knowing that) or face being ostracized from society because you will be alone in thinking what you are thinking.

2) You must exercise. If you think we shouldn't exercise, it is because you don't realize that you must exercise, thus it proves that you need to exercise.

    This conclusion is trying to mess with your mind and your sense of logic. If you are not quick on your feet, or if you have somewhat of an inferiority complex vis-a-vis the person arguing with you (maybe it is your boss), then you might blame the feeling of confusion on the conclusion of this argument on you rather than on the other person's faulty logic. "If you think we shouldn't exercise, it is because you don't realize that you must exercise, thus it proves that you need to exercise." This sentence is not logic. The first part is logic yet points at a possible blind spot you might have: if you think we shouldn't exercise, it is because you don't realize that you must exercise. If you think that this should not be done, it is because you do not know that it must be done could make sense in some circumstances. For instance, a coach might see in you the capacity to exercise at a certain level, but you do not believe you can do it. Thus, you think it should not be done (because you think you cannot do it), yet, your coach, thinks you do not believe that you can do it, and that is why you do not want to do it. Your coach is going to open your eyes to the possibility that you can exercise, and you will trust your coach and try it. But our conclusion adds, "thus it proves that you need to exercise." Be careful with the word "prove" in any text you read. To prove something is a very, very high threshold. In most cases, scientists have strong evidence that leads them to believe that something is significantly different than what we think, and that's as far as they will go. As you know, science evolves every day with new discoveries that make the previous "truth" not true anymore. Nothing "proves that you must exercise." Maybe a doctor could assess that if you do not exercise and continue to live your life the way you are currently living it, then you'll possibly hurt your health. The doctor might be right, is probably right, but still, you need to first believe that the exercise regime will significantly improve your health before you undertake it. The logic in the conclusion of the argument will not simply be that your ignorance that everyone must exercise or your lack of belief in the fact that people must exercise is a proof that you, in particular, must exercise.

3) You must exercise and if you don't want to exercise, I will have to confiscate your phone and force you to exercise.

Here is a very threatening conclusion to the premise that you must exercise. It is clear and the consequences are laid out. It is simply a threat, it will not change your belief, it only appeals to your fear and how much you love your phone. If you love your phone a lot, you will exercise. But the minute you can escape that predicament and run free, you will.

The Qualities of a Good Premise

A good premise needs to be verifiable. You must exercise because it is good for your health. That is verifiable. How do you verify that exercise is good for your health? You look at the literature on exercise and health. Every day scientists are conducting experiments to show that a treatment has a positive effect on your health. Then they publish their findings in academic journals. These journals' conclusions are then picked up in the non-scientific press and you might read about the results in some newspaper or watch a video on You Tube explaining the results. The source of the information, the "popular press" (that's how scientists call the non-scientific media), use the academic journals. For instance, the New England Journal of Medicine, Nature, Econometrica, and so on. There are hundreds of them in all the scientific disciples from medicine to marketing ("real" scientists call marketing a pseudo-science, but that is another discussion).

Experimentation

Why would the results of an experiment be closer to the truth than anything else? It has to do with the controls put in place during the experiment in order to make sure (as much as one can) that the results one gets, the effect of a drug, or the effect of a treatment, are, more likely than not, due to the medicine (treatment) used. For instance, a drug company wants to know if a vaccine works. They conduct an experiment in which two groups of volunteers selected at random will live their lives, one group thinking they have the vaccine, but in fact receiving a placebo (something that looks like the vaccine, but that in fact has no effect), and the other group actually receiving the vaccine. If there are significantly more people with the vaccine that do not catch the flu compared to the placebo group, then the scientists will deem the experiment conclusive, i.e., the vaccine (seems to) work.

So, coming back to our argument: You must exercise because it is good for your health. What is the evidence, from reputable scientific sources, that exercise is good for your health? And do you also find evidence of exercise NOT being good for your health?

In the end, that evidence will allow you to make up your mind. To reassess your original belief and update it. Who knows? Maybe you will change your mind in front of the evidence and be convinced that exercise is good for your health.

Now get out of your chair and exercise!

Hold on! Could you not argue that other things besides exercise are good for your health? And that, therefore, maybe it is not only exercise that is good for your health, and that maybe in your situation exercise is not the best for your health?

You might also rebut your friend's attempt to make you get off the couch with a question about the validity of the conclusion "exercise is good for your health." For instance, you might ask, "What is good health?" or, "Is good health a necessity?" or, "Is exercising feasible?" You might even go further and question the motives behind the argument, "Is forcing people to exercise or being in good health something morally sound? Why are we forcing people to exercise?"

IN CONCLUSION

"Lead, follow or get out of the way"

Commencement

> *Gen Z POV: "I know for me especially, after graduation, like, I'm not kidding you, life hit like a brick, it was crazy."*

In his Stanford 2005 commencement address Steve Jobs, arguably an excellent public speaker, tells three stories from his life. Why three? That is part of a public speaking framing "trick" designed to make the speaker pace himself and remember to stay on topic while creating some sort of logical sequence that feels quite effective in projecting depth and breadth. After all, if the speaker has three stories from his life, he must have more, and if he shares these three, they must be important to his central message (think trinity). In addition to the well-crafted argument presented by Jobs, the timing of his address comes a year after he was diagnosed with pancreatic cancer and 6 years before his death at the relatively young age of 56 (See here for the full text and video: https://news.stanford.edu/2005/06/14/jobs-061505).

His three messages are:

1) Even if you drop out of college, do not despair, keep your motivation toward whatever you are trying to achieve, your

vision of you in the future. Revisit the visualization exercise done in Chapter 2. Steve says that you will connect the dots (your path in life from today to when you achieve your dream) in the future. You cannot connect the dots forward but have faith in yourself; it will connect.

2) When you will face failure (being fired, going bankrupt, getting divorced), do not despair either. Keep the faith (notice the similarities?). Failures are here for a reason. It is karma. It is destiny. It teaches you a lesson (learn the lesson, discard the experience). It will make you stronger.

3) His third story is about his battle with cancer and his realization that he is going to die sooner or later, and probably sooner than he wants. Therefore, he advises the graduates of 2005 to "be all that they can be" now, to seize the day (carpe-diem) (watch *Dead Poet Society* with Robin Williams), to listen to your inner voice more than listening to others. To stay hungry (do not rest on your laurels) and stay foolish (keep your child creativity, your inquisitive mind, your curiosity).

I am no Steve Jobs, yet I have a garage. I almost dropped out of school and failed to invent the Apple computer, but I used it to my advantage. I created businesses and got fired. So, I can relate to Steve's message. It is intemporal. You can relate to his message. We can all relate.

Life is made of a weird mix between opportunities that present themselves to you (destiny), and you using your intelligence, education, knowledge, intuition to choose a path, an opportunity from the choices that are in front of you. The struggle is real between your inner voice and that of what Jobs calls the "dogma" (your parents, teachers, bosses, society).

Keep calm and live your life.

APPENDICES

You must conquer your fear of using simple math you'll need everyday

Some of you might be in the predicament psychologists call a "fixed mindset." When you say something like: "I am not good at math" for instance, it creates a self-fulfilling prophecy, and you will tend to not be good at math. At least not as good as you could be. It is a little bit like having low self-esteem. It lowers your abilities by creating unnecessary worries or anxieties when confronted with a "math" problem. It can be something as simple as using a percentage in some real-life situation. For instance, you are trying to figure out an amount in dollars equivalent to a 10% discount on a $49 pair of shoes to know if you can afford the shoes after discount and save you the embarrassment at the cash register.

Basic Math Percentages

A percentage is a fraction expressed as a proportion of 100%. For example, ½ (the fraction) is the same as 50% (the percentage). To get the percentage you simply divide (using a calculator App on your phone) 1 divided by 2. You get 0.50. To get to a percentage you then multiply the results by 100. In our example you get 0.50 x 100 = 50. That is now 50%.

Imagine you are cooking a pizza at home and you have 3 friends with you. What is the percentage of the pizza each of you will get (if your cutting skills are good and you do not want to cheat your friends)? Answer: 1 pizza divided by 4 people (4 people because it is you plus 3 friends) as a fraction is 1/4. Which results in 0.25. Or 25% (0.25 x 100) as a percentage. Thus, each of you will get 25% of the pizza. No matter how large the pizza is. Notice that when you add the 4 people, 25%, you get 100% again (25+25+25+25 = 100).

You can reverse the calculation and get a fraction from a percentage. Let's assume that you are allowed to get 5% of a sum of money. And let's assume that that sum of money is $1,000. Then what you will get is 5% of $1,000, or $50. How do you calculate that? Two ways: first you can say that 5% is the same as 5 divided by 100. And that is 0.05 (use a calculator if you need). Then multiply 0.05 by 1,000 to get 50. The second way is to directly multiply 5 by 1,000, which would be 5,000, then divide that result by 100. 5,000 divided by 100 is 50. Either way you get the same result.

Fractions or percentages are very important in anything to do with money (and pizza). For instance, interest rates, inflation rates, growth rates are all expressed as percentages. Over time percentages allow us to also measure whether saving go up or down and by how much. That simplifies comparisons between different amount of savings and different investment strategies. For example, a stock we purchased at $100 is now valued at $120. Another stock was purchased at $50 and is now $70. They both increased by $20, but the question is which stock increased the most in percentage? The simple formula we use is:

([new value – old value] divided by old value)

or in the first stock example ([120-100]/100). We first deal with the calculation in the brackets [120-100] and find 20. Then we have (20/100) which is 0.20 or 20%.

The second stock increased by ([70-50]/50) or (20/50) or 0.40 or 40%. You get it, the second stock has had a much larger increase in percentage than the first one even though the absolute amount in dollars ($20) is the same. That is because the second stock baseline (starting point) was lower than that of the first stock.

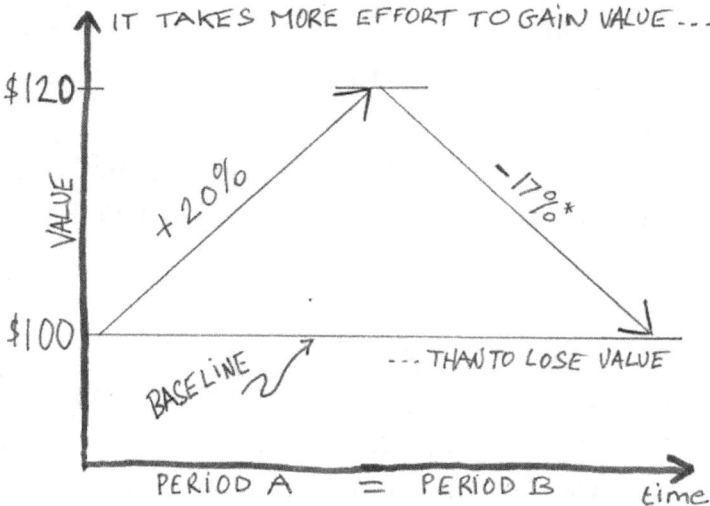

Figure 17   Visualizing Gains and Losses in Percentages

Image now that our first stock has gone back down to $100. What is the percentage decrease? You might rush into a wrong conclusion and say 20%. That would be incorrect. Let's do the math ([new value – old value] divided by old value). ([100-120]/120) or (-20/120). Notice the negative sign in front of 20, that is because the stock has decreased. 20/120= 0.166; we are rounding up to 0.17 or 17%. Let's not forget the negative sign, thus the stock has decreased by 17% or the change is -17%. Why is it not 20%? After all, we are dealing with the same numbers. It has to do with the baseline. In one case the stock was moving from 100 to 120, in the second case it was moving from 120 to 100. Since the baseline is different the percentages will be different.

The moral of the story is that it will always be more difficult to regain a loss. If you start with $120 and lose $20 or 17%, you will need a gain of 20% to be back to your starting point (See Figure 17).

Coming back to our introduction example. You are trying to figure out an amount in dollars equivalent to a 10% discount on a $49 pair of shoes to know if you can afford the shoes. If you only have $44 can you afford them?

10% is 0.10 (10/100). 0.10 x $49 is $4.9. The shoes will cost you $49 - $4.9 = $44.1. Oops! You can't afford them unless you find a dime on the floor.

Basic Cooking "Math"

Cooking is a good way to survive. It is also a good way to find pleasure when the food you are cooking is cooked properly and not raw (kinda defeats the purpose of cooking it in the first place, unless you are into salads or sushi) or not burnt. Here are a few pointers.

Basic Recipe Portions

Meat or Fish, count 6 oz per person (a little more if there is a large amount of waste or bones)
Rice or pasta, count 2 oz of uncooked, dry rice or pasta per person
Fresh pasta, count 4 to 5 oz per person
Vegetables, count 5 oz per person, then divide that amount by the number of veggie varieties you serve. For example, if you serve potatoes, carrots, and green beans on the same plate, then round up the quantities to 2 oz of each veggie per person or 6 oz total.
You need 3 eggs for an omelet per person

Cooking Times

Hardboiled eggs, 10 min (start in boiling water)
Pasta (dry) boiled "al dente," 17 min (average time for spaghetti, check often if you use smaller or larger pasta)
Pasta (fresh) boiled, 4 to 6 min
Rice boiled, 15 to 20 min (start in cold water)
Potatoes boiled, 15 to 20 min (start in cold water)

Cooking Temperature (in the center - use a thermometer)

Red Meat: Rare 125F; Medium 145F; Done 160F
Pork/Chicken/Poultry: 165F
Fish: 140F

INDEX